EVERY

GOOD

THING

TALKS FROM THE 1997
BYU WOMEN'S CONFERENCE

EVERY
GOOD
THING

TALKS FROM THE 1997
BYU WOMEN'S CONFERENCE

EDITED BY
DAWN HALL ANDERSON
SUSETTE FLETCHER GREEN
AND DLORA HALL DALTON

DESERET BOOK COMPANY
SALT LAKE CITY, UTAH

Library of Congress Cataloging-in-Publication Data
  BYU Women's Conference (1997)
      Every good thing : talks from the 1997 BYU Women's Conference /
  edited by Dawn Hall Anderson, Susette Fletcher Green, and Dlora Hall
  Dalton.
        p.   cm.
      Includes bibliographical references and index.
      ISBN 1-57345-367-6 (hb)
      1. Mormon women—Conduct of life—Congresses. 2. Women—Religious
  life—Congresses.   I. Anderson, Dawn Hall.   II. Green, Susette
  Fletcher.   III. Dalton, Dlora Hall.   IV. Title.
  BX8641.B89   1998
  289.3'32'082—dc21   98-10030
                                                                          CIP

Printed in the United States of America
10 9   8   7   6   5   4   3   2   1   72082 - 6317

CONTENTS

CONTENTS

THE UNEXPECTED LIFE

PARENTING GRAB BAG

BALANCING ACTS

COVENANT MAKING

TEXTS AND CONTEXTS

PREFACE

This book is the twelfth in the series from the annual women's conference sponsored jointly by Brigham Young University and the Relief Society of The Church of Jesus Christ of Latter-day Saints. The essays and poems in this volume were drawn from presentations given at the 1997 conference. We are grateful to the authors for working with us to tighten and reshape their oral presentations for this volume. Their extra effort allowed for more voices and topics to be included. We are proud of the way the contributors, few of them writers by profession, have captured in their articles not only the content but the spirit of the conference. The honest sharing of experiences and insights, the laughter and tears and joyous spirituality of this gathering of Latter-day Saint women can be heard in these pages.

We are especially grateful to the planners of the conference: the conference chair, Kathy D. Pullins, assistant dean of the J. Reuben Clark Law School at BYU; her executive assistants, Vicki M. Huebner and Anna Kennington; and their hardworking committee of BYU faculty members and Relief Society representatives. These dedicated women devote much prayer and thought to making this event the forum of learning and spirituality that it is.

Finally, we thank Suzanne Brady of Deseret Book. As editors, we look forward each year to working with her. Her warmth, expertise, and good sense guide us through the final stages of preparing the manuscript for publication.

PIECES OF PEACE

JANET LEE

I love the Smith Field House at BYU. I know it is just a gymnasium with a track and a few classrooms and offices, but to me it is much more. Despite its rambunctious purpose, this place brings me a peace you cannot imagine. It is a sanctuary, a haven, for me. My memories of experiences in this building provide a piece of peace as I look back through the years shared with my husband, Rex, and as I wonder about the years we will be apart.

As students, Rex and I attended devotionals and forums, basketball and volleyball games, and track meets in the field house. At lunchtime, we could buy hamburgers and brownies at the side of the track. At registration time, the entire building was filled with confused and frustrated students struggling to register for required classes before they filled up. With a little decoration and a big imagination, the field house was even turned into a dance hall. The first picture Rex and I ever had taken together was in this very building. I once wore my wedding dress here. No, we didn't have our reception in the field house, but Janie Thompson, who was in charge of BYU's annual Field House Frolics the year Rex and I were married, wanted a theatrical atmosphere. We sang "Love and Marriage" as we stepped down a tall, winding staircase. A decade later,

Janet Lee, an educator and speaker, earned her B.S. degree in education from Brigham Young University. She is the wife of the late Rex E. Lee, the mother of seven children, and grandmother of twelve. She serves as a member of the Young Women General Board.

President Dallin Oaks introduced Rex here as the founding dean of the yet-to-be-organized J. Reuben Clark Law School. Shortly thereafter, when we moved back to Provo, we came here often for family home evenings with our children. Here on this track I ran my first mile, then three, then five. I ran with Rex at my side, giving me encouragement, cheering me on. Sometimes I came in the daytime and settled my young children in the bleachers with paper and crayons or storybooks and the promise of a brownie if they were good while Mommy ran.

Years later, we returned to the same track after Rex's chemotherapy treatments. He walked slowly, holding my hand and gaining strength after a six-month hospital stay. For years we had been running long distances outside and thought we had graduated from a track, but that winter he needed the stability of temperature, and we enjoyed the comradery of friends. He loved greeting people as we walked the track. His voice boomed all through the field house. "Hi, Pete. How are you, Glen? I'll race you," he joked to runner friends as they passed him by. I thought he wouldn't want to draw attention to himself, with his chemically induced baldness and ponderous pace, but he loved their smiles as they passed. Some would stop and walk with him awhile to chat and then be on their way.

By spring, Rex was running two laps and walking one, and by early summer we were running outside together and all over Provo. The following summer, he became president of BYU, and once again, we returned to the field house for sporting events and winter runs when it was snowy outside.

How could I not love this building? My memories are one way I find peace. They have carried me, they brighten my life, and they are a wonderful blessing—a piece of my peace.

I have contemplated peace a great deal over this past year. I have thought a lot more about peace when I haven't had it than when I have. I have told myself, "As soon as I get the hospital bills paid, then I will feel peace . . . as soon as I figure out our finances and feel secure . . . as soon as I answer all the kind letters people have written . . . as soon as I get used to kneeling by our bed each night alone to pray . . . ." The list goes on and on. I foolishly put a condition on my peace.

Gradually I have learned not to postpone peace but to accept it as a gift when it comes piece by piece. If I look, I can find pieces of peace in each day—even in a bad day. Life does not have to be perfect to have moments of perfect happiness. They come with the smile of a child, the kindness of a co-worker, the satisfaction of a job well done, or the appreciation of a sunset, a blossom, a familiar melody, or even a well-scrubbed sink.

The Savior has promised us peace: "Peace I leave with you, my peace I give unto you: not as the world giveth, give I unto you" (John 14:27). The promise of peace is unconditional. He didn't say, "My peace I leave with you if nothing difficult ever happens in your life" or "My peace I give unto you unless you don't find the right person to marry, unless you have financial reverses, unless you experience poor health, or unless your children struggle."

The Savior didn't qualify his promise. He simply said, "My peace I give unto you," but note that he added "not as the world giveth, give I unto you." We must accept our Savior's gift of peace and recognize it as his peace, not the superficial peace of the world.

We can be relaxing on a beautiful beach, feeling the rhythm of the ocean, the sun in the sky, and a refreshing breeze and still not be at peace. By contrast, we can be anywhere in the workplace, the laundry room, or even in the car and feel a piece of his peace when we are in tune with the Spirit because, as we are told in Doctrine and Covenants 6:23, the Lord speaks peace to the mind. Some of my most inspirational moments have come while folding socks at midnight, making orange juice early in the morning, or praying alone in my car. Other pieces of peace come after action—we make a decision, accomplish a task, or work toward a goal.

We cannot remain in that state of peace forever. Daily concerns, mundane responsibilities, duties, and tasks creep into our sanctified moments of still assurance. Usually peace does not come without effort, and most of the time, our pieces of peace do not last very long. In my search for peace over the past year, I continue to return to John 14:27. That scripture has three parts that speak to me of peace: past, present, and future.

Past peace. Of past peace, the Savior tells us: "Peace I leave with you" (John 14:27). That was his gift to us as he left this earth—remembering him and all he has done for us will bring us peace. In my quiet moments of mourning, sometimes I succumb to questioning. Rex's death was untimely. Couldn't someone have done something to keep him here? I think of his pain during those last few years. I remember the agony of his last two weeks, and I wonder if even I completely understood his suffering. I wonder if anyone did. Then I remember the words of Elder Neal A. Maxwell: "Can we, even in the depths of disease, tell [our Savior] anything at all about suffering? In ways we cannot comprehend, our sicknesses and infirmities were borne by Him even before they were borne by us."[1] It is wonderful to know that no matter what happens to us on this earth, there is someone who understands everything. Thoughts of the Savior's love and compassion for Rex's suffering and my sorrow bring peace. I know that he understands all of our sorrow.

We can also find peace as we reflect on our own good memories. But what about memories that are uncomfortable or even painful? If we need ecclesiastical or professional help, we must seek it immediately so we can begin to move forward. Even then, our brief, daily pieces of peace can be part of the healing process. If our uncomfortable memories simply consist of things we wish we had or hadn't said or done, we must apologize or rectify our error. If we cannot improve the situation, then we need to let the memory go. That is hard to do sometimes. For those of us who lie awake nights rewriting the script of our past actions, peace can be elusive.

When Jesus came forth from the tomb and appeared to his disciples, his first greeting was: "Peace be unto you" (Luke 24:36). He did not ask, "Did you see how unfairly I was judged, how cruelly I was treated, or how brutally I was crucified?" He did not ask to be pitied or to have his enemies attacked. Christ knows that resentment and recrimination do not bring peace. They cause us to stagnate, leaving us unable to move ahead vigorously because we stumble when we constantly look back at what has been. "All crosses are easier to carry when we keep moving," Elder Maxwell counsels us.[2] During this past year, as my heart has yearned to cease grieving, I have prayed for peace, and I receive that blessing as I keep moving.

Present peace. When the Savior tells us, "My peace I give unto you" (John 14:27), he promises the continuation of his gift of peace while we struggle with all that is temporal. Sometimes we miss this gift. Recently, I found a letter I wrote to Rex in the fall of 1991. We often wrote letters or notes to each other, expressing feelings that were difficult to share in person during his nine-year struggle with cancer. Sometimes we delivered these letters in person, with a smile and a hug. Other times they were tucked into a pocket or purse to be discussed later. I must admit I wrote more than he did. I had a need to pour out my feelings.

I knew he read my notes; we often talked about them. But I never knew he saved them. During the past year, as I have gone through his things, I have found letters and notes in pockets, briefcases, drawers, and files. In this particular letter to Rex, I told of an experience with our daughter. I wrote: "This afternoon . . . I took Wendy home, and as we were driving she talked to me a little about how excited she was about the baby, but our talk ended with an account of all the aches

5

and pains and discomforts of pregnancy. She had an understanding ear as she recounted to me such things as a misshapen figure, swollen hands and feet, and a total off-balance, awkward feeling. 'Will I ever be the same again?' she asked as she got out of our car. I smiled and answered that she would, but as I was driving away, I thought, 'No! She will never be quite the same again.' Life is never the same after a big change of any kind in our lives.

"For a few seconds, as I drove along University Avenue, I began to feel sorry for myself and for you for the changes that have happened in our lives over the past four years. I was longing to be relieved of the constant worry, wishing you could be completely well again, wanting our lives to be like they were before you got sick. I took Wendy's question and applied it to you and to me. Will we ever be the same again? I startled myself when I answered 'No!' out loud at a stoplight.

"But as I drove up the hill toward the administration building, the most peaceful feeling came over me. I had been crying, but I stopped and listened as soothing thoughts poured into my mind. The thoughts were neither new nor profound, but what made them pierce my soul was that I felt the power of their source. 'Life's experiences are to be enjoyed and appreciated as they come,' I seemed to be hearing. Life is like a book, a play, or a puzzle. It is difficult to see it in its entirety until it is completed, but to look back or ahead too much takes away from the enjoyment close at hand, and besides that, we miss something important. . . . We must look for the good things about now and enjoy them with all of our hearts. 'No, we will never be the same again,' I thought to myself. And life will continue to change. But life will always be good."

My letter to Rex had been found to remind me of what I had momentarily forgotten. Love and peace overflowed in my heart that day, that moment, as I read.

Future peace. But what of our tendency to worry about the future? Our Savior's words assure us: "Let not your heart be troubled, neither let it be afraid" (John 14:27). This is my hardest challenge now. If I spend too much time thinking about the past or the future, I will miss the peace that comes from the present. But I cannot enjoy the present to its fullest unless I feel at peace with the past and the future, trusting that like the apostle Paul, I will have strength to face all conditions by the power that Christ gives me (see 2 Corinthians 4:14–16; 12:9).

My niece Mollie is a young missionary. Her ups and downs are perhaps intensified by her missionary experience and her youthful exuberance, but in a miniseries sort of way her letters represent all of us in our struggle for peace. She writes to her family: "It's so funny, a missionary's life. I feel so happy with just me, my ability to talk and pray to God. . . . Last night as I packed my three huge suitcases filled with a ridiculous overabundance of things, I almost felt SICK at how much happiness I had placed on *things*. Razors, lotion, soap, clothes, shoes. I mean, yes, they are essentials, but why did I have to bring SO MUCH? I hope you don't mind, but I have given SO much away. The people here just don't have anything."

Is this the same Mollie who made an emergency call the day before she left the MTC requesting four extra bottles of Victoria's Secret pear-scented lotion?

She continues: "I'm glancing out my window on the bus— yellow sun, green trees, fields, huge sky. Oh, how beautiful life is. I take joy in loving the Savior. I want to praise him in everything I do. I want my life to glorify him. I love the simplicity of happiness." She was in a really peaceful mood right then.

But four days later, Mollie was transferred, received a new companion, and suddenly faced the challenges inherent in change. She writes: "I'm struggling. . . . It's hot, about 115 degrees. I hope we can be in tune enough to find the souls that are ready." She adds: "I can feel the boards of the wooden bed on my bum through the two-inch mattress. I remember my fluffy feather bed, folded over double, and white satin, down comforter at home. It's wonderful, though, and I appreciate my life here and at home so much more."

Two weeks later she writes: "Do you know what? I'm being refined. Do you know what else? It hurts."

In Mollie's next letter the opening line is: "I got lice, and I cried! I told my companion I just couldn't do this anymore. I hit a wall. I was crying and sitting there, wet hair, bugs all over my scalp, wondering how I was going to live through the day. As I was crying, I looked at the wall. The picture of Christ in his red robe looked back at me. . . . I just cried, 'What can I do? What more can I give?'"

Later in the same letter she writes of finding resolution and peace: "Last night I read in the B of M a line, 'Thy will and not mine be done.' I have been trying to squeeze the Lord's will into mine. And yes, it fit, but like a puzzle piece in the wrong place. There were gaps and places where it was overlapping or too tight. I realized that I need to do the Lord's will and let my will go."

Like Mollie, I too have had to learn about the error of trying to squeeze the Lord's will into mine. When Rex was diagnosed with cancer in 1987, for days I begged and almost demanded of the Lord that Rex be made well. But my heart ached, and I could find no peace. I then began to reason and bargain, but still I felt no peace. Finally, one day my prayer began, "Thy will be done," and the peace I was searching for filled my heart. I thought I would never forget that lesson.

Yet, two weeks before Rex's death, I had to learn it once more. Again I had been trying to squeeze the Lord's will into mine. Again I had to let go of my will to find peace. The Lord didn't need my permission, but in allowing me to submit my will, a gift of peace was given to me by a loving Father in Heaven. He knew it would be easier for me to let Rex go if I could be allowed to do it willingly. Like children who resist being pulled away from play without warning, we struggle, but we can go willingly when allowed our agency. By putting my trust in the Lord, I gained a peace that would have been impossible had I continued to struggle against his will. At times like these, we arrive at a new understanding, and peace accompanies us for a time. Yet, we so often need reminders, guidance, and strength. We so often have to learn and relearn life's lessons.

Some days we think we would have greater peace if we were granted our heart's desire. On other days, we think peace would come if we could simply escape our current burdens. In one of my favorite fantasies, I have returned to the Garden of Eden. The way is so easy. My needs melt away. I bask in the beauty of God's finest creations and walk in the constant, calming presence of the Father and his Son. I feel unprecedented peace.

Yet, I realize that every act of God is purposeful, including the fall of Adam and Eve. They and their posterity had to fall away from permanent peace. We, as the children of Adam and Eve, also face challenges inherent in a fallen world. We spend sleepless nights surrounded by confusion, worry, fear, and discouragement. We struggle, and we ache for others who struggle. We encounter mistreatment and prejudice, injustice and unforgiveness. Sometimes we feel we are either failing or falling short of what is expected of us. Often we long for an easier way. In essence, we are longing for a Garden of Eden. We are asking to live as Adam and Eve once lived, surrounded simply by peaceful circumstances. At a glance, such conditions would seem to provide permanent peace; however, "Adam fell that men might be; and men are, that they might have joy" (2 Nephi 2:25). I find a connection between the Fall and finding joy, or eternal peace.

With all my heart, if I could change the course of these past ten years as our whole family has experienced the pain of Rex's cancer, I would do so. And yet, I would never want to give up the growth: the understanding, the insights, the compassion, or the increased love for each other and for our

Savior. Without the Fall, we would remain as children, without spiritual maturity, without knowledge, without realizing our ultimate potential of becoming exalted sons and daughters of God. My occasional desire to return to the Garden of Eden or escape to a life of ease is a misdirection, not the way to everlasting peace.

Christ healed bodies, minds, and souls. But after he healed the lepers, were they free from other struggles? After he restored sight to the blind, were they free from fear? Were the five thousand Christ fed ever hungry again? Was the sea calmed by Christ's hands stirred by future storms? Yes. As Helaman warned his children, the winds will continue to blow (see Helaman 5:12).

I often think of the tender last moments Christ shared with his apostles. Concerned, Christ tells his disciples that the time has come for him to leave. Full of heartache, the apostles turn to their Lord, who senses their sorrow. He replies, "Nevertheless I tell you the truth; It is expedient for you that I go away; for if I go not away, the Comforter will not come unto you; but if I depart, I will send him unto you" (John 16:7). If we expect mountains to move, seas to part, thunder to cease, and blinding light to point the way, we will miss the Savior's offering, his gift of comfort and peace. Peace comes as we truly rely on the Holy Ghost.

Like the fall of Adam and the crucifixion of Christ, there is something very significant, even essential, in being surrounded by conflict and finding peace in the midst of, or even because of, tribulation. "It is expedient for *you* that I go away," the Savior said (John 16:7; emphasis added).

The Lord promises safety and protection. He offers to all the gift of peace. Sometimes peace comes dramatically, like the calming of a raging sea (see Mark 4:39). Most of the time, however, peace comes quietly, as a subtle feeling of wellness, a renewed sense of God's omnipotent power, and the still, small voice whispering God's messages: words of comfort, thoughts of hope, feelings of strength, and a reassurance of love—the language of peace.

In the last days of Rex's life, he was given medication to ease his pain. As a result, he was sedated and could not talk, and I was not sure how much he could hear. I began to feel an almost desperate need to speak with him, to hear and be heard. I felt a sense of panic and insecurity. I felt out of control, as if I were falling away from all that was familiar to me. Desperate with heartbreak and weariness, I fell to my knees and prayed. As I expressed my urgent concerns to my Father in Heaven, I began to understand that the words I needed to speak to Rex and hear from him had already been given to me. I began to recall past conversations with Rex—conversations we had shared over many years. I sensed the comfort of the Holy Ghost as feelings and thoughts lifted me to a higher sphere, where souls could communicate without conventional conversation. Peace was being spoken to my mind. I was on sure ground again. Words unspoken now seemed insignificant and unnecessary. A lifetime of sharing each other's triumphs and sorrows had been stored in our hearts.

Now, in his hospital room, I thought about the many things he had been asked to do, and I was aware that what we were about to do was the most difficult of all. Memories flooded over me, and I concentrated on tender moments as well as milestones in our lives. Each time we had faced a turning point, I asked Rex what I could do to help him. His answer was always the same and always unequivocal: "Just be happy, Janet." Now, in the midst of our final challenge together, his words came back to me, and I knew what he would tell me if he could. I had never considered peace as part of the process of letting go. Yet when his final moment came, and I knew he was free from his pain, I felt his joy. Unexpectedly, my personal sadness was subdued as we shared his final triumph. I whispered: "I am so happy for you, Sweetheart." As I walked out of the hospital that afternoon, his words filled my heart:

"Just be happy, Janet," and I felt a moment of peace in my mighty whirlwind.

The Lord can speak peace to our minds wherever we are. We don't have to be in the temple or on a beautiful beach. Sometimes we are in the midst of trials and strife. It is the gift of peace that brings joy, surety, and solace—the kind of peace that can never be taken away. Piece by piece throughout a lifetime, we will long to return to the presence of the Prince of Peace. Our pieces of peace will fit together like a puzzle as our life takes shape after the pattern of our Savior. Because we are mortal, at times we will be unable to find the peace that is our gift, but our Savior's love can lift us soaring to new heights. In three short lines, Victor Hugo sings my theme song of this past year:

> Be like the bird who, halting in [her] flight on a limb too slight
> Feels it give way beneath [her],
> Yet sings knowing [she] hath wings.[3]

The boughs beneath us break sometimes. We will not fall. We have wings of truth, wings of faith, wings of glory—gifts of peace from our Savior, Master, and King.

NOTES

1. Neal A. Maxwell, *Even As I Am* (Salt Lake City: Deseret Book, 1982), 116–17.

2. Neal A. Maxwell, *Deposition of a Disciple* (Salt Lake City: Deseret Book, 1976), 30.

3. Victor Hugo, quoted in Marilyn Arnold, *Pure Love: Readings on Sixteen Enduring Virtues* (Salt Lake City: Deseret Book, 1997), 389.

THE BUNDLE OF LIFE

NANCY BAIRD

As winter deepens, the loss of light saps spirit from even the sturdiest souls. It is a critical time of year—the earth has tilted as far as it will go in its orbit and sent the bright winter stars sliding over the western horizon. Days are short; the midday sun is low and weak. It is easy to feel despair, or at least a nagging uneasiness in the waning light. Could not day disappear altogether and we be left in darkness? Each morning, out running on the streets in December, I impatiently count down the days to the moment when the planet makes its final great arc downward and joyously tilts back at the winter solstice. It is a private celebration for me, a magical, mysterious moment when the war with darkness is once more won and again the earth turns its beautiful, flawed face from death.

How deeply human beings long for light. If only we could always turn toward it, as does the earth at winter solstice, stopping in our self-destructive orbits. The miracle—the gift we are given—is that we can.

Mormon tells us that every man and woman is given the light of Christ and that this is the light by which we are to know, and judge, good from evil (see Moroni 7:16–19). He pleads with us, beseeches us, to search in that light and then to choose the good, that is, to "lay hold upon every good

Nancy Hanks Baird was named Utah Poet of the Year in 1996. She received her bachelor's degree in English from Brigham Young University and has worked as a freelance writer and editor. She and her husband, John K. Baird, are the parents of five children.

thing" (Moroni 7:19). Thus we are given two gifts: the light of Christ with which we are born, and the freedom to choose or reject that light. This is, of course, the crux of life. We are free to choose, and we do choose, using whatever portion of that light we manage to tap into.

Every moment of our lives we make choices—we turn between good and evil, light and darkness, life and death (see Moses 6:56). The choices define us: there is no escaping the decisions reflected in the shape and contour of minds, the brokenness of hearts, the stability of souls. Our choices are cast on our faces, released on our tongues, shaped on our bodies.

Bodies! Let me talk about bodies for a moment. For six months, recently, I watched my body thin and begin to waste away through disease; then, after medical diagnosis and treatment, thicken and fill with life. Too much thickening, too much life! It was a strange experience, confusing and provocative. It was as though my body, with a mind and perverse will of its own, was itself in darkness—unable or unwilling to absorb nourishment, and then, healing, unable or unwilling to stop.

As I have struggled to be disciplined about what I take into my body, I have thought a lot about being nourished by the bread of life instead of mortal bread. Adam and Eve were literally changed to mortal beings when they ate from the tree of knowledge. Is it not possible for us, in some limited way, to reverse this process and through schooling our minds and our bodies nourish ourselves with light? to take, as Brigham Young says, "a firmer hold on that enduring substance behind the vail, drawing from the depths of that eternal Fountain of Light gems of intelligence . . . a halo of immortal wisdom"?[1] There are many intriguing references in the scriptures to ingesting spiritual matter. Alma says we can taste light (see Alma 32:35). Joseph Smith wrote in Doctrine and Covenants 131:7–8 that all spirit is matter. Christ speaks of himself as the bread of life, the water of life (see John 6:35). And there is this fascinating statement by Brigham Young: "I want to see men and women breathe the Holy Ghost in every breath of their lives, living constantly in the light of God's countenance."[2]

Could we actually breathe in God's Spirit with every breath and desire to be fed more with light than food? Surely this is the place approached by those souls, so illuminated from within, that God is reflected out of their faces. I once read a remarkable statement by an unknown author: "One can see much in the face of a man as the years pass by. Something happens to the features of the relativist: a slackness, a weakness, a futility seems to stamp itself on them. But the man who has stood unflinchingly for great principles shows an increasing firmness, a nobility and a majesty in his face as time goes by."

At some level, human beings are always monitoring themselves—their thoughts, words, and deeds. Who has not gone through a day without some internal commentary and conversation? People internally register their choices—choices made by that light in every person—and reward themselves for strength, punish themselves for weakness. To be mentally healthy obviously requires choices consistent with one's moral values. And making such choices takes discipline not only of body but of mind. How clearly Moroni spoke so long ago: "Despair cometh because of iniquity" (Moroni 10:22). Perhaps someday we will fully understand the connection between choices and wellness not only of the body but also of the mind and spirit.

I was married with children before I woke to the fact that my mother was one of those truly rare people who "lay hold upon every good thing" (Moroni 7:19). Doesn't everyone come home from school to opera blowing through the house, dinner started, and clean sinks? Doesn't everyone's mother take them to see artists working in the jungle who make their own paper; invite total strangers to lunches of tacos, mangos, and coconut (from her own trees); have little red sweaters with beads and sequins made for them in Hong Kong? My mother is uninhibited, direct, and loving. Workmen follow her around like pets, hoping to (afraid not to?) please her.

Instead of bringing me dinner when I had babies, she brought me new dishtowels, sturdy hangers, soap dishes, and nature music. Her idea of a good TV show is Zubin Mehta at the Met; her bedroom is piled with books—biographies, history, classics, historical novels, inspirational magazines.

All her life, my mother has searched diligently for good things until layering them over her life became a natural instinct. Seeking light, she has, with intent, discarded pretension, dishonesty, and unhappiness.

About the year 960, Abd-er-rahman III of Spain wrote these words: "I have now reigned about fifty years in victory or peace, beloved by my subjects, dreaded by my enemies and respected by my allies. Riches and honors, power and pleasure have waited on my call, nor does any earthly blessing appear to have been wanting to my felicity. In this situation I have diligently numbered the days of pure and genuine happiness which have fallen to my lot: they amount to 14."[3] My mother has never agonized over her happiness; she has instead chosen to be happy and chosen to live a life of quality. She has nurtured her spirit and her mind, giving them what Einstein called "the deep shudder of the soul in enchantment."[4]

To live such a life is to be blessed. And I want such a blessing. I want the light of Christ. Without its constant presence, I will never be able to change, to act on my fragile decisions. We are such sorry children! Every day, as I battle myself and despair in my weakness, I think, as did Paul, "what I would, that do I not; but what I hate, that do I" (Romans 7:15).

In his book *In Heaven As on Earth*, Scott Peck makes the very interesting observation that what causes burnout in psychotherapists is not the tragedy in their patients' lives but their patients' attachment to their tragedy. People sought help, claiming they wanted to change, but no sooner was it under way "than they started behaving as if the last thing on God's earth they wanted to do was change."[5] How we cling to our sins and our comforts, like a child with her blanket, instead of putting aside our fear and choosing faith.

I know it is possible to change, to begin making good choices. Sometimes it is simply a matter of taking slow, gradual steps, making small decisions that then multiply on themselves, such as being particular about what we read and see. Every writer knows that what he reads, he will write, or, as Annie Dillard said, "he is careful of what he learns, because that is what he will know."[6] We have to search for what we value and then lay hold upon it. Only then will we be lifted "from one cleave of being to another."[7]

In December, as winter presents its longest, deepest days, I am not the only living thing aware of the earth's turning. Everywhere I look—at the peach tree knobbing outside my bedroom window, the aspens thickening in the yard, the bulbs swelling in the frozen ground—the energy, the flesh of life, is gathering strength to peel and explode out of death. And every year I am ready to join the parade, cut open the darkness, reel out of my long sleep. Not for me the regret of Augustine, written so beautifully and sadly long ago: "Too late did I love Thee! For behold, Thou wert within, and I without, and there did I seek thee; I unlovely, rushed heedlessly among the things of beauty Thou madest. Thou wert with me, but I was not with Thee."[8]

We can choose life. We can act upon our choices. The source of goodness and strength lies within us. It was a gift given us the day we broke the veil and entered this golden but broken world:

> And always the light is borne; cupped
> in steady palms and steadfast faces
>
> . . . .
>
> By its embrace we are bound in the bundle of life,
> and by darkness are never mastered.[9]

17

NOTES

1. Brigham Young, in *Journal of Discourses,* 26 vols. (London: Latter-day Saints' Book Depot, 1854–86), 9:288.

2. Young, in *Journal of Discourses,* 9:288.

3. Abd-er-rahman III, quoted in Jo Ann Larsen, "Life's Full of Happiness If You Know Where to Look," *Deseret News,* 27 August 1995.

4. Albert Enstein, quoted in Judith Groch, "Life After Work," *American Health,* March 1989, 100.

5. M. Scott Peck, *In Heaven As on Earth: A Vision of the Afterlife* (New York: Hyperion, 1996), 61.

6. Annie Dillard, *The Writing Life* (New York: Harper & Row, 1989), 68.

7. Gerard Manley Hopkins, quoted in *The Interpreter's Bible*, 12 vols. (Nashville, Tenn.: Parthenon Press, 1980), 5:915.

8. St. Augustine, *Confessions* X.27.38, quoted in *Interpreter's Bible,* 5:902.

9. Nancy Baird, "Christmas 1994," in *The Shell in Silk* (Salt Lake City: Publishers Press, 1996), 6.

BECOMING A DISCIPLE OF CHRIST

MARILYN S. BATEMAN

From the beginning of time, God has reserved choice lands and promised great blessings for his righteous followers. In the Book of Mormon, the prophet Lehi speaks of a land of promise, a land that is choice above all other lands (see 1 Nephi 2:20). Lehi's journey with his family to the promised land is symbolic of our journey through life to our promised land. Ultimately, it is our return to the land in which God and his Son, Jesus Christ, dwell.

To receive an inheritance in the heavenly city of God, we must learn how to put off the "natural man" and "[yield] to the enticings of the Holy Spirit" (Mosiah 3:19) while journeying through the wilderness of mortality. We must "search diligently in the light of Christ . . . and . . . lay hold upon every good thing" (Moroni 7:19) so the Spirit will bear a personal witness to us of the truth of all things. The Good Shepherd will call us (see Alma 5:38), and if we put aside the things of the world, we will hear his voice and follow him. We will become one of his disciples.

In our journey to this land of the heavenly city, whose builder and maker is God, we will encounter many obstacles and challenges. There will be ruts and holes of grief and

---

Marilyn S. Bateman, the wife of Brigham Young University president Merrill J. Bateman, is a mother and grandmother. She has served in leadership and teaching positions in ward and stake auxiliaries. The Batemans are the parents of seven children and have twenty grandchildren.

despair, rivers of tears, and mountains of sorrow, and each person will travel a different road. Each must blaze her own trail. My sister-in-law Maryland Scholes writes:

"We are the solitary pioneer of our own lives.

"No one has journeyed our path before us.

"No one began the trek with our particular assets and liabilities.

"No one will endure our exact set of hardships.

"No one has challenged our meanest enemies or stilled the terror of our darkest moments.

"Only we can struggle toward our own frontier—and our own safety and our own personal promised land."

But we need not travel the road alone. President Gordon B. Hinckley entreats us to develop a "simple faith, an unquestioning conviction, that the God of Heaven in his power will make all things right and bring to pass his eternal purposes in the lives of his children."[1]

When we believe that we "can do all things through Christ" (Philippians 4:13), our burdens will become lighter, and we will find that "peace of God, which passeth all understanding" (v. 7) as we travel the road in the fellowship of our brothers and sisters in the gospel.

In 1843, my great-great-grandparents James Lewis Burnham and Mary Ann Huntley Burnham, along with their four little children, joined the Saints in Nauvoo, Illinois. James and Mary Ann had joined the Church earlier that year while living in Beaure County, Illinois. James had been a minister of the Christian church, but upon hearing the "good news" of the gospel he could only acknowledge that he had no authority to preach. He and his wife, Mary Ann, were baptized into The Church of Jesus Christ of Latter-day Saints. He preached and advocated its doctrine faithfully until the day he died.

James and Mary Ann's youngest child, a little girl named Maria Antoinette, died the year after their arrival in Nauvoo. At the time, James was also failing in health: he was afflicted with a lung disease. Nevertheless, he labored quarrying rock for the Nauvoo Temple. He and Mary Ann were anxiously looking forward to the temple being completed so that they could receive their endowments and be sealed together for eternity.

In the summer of 1845, James's health grew worse. In October, he passed away. His death preceded the birth of another baby daughter by four days. That daughter, Mary Ann Burnham Freeze, later wrote: "This was a trying time for my mother, being left in sorrow and destitute of all worldly goods. She had no relatives near to help her. But the Saints were very kind to her in her afflictions. Her relatives in the East would gladly have sent means to take her back but it was no temptation to her. She had cast her lot with the Saints of God and would rather remain with them in poverty than have the wealth of the whole world elsewhere."[2]

In February 1846, the famous exodus from Nauvoo began. Mary Ann had no means to move herself and her family from the city, so they remained while the mob took over Nauvoo. They were then forced to leave or lose their lives. She received a wagon in exchange for her city property, was lent a yoke of cattle, and began that memorable, toilsome journey with her four young children. She later told of the mob searching their wagon for arms, the obscene language that they used, and how terribly she suffered from fear. She arrived in Winter Quarters late in the fall of 1846 and remained there for a year and a half. Then she, along with others, was compelled by the government to move back to the east side of the river out of Indian Territory.

In the depths of poverty, she let Brother Daniel Wood take her second son, Wallace, who was ten (and who is my great-grandfather), and her third son, George, who was eight, to the Valley with him. This was a severe trial for Mary Ann. She was separated from her young sons for five years because it wasn't until 1852 that she was able to start her trek west. Through the kindness and help of some of the brethren and sisters, she was

21

finally able to cross the plains with the rest of her children. They arrived in Salt Lake City on 8 October 1852.

As I think of Mary Ann's life, my heart confirms the truth of Elder M. Russell Ballard's observation regarding our early pioneers: "Each wagon and handcart was heavily laden with faith—faith in God, faith in the Restoration of His Church through the Prophet Joseph Smith, and faith that God knew where they were going and that He would see them through."[3] My pioneer forebears paid a heavy price for their discipleship. But they came to know their Savior.

In January 1847, while the Saints were at Winter Quarters preparing to begin their westward journey, the Lord told the prophet Brigham Young: "My people must be tried in all things, that they may be prepared to receive the glory that I have for them, even the glory of Zion" (D&C 136:31).

Much the same message has always been given to the children of God. In Isaiah 48:10 we read: "I have refined thee, but not with silver; I have chosen thee in the furnace of affliction." Elder Orson F. Whitney many years ago said: "No pain that we suffer, no trial that we experience is wasted. It ministers to our education, to the development of such qualities as patience, faith, fortitude and humility. All that we suffer and all that we endure, especially when we endure it patiently, builds up our characters, purifies our hearts, expands our souls, and makes us more tender and charitable, more worthy to be called the children of God . . . and it is through sorrow and suffering, toil and tribulation, that we gain the education that we come here to acquire and which will make us more like our Father and Mother in heaven."[4]

So often the things that teach us the most and give us the greatest insights into God's ways happen while we are struggling. If we turn to God for strength, feelings and sure knowledge pour into our thinking through the light that quickens our understanding. Recently I was pondering how I could be a better friend to my mother. She is a great lady, very active and healthy, living an independent life. But she is alone. My father died a number of years ago, and she has become widowed again in recent years. Loneliness is her greatest challenge.

As I was thinking about my mother, I felt a great sorrow for the difficult life she has had. She was only three when her mother died and nine when her father passed away. She was sent to live with an aunt who was kind but not motherly to her. My mother has been forced to fend for herself throughout most of her life.

As I thought about this, I knew that the Lord is aware of the trials Mother has endured and that he loves her. I also became aware that my grandmother felt great sorrow that she hadn't been able to mother and nurture her daughter in her growing years. I felt my grandmother's presence, and it was made known to me that as I loved and cared for my mother (her daughter), so my grandmother would be by my side and care and watch over me throughout my life.

In this life, we can have help from both sides of the veil. The Lord tells us in the scriptures: "I will go before your face. I will be on your right hand and on your left, . . . and mine angels [will be] round about you, to bear you up" (D&C 84:88).

If we remain true and faithful to the gospel of Jesus Christ and endure to the end, the Lord tells us that the promised land will be ours. The blessings and the riches of eternity will be our inheritance (see D&C 78:18). It is through meeting the challenges of our mortal journey that we become disciples of Christ. As we put our trust in him, he will bless us according to our faith. As we go through pains, sicknesses, afflictions, and temptations of every kind, our Savior will be there to succor us. He has paid the price through his atoning sacrifice to know us and to know how to help us. He knows how to deliver us safely back home. He is our Deliverer—our all!

23

NOTES

1. Gordon B. Hinckley, "Faith of the Pioneers," *Ensign,* July 1984, 6.

2. Burnham family records, in possession of author.

3. M. Russell Ballard, "You Have Nothing to Fear from the Journey," *Ensign,* May 1997, 60.

4. Quoted in Spencer W. Kimball, *Tragedy or Destiny,* Brigham Young University Speeches of the Year (Provo, 6 Dec. 1955), 7.

The original presentation of this essay is available on audiocassette from Deseret Book or on the Internet at http://coned.byu.edu/cw/womens.htm

WITH HEART AND MIND

MERRILL J. BATEMAN

The theme of this women's conference volume is taken from Moroni 7:19. In this passage, Mormon describes two steps along the path of life which, if taken, will spiritually transform a person into a begotten son or daughter of Christ. The first is to "search diligently in the light of Christ" so that good may be distinguished from evil. The second is to "lay hold upon every good thing, and condemn it not."[1]

Mormon's first step of searching diligently describes the quest for truth, for the good. His second command, to lay hold upon every good thing, means to live every good truth once it is found. In both the searching and the living, diligence is required. In the Lord's plan, diligent effort involves both the heart and the mind (see D&C 4:2). Diligently seeking truth and living gospel principles with all one's heart and mind opens the door for the Holy Spirit to transform us. We put off the natural woman or man because of the truths we value. With a humble heart, we "[yield] to the enticings of the Holy Spirit," partake of the Atonement, and become the "children of Christ, his sons, and his daughters" as we are spiritually reborn (Mosiah 3:19; 5:7).

Merrill J. Bateman is president of Brigham Young University and a member of the First Quorum of Seventy. He has served as Presiding Bishop of the Church and as dean of the College of Business and School of Management at BYU. He and his wife, Marilyn, are the parents of seven children and the grandparents of twenty.

SEARCHING WITH ONE'S HEART AND MIND

A wonderful example of the power inherent in connecting the heart and mind while searching for truth is related by Nephi the disciple at the time the resurrected Savior appeared to the people in the land Bountiful. Approximately twenty-five hundred people were gathered near the temple, marveling at the changes associated with the three days of darkness and discussing the sign given concerning the Redeemer of the world (see 3 Nephi 11:1–2). While conversing with each other, they heard the Father's voice introducing his Son on three separate occasions. They did not understand the voice the first two times, but they did feel the power of the Spirit piercing their hearts to the center, causing their frames to quake and their hearts to burn. They knew something special was about to take place, but their minds did not grasp the meaning of the Father's words. Moreover, the feeling in their hearts registered the importance of the message but not its content (see 3 Nephi 11:1–4).

On the third occasion, the Nephites opened their ears and understood the voice, which said, "Behold my Beloved Son, in whom I am well pleased, in whom I have glorified my name— hear ye him" (3 Nephi 11:5–7). The events that follow suggest that even though they understood the words spoken on the third occasion, they did not comprehend their full meaning. They looked into the heavens and saw a Man descending, clothed in white. Upon reaching the ground, he was encircled by the Nephites, who were speechless, believing they were in the presence of an angel (see 3 Nephi 11:8). The thought processes of the mind and the spiritual witness in the heart had not yet combined to help them understand who stood in their midst.

The Savior then introduced himself as Jesus Christ, the light and life of the world. The Nephites learned that he had "drunk out of that bitter cup" given to him by the Father and had "glorified the Father in taking upon [himself] the sins of the world" (3 Nephi 11:11). Before this moment, the thoughts and feelings of the people were disjointed, and they remained confused about the person descending out of the heavens. Despite being told "This is my Beloved Son," their thoughts were not clear, and their reaction remained one of awe rather than of humility. As the Savior's words registered in their minds and hearts, awe and wonderment changed to worship, and the multitude fell to the earth, knowing they were in the presence of Deity. The power that comes with a clear message in the mind combined with the spiritual burning in the bosom is illustrated by this change in their demeanor.

Searching diligently in the light of Christ can have that same effect on each of us as we put off the natural woman or man, humble ourselves, yield to the enticings of the Holy Spirit, become submissive as a child, and receive the fruits of the Spirit. Like King Benjamin's people, we too may have a mighty change of heart come to us, and we will "have no more disposition to do evil, but to do good continually" (Mosiah 5:2). Spiritual rebirth requires us to search diligently in the light of Christ that we may know truth. Sacred truths come when both the heart and the mind are active participants in the process.

LAY HOLD UPON EVERY GOOD THING

The second step along Mormon's path of discipleship is to lay hold on every good thing, to incorporate sacred truths into our lives. This involves faith, repentance, participation in sacred covenants, companionship of the Holy Spirit, and enduring to the end. It does not mean laying hold on every good thing all at once. The principle is "line upon line, precept upon precept, here a little and there a little" (2 Nephi 28:30). Also, the command to serve God with "all your heart, might, mind and strength" (D&C 4:2) should leave one exhausted at the *end* of life, not midway through the journey. The Lord expects us to pace ourselves, to "run and not be weary, and . . . walk and not faint" (D&C 89:20).

The prophet Nephi explains what it means to serve God

with all one's heart. He states that the objective is to serve with "full purpose of heart, acting no hypocrisy and no deception . . . , but with real intent, repenting of your sins, witnessing unto the Father that ye are willing to take upon you the name of Christ, by baptism . . . then shall ye receive the Holy Ghost; yea, then cometh the baptism of fire and of the Holy Ghost" (2 Nephi 31:13).

To serve with all one's heart is to serve with full purpose of heart. The concern is with direction, not speed. The process allows for repentance. What counts is one's desire and determination, not an extraordinary burst of energy. Although the Lord expects us to do our best, he is looking for steady candlepower on a hill and not bright flashes in the sky that briefly illuminate but then fade.

The woman who touched Christ's garment and was healed is a wonderful example of faith, determination, and resolution. Her motives were pure. There was no hypocrisy or deception in her hoping her actions would go unnoticed. She did not want to inconvenience the Master or disturb those listening to him. The woman had spent all her income on physicians, hoping to be cured of a blood disease, but to no avail. With great faith, this sister disciple sought out Jesus and in the midst of a crowd "came behind him, and touched the border of his garment" and was healed. Jesus experienced the withdrawal of spiritual power. He inquired of his disciples, "Who touched me?" The disciples pointed to the multitude thronging him and suggested that it could be any number of persons. Jesus persisted, sensing the special person in his midst and the nature of the event. The woman then came forward, "trembling, and falling down before him, she declared unto him before all the people for what cause she had touched him, and how she was healed immediately. And he said unto her, Daughter, be of good comfort: thy faith hath made thee whole; go in peace" (Luke 8:43–48).

The story teaches at least two lessons. One concerns Christ's spiritual sensitivity to the individual woman. In the midst of the multitude pressing against him, he was aware that one person had not only touched him physically but had made contact with the garment of his soul. The other lesson is the depth of the woman's faith. Because of her faith, she was healed both physically and spiritually. The phrase "thy faith hath made thee whole" often refers to a spiritual healing. It is the same phrase Christ used to bless the one leper who returned to express thanks. All ten lepers were cleansed of leprosy, but only one was made whole—only one was cleansed from within (see Luke 17:11–19). It is also the phrase used by the Lord in answering Enos's question regarding forgiveness of sin. When the voice said, "Enos, thy sins are forgiven thee, and thou shalt be blessed," Enos inquired as to how it was possible. The answer was "thy faith hath made thee whole" (Enos 1:5–8). Enos's spiritual cleansing came through faith. His faith had the power to produce humility, repentance, and a baptism of water and fire. The woman's faith brought the same power enjoyed by Enos and by the leper. Her faith produced a spiritual rebirth in addition to solving her physical problem. Her faith and determination allowed her to lay hold on two good gifts.

As mentioned earlier, the race is not necessarily to the swift but to those who endure—those who continue in the quest to lay hold on good things, those who are facing in the right direction, those still striving to eliminate a few discordant notes in their lives. In the tenth chapter of Moroni, the prophet states that Christ's grace is sufficient, that we will be "perfected in him" if we deny ourselves of ungodliness (v. 33). The capacity of the Atonement is more than sufficient to wash our garments white though they be as scarlet, to lift and change us from mortality to immortality, from corruptible to incorruptible beings (see Isaiah 1:18; 1 Corinthians 15:42–44). For most of us, this spiritual rebirth process stretches across a lifetime and into the next, as we are refined one step and one principle at a time.

THE BLESSING OF ENDURING

Living and serving faithfully with all one's heart, might, mind, and strength is really a function of steadily enduring, of doing one's best each day, in contrast to great bursts of energy that one tries to prolong. Almost thirty years ago I met a wonderful sister who, in the intervening years, demonstrated the power of enduring to the end. Her name is Virginia Cutler. She is now deceased, having passed away four years ago. During the summer of 1969, Virginia and I met in West Africa, where she was serving as a Fulbright Fellow at the University of Ghana developing a home economics department for the university. I was a member of a World Bank team advising the government on economic matters. The two of us plus one other were the only members of the Church in the country at the time. We met on occasion to discuss the gospel, our common interests, and our work. I was struck by Virginia's wonderful laugh and quick mind, by her generosity and quick acceptance of all people as brothers and sisters.

Born in Utah, she had attended the University of Utah on a four-year scholarship, graduating in 1926. She taught for a short time and then married Ralph Cutler, a farmer. Within two years of the marriage, her husband came in one day deathly ill. Within a few hours he was gone. At the time, she had one little son and another soon to be born. It was 1931, the depths of the Depression. She returned to teaching to provide for herself and her two sons. Within a short time, however, she felt a strong desire to improve her circumstances. With the encouragement of her bishop and former faculty members at the University of Utah, she applied for a scholarship at Stanford. There she completed her master's degree and went on to Cornell for her Ph.D. She finished at Cornell a full fifteen years from the time she entered Stanford, but that pace was deliberate: she managed the programs so that the two boys were an integral part of her life.

In 1946, she returned home to head the Home Economics

Department at the University of Utah. Once her boys were grown, she accepted an appointment with the United States State Department as an education advisor in Southeast Asia. Seven years later she returned to Utah to become dean of the College of Family Living at Brigham Young University. When we met near the end of her career, she was a Fulbright scholar, establishing a program to train young West African women to become better mothers, teachers, and homemakers.

Toward the end of the summer, as both of us were preparing to return to the United States, she shared one regret that had occupied her thoughts for some time. For most of the years since her husband's death, she had lived in places where Latter-day Saints were sparse and temples did not exist. Consequently, temple worship was missing in her life. She believed that there was one more good thing she should lay hold upon. She then told me of her plan. She would return to her small Provo apartment, and when the new Provo Temple opened she would begin serving. Her goal was to perform as many endowment ordinances as there had been weeks since receiving her first recommend as a young woman. It had been almost fifty years, and her goal was twenty-five hundred.

Our paths did not cross for another eleven years. In 1980, I was called as president of the Provo Utah Sharon East Stake. One of the first members to seek renewal of a temple recommend was my friend, Virginia, a member of the stake. After the interview, as we were reminiscing about our African odyssey, she said, "President Bateman, do you remember our conversation in which I shared my temple goals with you?"

I remembered. How could I forget?

She then said, "I have almost reached my goal. May I share with you a special experience I had in the temple recently? During one of the sessions I was thinking about the sisters for whom I had performed vicarious ordinances. I began wondering if they were aware of the work I had done. Was someone on the other side helping them? I wondered if my husband was

31

aware of my efforts and if he was preparing the sisters to receive their blessings." Typical of Virginia, she then said, "He better be!" She continued, "As those thoughts passed through my mind, I suddenly saw a man's hand pierce the veil of mortality from the other side. I recognized the hand. It was my husband's. I had not seen it in sixty years. I knew he was there. I knew that he knew of my work and that he was assisting sisters on the other side of the veil. I was so glad to be in the temple that day. I can hardly wait to greet him and the sisters he will introduce to me."

Sister Virginia Cutler was faithful to the end. By laying hold upon one more good thing, she took hold of her husband's hand and became his partner in the work beyond the veil. One more good thing brought much happiness to her in her later life. Today, she counts twenty-five hundred women among her best friends.

I am grateful for a Savior and Redeemer. I appreciate his teachings and the great plan of happiness. I am grateful to know that we are spirit sons and daughters of an Almighty Father and that we can become begotten daughters and sons of the resurrected Lord through diligently searching in his light and applying his truths in our lives. May each of us continue the quest for eternal life by "lay[ing] hold upon every good thing" (Moroni 7:19).

NOTE

1. Earlier in the chapter, Mormon notes that every woman and man receives the light of Christ as a gift to differentiate right from wrong. A more common name for this light is conscience, a discerning power by which individuals know good from evil (see Moroni 7:15–17).

The original presentation of this essay is available on audiocassette from Deseret Book or on the Internet at http://coned.byu.edu/cw/womens.htm

A FIRE BURNING

SILVIA HENRIQUEZ ALLRED

His word was in mine heart as a burning fire.
—Jeremiah 20:9

I was born and raised in a Catholic home in El Salvador. My parents were average Catholic members, so our family went to church for baptisms, confirmations, communions, weddings, deaths, and anniversaries. As children we learned the appropriate rituals and prayers and had the proper ordinances performed at the recommended ages. Because we lived in a large city, we did not belong to any particular small parish but instead attended different churches every time we went and never developed close relationships with the priests or nuns in our community. Still, I was very spiritually oriented. I recited my prayers with much devotion and belief. I enjoyed reading about the lives of the martyrs and sometimes secretly wished I were one.

My parents and my six brothers and sisters and I lived with my maternal grandparents. My grandfather, who was in the military, owned a new house in a subdivision. We had lived in this house for just a few months when on a beautiful August morning, two young missionaries knocked at our door. Normally they

Silvia Henriquez Allred, who was born in El Salvador, is a member of the Young Women General Board. She served a full-time mission in Central America and accompanied her husband in presiding over the Paraguay Asuncion Mission. They are the parents of eight children.

33

would have found only my grandmother and mother at home; the rest of us would have been either at work or school. On this particular morning, however, my sister, who was seventeen, my aunt, who was nineteen, and I, who was fourteen, were studying for semester finals. We answered the door, and out of courtesy, all five of us sat down to listen to the missionaries' message.

One elder was new and spoke very little Spanish. (In those days, before there was the Missionary Training Center, missionaries didn't learn language skills before they traveled to their missions.) The other missionary was very fluent. He spoke to us about the Godhead and the nature of God. They gave us some pamphlets, and we agreed to let them come back in about three days.

This experience was totally new for us. We had never met anyone who was not Catholic. In my all-girl school, in our neighborhood, and in my family, everyone was Catholic. Religious discussions were totally foreign to us. After the missionaries left, we all agreed that we had felt something during the forty-five minutes of conversation with these missionaries. We didn't know how to explain our feelings, but they were unlike anything we had ever felt before.

Because we were curious, we read the pamphlets before the missionaries returned. They came in the evening when the whole family was at home. We all sat down and listened attentively to their message. This time they talked to us about the early Christian church and the Great Apostasy that followed the death of the apostles. Again they left pamphlets, but this time they also invited us to come to church—a very special meeting on Sunday that they called a district conference. Members from all over the country would be there. This was in 1959, when missionary work in El Salvador had just begun and LDS Church membership was very small. After much pondering, my sister, aunt, and I—not knowing what to expect—summoned the courage to go.

We had to take two buses and walk a little way to a large,

old but classy, rented house. Just as the missionaries said, people had traveled from many other places. The missionaries were right there at the door, waiting happily for us. They introduced us to other missionaries and to some young members, and then we sat down in the overflow area on the patio. (The living room-dining room was used for the main seating area.)

We liked what we experienced. The songs seemed happy, unlike the ones I remembered from the Catholic church. The mission president spoke about the growth of the Church and his recent visit to Maracaibo, Venezuela. I understood very little of what was going on, but I remember the feeling, just like I had felt when those missionaries had been at our home.

On their third visit, the elders talked to us about the Restoration and mentioned for the first time Joseph Smith and the Book of Mormon. Would we be interested in buying a Book of Mormon? they asked. We were. The whole family was home, but by this time some members had decided they were not interested. Little by little during the discussion, first my grandparents, and then my mother, excused themselves—until only a few of us remained. But we bought the Book of Mormon, and the missionaries left more pamphlets.

My sister and I raced to see who could read the book first. Neither of us had ever read or even held a Bible before. This was common in a Catholic family then. We were fascinated to be able to open this book and read things about God. We had one book for us to share, and we read it in two weeks. School was forgotten because we were more interested in this brand-new experience. I read with intensity, soaking up this new knowledge.

When we shared our new interest in the Church with our extended family, they were outraged. How could we betray our faith? They put pressure on the family; that may have been one reason why my grandparents stopped listening to the missionaries then. My sister and I started praying as the missionaries had taught us. I don't know when during those first experiences of reading the Book of Mormon that I felt that it was true. But I remember a certain feeling when I was reading in Alma 29:1. Like Alma, I wanted to have the voice of a trump, like an angel, to shout out what I was discovering. I wanted everybody to know. Why couldn't they see that Heavenly Father had a body just like ours? Or that the Trinity was three separate beings? Why couldn't they see the possibilities of a relationship between God and us—that we could pray to him and he would answer?

By this time, my sister Ana Dina and I started going to church twice on Sunday and twice during the week for Mutual and Bible study classes. We became thoroughly immersed in our new activities in the Church. Though my aunt stopped attending, a couple of my younger brothers and sisters joined us.

When we finished the Book of Mormon, we bought a copy of the Doctrine and Covenants. That only took us one week, so the missionaries told us about the *Articles of Faith,* which we bought and started to read. Next we took on *A Marvelous Work and a Wonder,* which became my favorite because I could use it to answer any questions my friends or family had about the Church. It became my missionary tool, and I wasn't even a member.

Two months had passed since the missionaries had first knocked at our door. We wanted to be baptized, though the missionaries had never even mentioned baptism. At that time, investigators had to wait a year before they could receive baptism. I didn't know about this requirement. When we asked to be baptized, the missionaries said, "Yes, but since you are just fifteen and your sister is seventeen, you need written permission from your parents." We asked our parents. My father promptly said yes. He preferred religious studies to wild parties or boys and was happy for us.

But my mother was receiving pressure from her family. How could she let us betray our faith? Surely those missionaries had fooled us. Who knew what we were doing there! She would not give her permission. For the next month we begged and begged. Even the missionaries and branch members wondered if we were pushing things too quickly. Although we had read almost all the LDS books that had been translated into Spanish, they still wondered if we were really interested in becoming Church members. We were. Finally one day when my mother was sick in bed, we caught her in a weak moment and she signed the permission form.

In our Catholic tradition, ordinances were major events to be shared with all relatives and friends. (We had no idea what to expect from a Mormon baptism.) "You have to be there," we told our mother. "Parents are always at baptisms." We finally convinced her that since she had signed the permit, she had to be there. My father did not come, but my mother brought my younger brothers and sisters. The evening of November 24, all the missionaries, investigators, and active members of the branch were present. We were baptized in the old rented building and confirmed. The missionaries then asked if we would share our testimonies. My heart just pounded. As I began to speak, a warmth filled my whole body. I could feel a fire burning, and that fire has never left my heart.

As I began speaking, the only thing I could see in the congregation was my mother's face. I wanted her to know and feel what I was feeling. The Spirit touched her, and right after the meeting she approached the missionaries and asked them to resume teaching her the discussions. A month later, she and my younger brothers and sisters were baptized. The whole family, except my father, was then committed to the gospel.

I realize, however, that conversion can bring very real challenges and trials. My husband and I have seen young men who have had to look for another home because they have been disowned by their families. We have seen husbands beating their wives because they go to church. We have seen parents abusing and beating their children for going to church. All this is real. I thank my Heavenly Father it has been easy for me.

SEARCHING DILIGENTLY
IN THE LIGHT OF CHRIST

WENDY L. WATSON

When I was growing up, I read and studied in various places in our home. It didn't matter where I was—in the front room, at the kitchen table, or in my bed—my mother would always find me and say, "Would you like a little more light on the subject?" Actually, I usually wanted a lot more light on the subject. I needed increased illumination—of the pages, of my mind, and of the topic.

She would then turn on a light. Her consistent interest and comforting presence would tell me that even the seemingly impossible task before me was indeed possible, that with continuing effort on my part and the increased light she had provided, I would succeed.

Our theme for this women's conference volume is Moroni 7:19: "Wherefore, I beseech of you, . . . that ye should search diligently in the light of Christ that ye may know good from evil; and if ye will lay hold upon every good thing, and condemn it not, ye certainly will be a child of Christ."

Here Moroni is giving us the words of his father, Mormon, at a time when Moroni hadn't thought he himself would still be

Wendy L. Watson holds a Ph.D. in family therapy and gerontology from the University of Calgary in Calgary, Alberta, Canada. She is a professor in the Department of Family Sciences at Brigham Young University and serves as chair-elect for the 1998 BYU Women's Conference.

alive, let alone writing more on the plates. He begins his final addition to the record: "I had supposed not to have written more, but I have not as yet perished" (Moroni 1:1).

That puts a whole new spin on "publish or perish," doesn't it? These are some of the last recordings of a man who had thought he would be dead by then. Marilyn Arnold notes: "Not only did [Moroni] conclude and conceal the record, but he made of his very life a shield around it." I like that. "Preserving it became perhaps the primary purpose of his existence. We cannot begin to contemplate its preciousness to him who had lost everything but his life and his resolute faith."[1]

What words of great price does Moroni carefully select to conclude his record? Among them are these: "Search diligently in the light of Christ" and "lay hold upon every good thing" (Moroni 7:19). These two admonitions are, of course, related by their connection to Christ. In Moroni 7:24, Mormon tells us, "All things which are good cometh of Christ."

When Mormon admonishes us to search diligently in the light of Christ so that we can know good from evil, I hear his wisdom about these last days—our days—in which some people do indeed "call evil good, and good evil," and some "put darkness for light, and light for darkness," and some "put bitter for sweet, and sweet for bitter" (2 Nephi 15:20). Some call the prophets men without vision; and others call wickedness a right. Distinguishing good from evil, light from darkness, is critical in these latter days.

Many may say, "Good from evil? That's not a problem for me. I'm trying to figure out 'better from best' these days." We may need, however, to discern other subtle but significant distinctions that either invite more light into our life or dispel the light that is already there. Our spiritual wattage will often be increased or diminished, depending on the distinctions we make and hold to.

Sometimes we as Latter-day Saint women make distinctions about each other that are not useful. We distinguish between those women who do crafts, and those who don't; those who work outside the home, and those who don't; those who are married, and those who aren't; those who do their visiting teaching, and those who don't; those who are presently participating in church activities, and those who are not. These deeply ingrained distinctions come complete with embedded assumptions, expectations, and permission to behave in certain ways toward the groups so distinguished. Should we go so far as to say that these distinctions—which subtly imply that some of us are "good Latter-day Saint" women and others are "bad Latter-day Saint" women—should we say that these very distinctions are in themselves bad—even evil? These distinctions certainly do not knit our hearts together nor make us His.

Mormon proposes that once we discern good from evil, we then commence to "lay hold upon every good thing" (Moroni 7:19). Before we can lay hold upon good things, however, I believe that we have to lay down some other things first. Let me offer you six beliefs that I find prevent women from laying hold upon every good thing:

1. The belief that we have to lay hold upon every good thing all at once. The grand smorgasbord of life is before us. It all looks so good. What do we choose? Can we have it all? More important, can we have it right now and all at once? Most women who appear to have it all, all at once, confess that they usually pay quite a high price with their own or their family members' physical, emotional, mental, or relationship health. One woman lamented, "I wish someone had told me I had to make a choice."

So what's a woman to do? The scriptures tell us, "To every thing there is a season" (Ecclesiastes 3:1). We all know that the season is in "the own due time of the Lord" (1 Nephi 10:3). There will be times that we need to "run with patience the race that is set before us" (Hebrews 12:1), and at the same time we are not supposed to run faster than we are able (see Mosiah 4:27). And there will be many times that we need to stand still (see D&C 5:34), to "be still and know that [he is] God" (D&C 101:16).

That leads us to the next constraining belief.

2. The belief that we know how our life should be and will be and that we are the captain of our ship. Being so certain about how our life will be, how our life will turn out, may constrain us from being open to continuing personal revelation from the Lord that can shift the direction of our life—even in a moment—moving us away from our destination and even away from our shipmates.

Made-to-measure ironies are part of each woman's compressed, personalized curriculum of life. The constraining belief that our plan for our life is the only one that counts causes problems when our life-ironies challenge our five-year plans—and some weeks, even our five-day plans. Diligently searching for more light and responding to these ironies with humility and resiliency allows us to live fully the perpetually unexpected life.

My mother loved the lights in the firmament. Each comet, each planet, each star—falling or not—each phase of the moon, was something to celebrate. She would phone from 150 miles away and excitedly invite me to "run out and look at the moon!" She wanted to share the good light she was seeing. One of my mother's life-ironies was that in the last months of her life, she lost her physical vision. She was blind. She, who had taught others to see more clearly, widely, and enthusiastically, now had her eyes veiled until she passed through the veil.

Her trial brought sorrow and anguish into my life. I needed extra light to understand and endure; however, enduring—rather than just persevering—often tutors us into remembering who we really are—perhaps even jogging loose a premortal memory of a commitment or two.

3. The belief that we are more correct than others: the sin of certainty! [2] Believing that there is one right way to look at something and we have it does not invite others or more light into our life. Wives have found that when they "know" the one right way to view everything and do everything, husbands are not invited to intertwine their lives, to really forge a marriage relationship.

When we hold to the belief that we are right and others are wrong, there is no room, let alone need, for further light. We already have it all—or so we believe. Our sin of certainty and subsequent actions allow no room for others to co-create with us even more good things.

What there is room for, however, and what is invited in, is unrighteous dominion. And as Elder H. Burke Peterson has pointed out, women can exercise unrighteous dominion just as well as men can.[3]

4. *The belief that words don't matter, that words can't hurt.* This belief is promoted by that old childhood rhyme: "Sticks and stones may break my bones, but words will never hurt me." What a terrible thing to teach a child in the name of building thick skins. Thick skins, yes; thin hearts, absolutely.

In 1 Peter 2:1, the apostle Peter speaks to the importance of words. He counsels us to "[lay] aside all malice, and all guile, and hypocrisies, . . . and all evil speakings."

Words do matter. They lodge in our cells and in our souls.

One woman told me: "My husband's words hit me, and they hurt me so much. I think the word *stupid* is the meanest word in the whole world because I've heard it so much. I'm not stupid. I know I'm not, but the word still hurts because this is the person I love, and when he calls me that, it makes me feel so bad. It hurts. It hurts my soul. My soul wants to run away and hide. But I can't because this is my marriage."

This young couple who came to me for marital counseling had been struggling with difficulties in their relationship from the beginning of their less-than-two-year marriage. They were successful in resolving their difficulties once they worked together on dissolving the barrier of words they had unwittingly co-created.

Over time, individual cutting words build into full conversations of accusation and recrimination.[4] These conversations are filled with complaints of unfulfilled expectations: "You never . . . "; "You didn't. . . . " Each person suffers emotionally and even physically, and the relationship disintegrates.

At the same time "building" words strengthen relationships, just words alone are not enough. In 1 Peter 1:22 we read about the need for unfeigned love. Feigned love occurs when the words of love are present but the behavior of love is not. I met with a young couple contemplating marriage whose relationship had drifted into trouble. In that anguishing interview, they repeatedly threw venomous words—*hate, trapped, violated, oppressed*—back and forth at each other, juxtaposing all those hateful words with the sacred word *love*.

Instead of "I love you," this couple should have added a few more words between *I love* and *you*. "*I love* oppressing *you*." "*I love* how you squirm when I berate *you*." "*I love* seeing *you* suffer." "*I love* being more right than *you* are—and showing you that!" These sentences would represent more accurately their experiences in the relationship. Using the word *love* is not enough. If the word *love* doesn't match your behavior or fit the experience of the one you claim so to "love," please use another word.

So, again, words do matter. They lodge in our cells and in our souls. Maya Angelou, past United States poet laureate, has written of words that lodge in the walls of our homes. If words lodge in our cells, souls, and walls, we need words—and tones that accompany those words—that build and maintain the temples of our bodies and the temples of our homes.

Elder Jeffrey R. Holland spoke of a hopeful, encouraging, peaceful word in a recent general conference. That word was *repentance*. He said: "The very beauty of the word *repentance* is the promise of escaping old problems and old habits and old sorrows and old sins. It is among the most hopeful and encouraging—and yes, most peaceful—words in the gospel vocabulary."[5]

His thoughts on repentance suggest a fifth constraining belief:

5. *The troublesome belief that sounds like this: "My past, which was filled with wrongdoing, predicts and determines my future. I am not worthy to lay hold upon any good thing, let alone every good thing, because I am bad, tainted, unclean, beyond hope!"* Does that sound familiar? For far too many women, it does.

This constraining belief needs to be laid on the altar of repentance. The guilt and grief we feel are a good sign, an indication of our continued goodness, in spite of our sins. We should congratulate ourselves on still being able to feel guilty! The light is still there. Guilt has had a lot of bad press in the past, yet for most of us, guilt—if used well—is exactly the help most of us need to stop sinning and start toward full repentance.

Let guilt start us on the path of the sincere, heartfelt, and therefore heart-changing process of laying down our sins, even giving away our sins to know the Lord (see Alma 22:18). And as we come to know him, and come unto him, we will also come to know our real selves, unshackled and free from the past. The Savior really did mean it when he said, "Though your sins be as scarlet, they shall be as white as snow; though they be red like crimson, they shall be as wool" (Isaiah 1:18).

The Savior and our ecclesiastical leaders will lead us along, helping us cast off constraining beliefs about repentance. My heart still aches for the woman who told me she believed that sin was like pounding nails into a beautifully smooth board and repentance was like pulling the nails out of that board. After repentance, the nails would be gone, but the board would still be left marred with holes from the nails, never to be as it had once been. She indicated she had learned this from a Primary teacher. (I say "learned" because I am not sure what the teacher believed or intended to teach.) But this woman, from her childhood on, had held that image of sin and repentance and as an adult saw herself as permanently unclean and unworthy. Oh, how we need to be careful about our metaphors when teaching children! The only board and nails that are important in teaching about repentance are the ones that formed the cross upon which the Savior was crucified for our sins.

This particular woman's belief that nothing she could do would ever make the board whole again is partially right. She can't do it, especially on her own. That's why she needs to take the board to the Savior. His grace is more than sufficient, not just to remove any nails but to remove the holes and make the board whole again, as though the nails had never been there. The Lord says he will remember our sins no more (see Hebrews 8:12), so why would he leave nail holes in the board to remind us of those sins? It is the prints of the nails in his hands and feet that he wants us to remember.

I love his words: "I, the Lord, forgive sins, and am merciful unto those who confess their sins with humble hearts" (D&C 61:2). *Please believe me,* I hear him saying, *I forgive sins. Come to me. Bring your humble heart. Confess your sins. I am full of mercy.*

As we take responsibility for our wrong choices, experience sincere remorse, and deeply desire to turn away from our sins (even our favorite ones)—choosing instead to keep the commandments and devote time to building up the kingdom—we each can experience the Savior saying, "Daughter, be of good comfort; thy faith hath made thee whole" (Matthew 9:22). He said it to the woman who touched the hem of his garment, and he will say it to me and to you as we come unto him.

6. The constraining belief that involves unforgiveness and sounds something like this: "I don't have to forgive evil, cruel, or corrupt people."

45

Many of us act as if forgiveness and repentance are only for the righteous: "Oh, she's a basically good person. I forgive her." What about those who have caused us physical, emotional, mental, or spiritual pain and suffering? What about those who have broken seemingly every commandment and who have profoundly affected our life through their choice to sin? What about hypocrites? What about the unrepentant? Do we have to forgive them?

Let's see what the Lord says. In Doctrine and Covenants 64:10 we read: "I, the Lord, will forgive whom I will forgive, but of you it is required to forgive all men." A lot of us act as if this scripture reads in the reverse: God will forgive all; we as mortals will pick and choose whom we will forgive, based on our own standard of forgiveability. And the ultimate criterion of what is or is not forgiveable seems to be that the sinner must first suffer more than those who have suffered at the sinner's hands.

And what happens if we don't forgive another who has wronged us? The Lord is very clear about the outcome: "For, if ye forgive men their trespasses your heavenly Father will also forgive you; but if ye forgive not men their trespasses neither will your Father forgive your trespasses" (3 Nephi 13:14–15). And "wherefore, I say unto you, that ye ought to forgive one another; for he that forgiveth not his brother his trespasses standeth condemned before the Lord; for there remaineth in him the greater sin" (D&C 64:9).

Could this possibly mean that if we do not forgive someone who has wronged and harmed us that we become more sinful than the initial sinner? I believe the Lord means what he says. He hasn't provided his words just to give us something to read at night. He has said that "the greater sin" is to remain unforgiving, and he means just that.

In my clinical practice I see almost daily the outcome and effects of unforgiveness. Unforgiveness increases suffering. Unforgiveness is lethal. Bitterness, resentments, and malice, like dark words, lodge in our minds, hearts, cells, and souls and wreak havoc, causing more mental and emotional pain, more physical and spiritual agony, than even the initial sin brought about.

The Lord's plea that we quit hanging onto the sins of others in no way lessens the gravity of sin or the culpability of the sinner. As the 1995 proclamation to the world on the family states: "We warn that individuals who violate covenants of chastity, who abuse spouse or offspring, or who fail to fulfill family responsibilities will one day stand accountable before God."[6] But if we find ourselves drumming our fingers and saying to the sinner, either out loud or under our breath, "Your day will come," we just may have a little more soul work to do on forgiveness.

In Doctrine and Covenants 64:8, the Lord tells us that we are to forgive one another in our hearts—not in our mouths, not in our minds. This kind of forgiving is not easy, not something that happens overnight. To forgive in our hearts involves a deep spring-cleaning of our souls, even a change of heart so that all the acid constraints of unforgiveness are gone and can never come back. It may be a long process, but it is possible or the Lord would not have commanded us to do it. He will help us find the way if we ask him.

Now that we have laid aside six constraining beliefs, let's consider Mormon's words: "Lay hold upon every good thing" (Moroni 7:19). To "lay hold" upon something implies focusing and permanence. When we "lay hold" upon something, it becomes real to us. We embrace it and it becomes ours.

What happens if, instead of laying hold upon the good we find, we just touch it lightly?

What's the effect of superficial readings of the scriptures?

What's the effect of service that is done to be seen of women?

What happens when we join or belong to the Church in the same way that some of us join a gym, showing up only sporadically and without real commitment and sustained involvement?

What happens when year after year we do not lay hold upon the good things but continue to touch them only lightly?

After a while, we may find that we are not losing our life in His service and for His sake, but rather that we're just losing our life, losing our heart's former desires, losing our stamina, and sadly, even losing our interest in good things (see Matthew 10:39). Thinking we have "been there, done that" with good things, we may move from touching them lightly, to dabbling occasionally, to taking them for granted, and even sometimes to making fun of them.

As our spiritual life wanes, discouragement and despondency may set in, and we may wonder what is wrong when we are "doing everything right," albeit superficially. We're doing good things, aren't we? Yes, but without depth, without passion, without deep love, without vigor, without commitment, and without ever really laying hold upon the good things. And thus the joys that come from laying hold upon good things continually elude our wavering grasp.

Thus Mormon's words are rivetingly true: For our own happiness and salvation, we must "lay hold upon every good thing."

What are the good things that you need and want in your life? What are the good things that you already have in your life—that you do not want taken from you? In your deepest heart of hearts, what constitutes "good things" for you these days?

How about your family? We are all members of a family. Is yours a good thing? Are you laying hold upon every good thing in your family?

What good quality about your husband have you been noticing these days?

What good thing about your sister has been waiting for you to notice and lay hold upon?

When was the last time your child overheard you talking on the phone to a friend, saying, "I don't know what I ever did to merit having a daughter who . . ." or "I'm so blessed to have a son who . . . "

But what about family members with obstreperous behavior or borderline—perhaps even full-blown—prodigal-son ways? Now more than ever is the time to study them and lay hold upon every good thing about them. Secure their goodness. Make it real—for you and for them.

When we recognize and lay hold on the good things in our family, we actually increase the good; because in order to offer sincere commendations, honest compliments, and specific praise, we have to really study a subject. When we care enough to look closely, to get up close and notice, we will see our family members in a new light and be able to commend them on their goodness, their competence, their courage, their tenacity, perhaps even their patience with us. That means we need to be with them in a very different way, and that different way of being together will invite more light—and our ability to lay hold upon even more good things will increase.

One of the marvelous things about commendations, as opposed to condemnations, is that they increase the likelihood that our other words will be received with increased influence. Isn't that just what Joseph Smith told us? Listen to his words: "When persons manifest the least kindness and love to me, O what power it has over my mind."[7]

Is it any wonder that relationships start building naturally and securely in a commendation-saturated environment? The commendations build into conversations of affirmation and affection and confirm each family members' worth and value. These conversations assist in healing the mind, body, and spirit. When was the last time you had a heart-to-heart talk with a family member that in some way healed you?

Researchers have become very interested in what I am calling the commendation-versus-condemnation ratio. They have found that a certain ratio of positive to negative communication needs to be present in a marriage to keep it on a pathway to improvement and increased happiness.[8] I believe that their findings apply to all relationships within a family and to all relationships that feel like family.

The magic ratio the researchers found was 5:1. That is, as long as there are at least five times more affection, humor, smiling, complimenting, agreement, empathy, and active, nondefensive listening than there is criticism and disagreement, marriage and other relationships will prosper. So, what does the ratio in your home look like these days?

As we increase the number of conversations of affirmation and affection and decrease the conversations of accusation and recrimination and condemnation, every good thing about our family will become more palpable and therefore easier for us to lay hold upon. Not only that, but because there is such a connection between light and love, the increasing love in our family will invite more light, and the increased light will invite more love. Now, how's that for a virtuous cycle?

What other good things are you drawn toward? What other good things would you like to lay hold upon?

A greater understanding of the scriptures?

More peace in your life? More patience? More charity?

Mormon tells us, in the last verse of Moroni 7, to "pray unto the Father with all the energy of heart, that ye may be filled with this love [which is charity], which he hath bestowed upon all who are true followers of his Son, Jesus Christ; that ye may become the sons [and daughters] of God." Today is the day for us as Latter-day Saint women to search diligently in the light of Christ and to make choices that invite an increase of his light into our lives so that we can "lay hold upon every good thing." May we through our Lord's atoning power increasingly see as the Savior sees and love as he loves and become his own.

NOTES

1. Marilyn Arnold, *Sweet Is the Word: Reflections on the Book of Mormon—Its Narrative, Teachings, and People* (American Fork, Utah: Covenant, 1996), 345.

2. Humberto Maturana, *Biology, Emotions, and Culture* (videocassette 6), November 1992 (Calgary, Alberta, Canada: Vanry and Associates).

3. H. Burke Peterson, "Unrighteous Dominion," *Ensign,* July 1989, 7.

4. See Lorraine M. Wright, Wendy L. Watson, and Janice M. Bell, *Beliefs: The Heart of Healing in Families and Illness* (New York: Basic Books, 1996).

5. Jeffrey R. Holland, "The Peaceable Things of the Kingdom," *Ensign,* November 1996, 83.

6. "The Family: A Proclamation to the World," *Ensign,* November 1995, 102.

7. The Prophet Joseph Smith taught: "Nothing is so much calculated to lead people to forsake sin as to take them by the hand, and watch over them with tenderness. When persons manifest the least kindness and love to me, O what power it has over my mind, while the opposite course has a tendency to harrow up all the harsh feelings and depress the human mind." *Teachings of the Prophet Joseph Smith,* sel. Joseph Fielding Smith (Salt Lake City: Deseret Book, 1938), 240.

8. See John Gottman and Nan Silver, *Why Marriages Succeed or Fail* (New York: Simon and Schuster, 1994).

The original presentation of this essay is available on audiocassette from Deseret Book or on the Internet at http://coned.byu.edu/cw/womens.htm

THE BEACONS OF HIS LIGHT

MARY ELLEN W. SMOOT

Lighthouses have stood for centuries, signaling a true and consistent message to travelers. The Egyptians completed one of the world's largest lighthouses in Alexandria. Over four hundred feet high, it guided ships for more than fifteen hundred years until it was destroyed in an earthquake. Atop each lighthouse is a beacon of powerful and distinctive light. Special lenses in the beacon increase the intensity of light from the inner lamp and allow the light to travel further and communicate the position of the shore to ships. These beacon lights guide ships safely away from danger and to shore.

Beacons are used not only in lighthouses but anywhere there is a need to guide or warn. We have been given spiritual beacons to help us travel safely through our earth life. Each of these beacons relies on the same source of light or truth—the eternal truths of the gospel of Jesus Christ. Christ himself acted as a beacon of that light during his life here upon the earth. He was the perfect beacon. In fact, through his mission he became synonymous with light and truth: "He . . . ascended up on high, as also he descended below all things, in that he

Mary Ellen Wood Smoot was called to serve as Relief Society General President in April 1997. She loves family history and research and has written the history of parents and grandparents as well as a history of their community. She served with her husband, Stanley M. Smoot, when he was called as a mission president in Ohio, and they later served together as directors of Church Hosting. They are the parents of seven children and grandparents of forty-five.

comprehended all things, that he might be in all and through all things, the light of truth; which truth shineth" (D&C 88:6–7).

President David O. McKay wrote: "Statesmen, men of science, thinking men in all nations, laymen everywhere sense the need of something definite to which to look forward, some clear beacon that will guide the stranded nations to a safe harbor or permanent peace."[1]

I can bear fervent testimony that our prophet and the Church are a beacon to the world. During the past eleven years, my husband and I have been serving in Church Hosting. In this capacity, we have hosted people from all over the world, as they come to take counsel from our prophet and leaders and to understand what enables the Church to do all that it does. The Church has hosted royalty, leaders of nations, ambassadors, journalists, and business and religious leaders from throughout the world; thousands come every year. Let me share a few of the sentiments expressed by these visitors.

One religious leader inquired, "How do you get your missionaries to voluntarily go out, at their own expense, for two years or eighteen months, and set all their goals and desires aside? We can't even get our youth to attend church services." A member of the Quorum of the Twelve responded, "It's a miracle, isn't it?"

Another visitor asked, "Where do you find so many volunteers? Everywhere we go we see people volunteering. And where do you find all of these commodities to send around the world for people in need?"

One journalist said, "I bring the international writers to Salt Lake City because if they just visit New York or Washington, D.C., they leave the United States saying we are anti-religion and anti-family. I bring them to Utah to witness families, to see parents who are still having and enjoying their children. My mother country has youth, including my own, who have stopped having children; there will soon be no one to take care of the parents and grandparents."

People need not visit Church headquarters to see the beacon of the gospel light. President Gordon B. Hinckley said in the October 1996 general conference: "I wish to say that none of us ever need hesitate to speak up for this Church, for its doctrine, for its people, for its divine organization and divinely given responsibility. It is true. It is the work of God. The only things that can ever embarrass this work are acts of disobedience to its doctrine and standards by those of its membership. That places upon each of us a tremendous responsibility. This work will be judged by what the world sees of our behavior. God give us the will to walk with faith, the discipline to do what is right at all times and in all circumstances, the resolution to make of our lives a declaration of this cause before all who see us."[2]

Latter-day Saint women, as sisters in the gospel, can be powerful beacons of our Savior's light regardless of our position in life. One such beacon was Mary Stretton Blood. Born in Yoxall, Staffordshire, England, on 25 July 1811, Mary Stretton was the sixth of nine children, with five brothers and three sisters. Mary's parents were sturdy, frugal, and hardworking—the strength of the British Isles, according to a descendant, Mary Linford, who researched Mary Stretton's history.

Mary was about five feet six inches tall, had light hair, blue eyes, and a clear rosy-and-white complexion. She was quick in her movements and very methodical. Little or nothing is known of Mary's early life, beyond the facts that became evident in her later years. From these it is known that she was carefully reared and well trained to take up life as a homemaker and a provider of household needs. She was a baker. She also was adept with knitting needles, and each evening throughout her life she knitted.

The earliest recorded incident in Mary Stretton's life took place when she was employed as a dairymaid at Hare Hill Farm, a gentleman's estate near Sudbury in Derbyshire. William Blood was employed at the same place as farm foreman. They fell in love and were married in the parish church in the neighboring town of Church Broughton on 16 February 1836. Shortly after their marriage, William and Mary opened a bakery and small store. William took a position with the railroad as "plate-layer," and Mary ran the shop. While they resided in Barton-under-Needwood, four children were born—first Ann, then William, Thomas (who died in infancy), and Mary.

In 1842 William returned home one evening and said, "Mary, I have heard the truth tonight, and I want you to go with me tomorrow night." He had heard Mormon elders speaking on the street. Mary and William listened to the message of the restored gospel and were converted. On 1 March 1843, they were baptized into the Church. William's large family turned against them because of their new religion. Mary said, "We shall not bother any of them," and very soon they sold their business and most of their belongings and left for America. They sailed 23 January 1844 on the ship *Fanny*. The Prophet Joseph Smith himself met the boat and greeted the new Saints in Nauvoo.

Almost immediately after they arrived, William became ill with the fever that was afflicting many. He passed away on 4 May 1844, only three weeks after he landed in Nauvoo, leaving Mary with their three children: Ann, William, and Mary. Another infant was born only four days after her father died. Mary named her Emma, but little Emma only lived a few weeks and was buried beside her father.

More shocking news was soon to come for this young woman. Just eight days after the death of her baby, Mary was stunned to hear that the Prophet Joseph Smith and his brother Hyrum had been martyred. For the remainder of her life, Mary remembered clearly the horrors of this period. With her husband and baby gone and the leader of her chosen people murdered, Mary could have turned on her heel and gone back to her family in England, where she would have had security and help in rearing her three living children. A less resolute and self-reliant woman would have been unnerved and crushed by so many losses coming one after another. But she remained undaunted. At this point in her life, she became a beacon of light to her posterity. She looked forward instead of turning back. She was present that historic moment when Brigham Young stood up to address the Saints, and she always declared that he spoke in the voice of Joseph Smith and appeared as if he were Joseph as he spoke. Mary pressed on, sustained by her testimony of the gospel of Jesus Christ and her commitment to do his will. She did not compromise or apologize for her belief.

I am grateful to this stalwart woman; her radiance beams light into my life. She did not foresee that her decision would bring glory on her head and the heads of her posterity forever. She simply did her part in standing firm in the gospel of Jesus Christ and being obedient to the promptings of the Spirit. Mary later married Henry Woolley, who was a good father to her children. They followed William Kay and helped settle Kaysville, Utah. Mary's grandson Henry Blood[3] became a governor in Utah. The number of descendants from her three living children now number more than one thousand. To measure the magnitude of goodness that has emanated from the life of this faithful beacon would be impossible. I honor the heritage and guiding light left by this devout woman and look forward to meeting her beyond the veil. Mary Stretton Blood was my great-great grandmother. Her life illustrates the principle identified by Frederic W. Farrar: "Christ came to convince us that a *relative* insignificance may be an *absolute* importance. He came to teach that continual excitement, prominent action, distinguished services, brilliant success, are not essential elements of a true and noble life, and that myriads of the beloved of God are to be found among the insignificant and the obscure."[4]

Beacons, however, can be obscured. Haze, smoke, fog, rain, or snow can dim the signal. Spiritual beacons sometimes fall prey to similar obstructions. The trends of the world can distract us from the light of Christ and lead us into dangerous waters. In recent decades, families have been deteriorating with alarming momentum. All of us have felt the repercussions. President Spencer W. Kimball stated: "Society without basic family life is without foundation and will disintegrate into nothingness."[5]

No activity has a more profound effect for good on society than a mother and father spending loving time nurturing and training a child in the true principles of the gospel of Jesus Christ. And there is no greater void than the absence of a mother from her child during the formative years of that child's life. Please guard against any influence or circumstance that would take a mother from the side of her child more than is absolutely necessary.

During my early childhood years, my world fit neatly within a several-block radius of my home in the small community of Clearfield, Utah. On one side of my home was the church house, built while my paternal grandfather, James G. Wood, was the first bishop of the Clearfield Ward. On the other side was the Smith Canning Factory, built by my maternal grandfather, Albert T. Smith, and across the street was the school. Life was peaceful and happy for my five sisters and me, daughters of Melvin and LaVora Wood.

The gospel of Jesus Christ was an integral part of our lives. My parents both served full-time missions before they were married in 1924. Family prayer was a ritual. Provident living and self-reliance were virtues instilled in us from an early age as we all placed seeds in the ground, watered, weeded, harvested, and canned or bottled in preparation for the winter months. We learned to fast every month and on special occasions to draw on the powers of heaven. We were taught love and respect for our grandparents and other relatives.

My sisters and I learned unconditional love for one another through our parents' example. We watched them love and serve others. Father was the bishop for nine of my growing years, and Mother taught Sunday School and Relief Society and later was both the ward and the stake Relief Society president. My parents taught us the fundamental principles of the gospel and bore testimony to us of their teachings by the way they lived.

As I grew and the boundaries of my world expanded, I had many opportunities to put to the test those lessons taught me by my parents. I learned for myself the truthfulness of gospel precepts. In marriage, I have experienced the sacrifice, trials, and supreme joy of rearing seven children. I have come to understand the divinity of the grand and glorious plan of salvation provided for us by our kind and loving Heavenly Father.

The beacons of the world lead us to practice selfishness, while the light of the gospel gently schools us in the discipline of selflessness. The outcome of these two paths is best described in Christ's own words: "For whosoever will save his life shall lose it: and whosoever will lose his life for my sake shall find it. For what is a man profited, if he shall gain the whole world, and lose his own soul?" (Matthew 16:25–26).

I humbly embark upon my new calling, having few credentials by the world's standards. But I am not on the world's errand. I am on the Lord's errand. I bring to this calling a lifetime of experiences as a daughter, wife, mother, and servant within the kingdom. Never once has the Lord let me down, nor have I ever regretted my obedience to the eternal truths of the gospel of Jesus Christ. To the contrary, the blessings of obedience have been overwhelming. Although the task that lies before me is daunting, I have peace in my heart because this is the Lord's work and his answers to life's challenges are profoundly simple and complete. As our Savior, he understands what each of us is going through, for he comprehendeth all.

President Hinckley stated: "This is a season to be strong. It is a time to move forward without hesitation, knowing well the meaning, the breadth, and the importance of our mission. It is a time to do what is right regardless of the consequences that might follow. . . . We have nothing to fear. God is at the helm. He will overrule for the good of this work."[6] I can envision four million women and more, who are members of Relief Society throughout the world, unitedly standing firm in the principles of the gospel as beacons for all the world to see.

I challenge you to rejoice in who you are and the work that we are all a part of. Radiate the Savior's light to all within your sphere of influence. We have within our power the ability to influence the world for good, to reaffirm the importance of the family as the foundation of society. May we rise up and be powerful beacons unto the world, pointing the way to that eternal harbor of peace and safety.

NOTES

1. David O. McKay, in Conference Report, October 1942, 69.

2. Gordon B. Hinckley, "'This Thing Was Not Done in a Corner,'" *Ensign,* November 1996, 51.

3. Henry was the son of Mary's only surviving son, William Blood.

4. Frederic W. Farrar, *The Life of Christ* (1874; reprint, Salt Lake City: Bookcraft, 1994), 89.

5. Spencer W. Kimball, *The Teachings of Spencer W. Kimball,* ed. Edward L. Kimball (Salt Lake City: Bookcraft, 1982), 324.

6. Gordon B. Hinckley, "This Is the Work of the Master," *Ensign,* May 1995, 71; also in Sheri L. Dew, *Go Forward with Faith: The Biography of Gordon B. Hinckley* (Salt Lake City: Deseret Book, 1996), 515–16.

The original presentation of this essay is available on audiocassette from Deseret Book or on the Internet at htt://coned.byu.edu/cw/womens.htm

HE KNOWS YOUR NAME

VIRGINIA U. JENSEN

I am a shy person who would rather be in the background, not up in front. As I have had occasion to sit on the stand as a counselor in the general Relief Society presidency, I have thought to myself, *What is a girl like you doing in a place like this?* My sense of being out of place began in April when I was in a dressing room trying on a blouse. My mobile phone rang, and when I answered, a voice on the other end said, "Sister Jensen, President Hinckley would like to meet with you and your husband tomorrow at 10:45." I can't remember what I replied, but I remember thinking, *Pull yourself together. Don't forget to pay for this blouse and get arrested for shoplifting.*

The next day when I left President Hinckley's office, I thought of the words of Psalm 8:3–4: "When I consider thy heavens, the workings of thy fingers, the moon and the stars, which thou hast ordained; What is man, that thou art mindful of him?" *And who am I that thou art mindful of me?* I wondered. Even to think that President Hinckley knew my name was almost beyond comprehending.

In 1820, a young, unschooled fourteen-year-old farm boy went into the woods to pray. God the Father and his Son Jesus Christ appeared to him, and God the Father called Joseph "by

Virginia U. Jensen is the first counselor in the Relief Society General Presidency. A home-maker, she and her husband, J. Rees Jensen, are the parents of four children and grand-parents of five. She has served in numerous volunteer and Church service missionary assignments and enjoys gardening, grandchildren, and family activities.

name, and said, pointing to the other—This is My Beloved Son. Hear Him!" (JS–H 1:17). The Lord knew Joseph by name, even though this was the first time Joseph had attempted to pray vocally. Joseph relates the experience of meeting the angel Moroni on 21 September 1823, and again he records, "He called me by name" (JS–H 1:33). Just as the Lord knew Joseph's name, so does he know your name and mine. He knows everything there is to know about us. He knows us better than we know ourselves. He knows the person in the most remote corner of the earth. He knew a boy of fourteen on a small farm in upstate New York. He knew that boy's capacities and strengths. He knows ours. And he knows our sorrows and our joys. We feel no hurt, no pain, no sorrows that he is not *very* familiar with. And he loves us.

In *The Promised Messiah,* Elder Bruce R. McConkie writes: "One of the sweetest and most tender terms by which the Lord was known anciently was that of the Shepherd of Israel. To a pastoral people who loved their sheep, who cared for them with tender solicitude, and whose very lives depended upon keeping them safe, this designation taught great truths about the relationship of the Lord to his people."[1]

In a 1988 general conference, Elder John Lasater, then a member of the First Quorum of the Seventy, told of visiting Morocco as part of an official United States government delegation. One day they visited some ruins, traveling in an impressive entourage of five large black limousines speeding across the lovely Moroccan countryside. "I was riding in the third limousine, which had lagged some distance behind the second," Elder Lasater recounts. "As we topped the brow of a hill, we noticed that the limousine in front of us had pulled off to the side of the road. As we drew nearer, I [saw that] . . . an old shepherd, in the long, flowing robes of the Savior's day, was standing near the limousine in conversation with the driver. Nearby, I noted a small flock of sheep numbering not more than fifteen or twenty. An accident had occurred. The king's vehicle had struck and injured one of the sheep belonging to the old shepherd." Elder Lasater's driver explained that by law the shepherd of the injured animal was "now entitled to one hundred times its value at maturity. However, under the same law, the injured sheep must be slain and the meat divided among the people. My interpreter hastily added, 'But the old shepherd will not accept the money. They never do. . . . Because of the love he has for each of his sheep.' It was then that I noticed the old shepherd reach down, lift the injured lamb in his arms, and place it in a large pouch on the front of his robe. He kept stroking its head, repeating the same word over and over again." The word was the injured lamb's name, the driver told Elder Lasater, adding, "'Good shepherds know each one of their sheep by name.' It was as my driver predicted," Elder Lasater remembered. "The money was refused, and the old shepherd with his small flock of sheep, with the injured one tucked safely in the pouch on his robe, disappeared into the beautiful deserts of Morocco."[2]

In *The Promised Messiah,* Elder McConkie tells more about sheep and shepherds: "In Palestine sheep are led, not driven. The American practice is for sheepherders to drive sheep; the Palestinian custom is for the shepherds to go before their sheep, to call them by name, and to lead them to green pastures and beside still waters. At night the flocks of several shepherds are sheltered and protected together in one sheepfold. In the morning each shepherd calls his own sheep by name, out of the larger intermingled flock, and they follow him into the places of food and water."[3]

In John 10:14, our Lord and Savior says plainly, "I am the good shepherd." In the parable of the good shepherd, he explains: "He that entereth in by the door is the shepherd of the sheep. To him the porter openeth; and the sheep hear his voice: and he calleth his own sheep by name, and leadeth them out. And when he putteth forth his own sheep, he goeth before them, and the sheep follow him: for they know his voice. And a stranger will they not follow, but will flee from him: for they know not the voice of strangers" (John 10:2–5).

Even though our Father in Heaven knows and loves us by name—even though he stands ready to lead us beside still waters and to bless us—he cannot shield us from all of life's storms. In 2 Nephi 31:20 we read: "Wherefore, ye must press forward with a steadfastness in Christ, having a perfect brightness of hope, and a love of God and of all men. Wherefore, if ye shall press forward, feasting upon the word of Christ, and endure to the end, behold, thus saith the Father: Ye shall have eternal life." My husband remarked of this scripture recently that it contains everything a person needs to know and do to live a good life: have hope, love God, love others, follow Christ, and endure to the end.

The life of my husband's great-grandmother Catherine Richards Stevens is a moving example of someone who, despite a particularly pronounced routine of adversity, endured with a steadfastness of hope that I find remarkable. She died in 1959, so she was a modern-day pioneer. She married her childhood sweetheart, George Stevens, when she was seventeen, and by the time she was twenty-nine had delivered five eleven-pound babies and endured with them smallpox, typhoid, whooping cough, diphtheria, and appendicitis. She and George ran a farm, and George was also a full-time schoolteacher and part-time bookkeeper and clerk who drove to neighboring towns on weekends to sell the produce and butter from their farm. Hard work did not diminish their enjoyment of life. In 1904, when she was twenty-nine, she wrote: "True joy, happiness, and satisfaction existed for us . . . the future glowed with promise, even as the present offered its established security and peaceful satisfactions . . . our hopes and plans were established."[4]

In May 1905, George was called on a mission to New Zealand. He worked very hard to provide for his family and prepare his farm to run without him for two years. This extra effort "wore him down in strength and health," wrote Catherine. Her diary records their mutual faith but does not gloss over the hardship. "Our faith continued strong and we trusted in the Lord . . . but there were so many things to get done. . . . We were humble and prayerful and felt that surely everything would be well, but our hearts were full and our thoughts were heavy." When he left, "neither of us saw the other for tears. . . . Maybe we shouldn't have given in to our feelings so much, but after all we were just human." In his own diary George wrote of his grief at this parting, and as he reached his mission and began his work, he writes of worsening health and his practice of tracting anyway. He copied into his missionary diary this passage from one of Catherine's letters: "Real love is eternal, and nothing can destroy it. Deep waters cannot wash it away; the storm of adversity cannot prevail against it . . . sacrifices but make the flame leap higher; opposition is fuel which feeds it, and absence and separation have no effect upon it." George's last journal entry was made on 8 July 1906: "I'm finally getting concerned about my health."[5]

On 17 August 1906, George's cousin picked up a copy of the *Deseret News* while on business in a neighboring town. In it he read that George Stevens, age thirty, had died in New Zealand on 26 July 1906 and that his body would arrive in San Francisco later in August. In her diary, Catherine copied Psalm 102: "O Lord . . . Hide not thy face from me . . . For my days are consumed like smoke . . . My heart is smitten, and withered like grass; so that I forget to eat my bread" (vv. 1–4).

Catherine learned in her early thirties to run the farm herself. Only five foot one inch tall and weighing just over one hundred pounds, she writes demurely, "I was not a big bodied woman and was not used to doing man's hard labor." Her diary details milking cows, stacking hay, and caring for livestock, two orchards, vegetable gardens, and her four surviving children. After thirty years, she sold the farm in 1935, when she was sixty-one, and retired to work in the Logan Temple for many years until her death in 1959 at age eighty-four. Her personal history closes with the Fortieth Psalm, a simple and poignant testimony of a woman whose brightness of hope endured: "I waited patiently for the Lord; and he inclined unto me, and heard my cry. He brought me up also out of an horrible pit . . . and set my feet upon a rock, and established my goings. And he hath put a new song in my mouth, even praise unto our God: . . . Blessed is that man that maketh the Lord his trust" (vv. 1–4).

Catherine Stevens's example of endurance and rejoicing reminds me that no matter what the circumstances of our life may be, we will ultimately look back, with the objectivity that time confers on past events, and see meaning and opportunity that are obscured by emotion when the events are taking place.

My oldest child, a daughter whom I love very much, always wanted to be a mother. But after her marriage, this deep wish of her heart did not become a reality. For years she went through intensive fertility treatments, all the time fearing that she would never bear children. This thought often seemed more than she could accept. Her only recourse was to persist in seeking treatment and pursuing all possibilities. She continued for six years before being blessed with one child and then two years later another. She tells me now that she recalls but no longer feels the pain of those six years and is enormously grateful to her Heavenly Father for what she learned along the difficult path to motherhood.

As I said before, the Lord knows us better than we know ourselves. His divine perspective is not blocked by mortal comparisons and insecurities. He knows the desires of our hearts, he knows our potential, and he knows how we can best serve those in our homes, and in our wards, stakes, and communities.

We were born with abilities and gifts. All the characteristics we need to help build the kingdom of God are inherent within us from our premortal existence. In Abraham 3:22–23, Abraham recalls his vision of that premortal state: "Now the Lord had shown unto me, Abraham, the intelligences that were organized before the world was; and among all these there were many of the noble and great ones; And God saw these souls that they were good, and he stood in the midst of them, and he said: These I will make my rulers; for he stood among those that were spirits, and he saw that they were good."

The story of Moses and the journey of the children of Israel out of Egypt is replete with miracles. The parting of the Red Sea and the plagues visited on the cruel Egyptians were amazing, but do not discount the miracle of the Lord's preparing a leader who would be equal to the task of leadership. Moses was asked to lead almost 650,000 Hebrew families out of Egypt to Israel, a land then inhabited by others. Along the way, he was to teach a people raised in an idolatrous society the word and ways of God. He was to prepare them to receive the holy priesthood and to anticipate the coming of our Savior.

In the wilderness, the Lord spoke with Moses "as a man speaketh unto his friend" (Exodus 33:11). After the children of Israel angered the Lord by making the golden calf, Moses pleaded with the Lord to "forgive their sin" (Exodus 32:32). The Lord agreed to continue leading their camp. Though disappointed with the children of Israel, the Lord reaffirmed to Moses his love for him, telling him, "thou hast found grace in my sight, and I know thee by name" (Exodus 33:17).

What qualified Moses for this task? He had been reared as an Egyptian prince. Egypt at that time was a very civilized society with achievements in writing, science, medicine, engineering, astronomy, and mathematics. As a prince, Moses was "learned in all the wisdom of the Egyptians, and was mighty in words and in deeds" (Acts 7:22). Josephus, an ancient historian, records that Moses "led a military expedition up the Nile and captured Meroe at the junction of the Blue and the White

Nile."[6] No doubt these experiences prepared Moses for the long journey which lay ahead. But the more important spiritual preparation and strength was unseen, even by Moses, who asked, "Who am I, that I should go unto Pharaoh, and that I should bring forth the children of Israel out of Egypt?" (Exodus 3:11).

We do not know our own capabilities as the Lord knows them. We do not always see ahead how we may contribute. As we receive new callings, we may find ourselves asking this same question: Who am I that I should lead the ward choir? Who am I that I can be an effective nursery leader? The Lord does not call us to fail. President Thomas S. Monson assures us that the Lord will not let us fail in his work when we do our part.[7] Our Heavenly Father needs each of us. Each of us brings our own offering to the Lord and in doing so contributes to the building of his kingdom. We all serve the Lord in our own way and in our own manner (see Luke 10:40–42). Too often we compare ourselves to others. And as we measure our own contribution against someone else's, we often feel that we come up short. The challenge for each of us is to focus on our uniqueness, our contributions—not our sameness: who we are, not who we are not.

In the Hong Kong Temple are three exquisite upholstery fabrics of intricate Chinese design, fashioned by a local textile artist, Cheng Hwa Seng. Cheng Hwa was born and reared in Taiwan, where she joined the Church sixteen years ago. After studying fine art for three years and then working as a designer in Taiwan for about twelve more years, she was admitted to the Philadelphia College of Textiles and Design. In the United States, she studied print design and jacquard weaving design—a weaving technique used to produce upholstery fabric. As a student there, on a visit to the temple in Washington, D.C., Cheng Hwa noticed the beautiful upholstery fabrics in the temple.

When the Church announced its plans to build a temple in Hong Kong, Cheng Hwa expressed to Larry Wyss, who worked with interior design for the temples, her desire to contribute to the Hong Kong Temple. Cheng Hwa's fabrics not only are beautiful but contain symbols important to the Chinese people. One of her weavings is a white piece of fabric with a water lily design, which has been placed in the celestial room of the Hong Kong Temple. Water lilies are very common in China. Their beauty graces ponds surrounding traditional Chinese buildings. Ironically, the beautiful water lily grows in dirty water. For the Chinese, the water lily represents our ability to rise above the temptations of the world and grow into a pure and righteous person. Cheng Hwa's thoughtful and highly skilled offering to the Lord will bless generations of temple patrons.

But what if our talents and contributions seem meager offerings compared to those of others? Alma taught that "by small and simple things are great things brought to pass" (Alma 37:6). My friend Vicki Huebner attended a small singles ward in Orange County, California. Frustrated with her job and after prayerful consideration, she decided to apply for a position at Brigham Young University. The Sunday after she applied, her bishop called her to be the Relief Society president, but she explained she had just applied for a job elsewhere. Did he still want to call her to be Relief Society president?

The bishop, despite her possible move, wanted to sustain her. He had been impressed that she was to be the next Relief Society president. She sought and also received a confirmation that the Lord wanted her to accept the call.

Soon afterward, she was offered the job at BYU, to begin as soon as possible. She and her presidency prayed to know their purpose. How were they to serve the sisters of the ward in only three weeks? The answer came: they were to organize their Relief Society's visiting teaching program.

The visiting teaching program had become disorganized, and visiting teaching supervisors, most of them recent high school graduates, lacked experience or training. In three weeks, the Relief Society presidency reorganized the visiting teaching districts, taught the supervisors and district leaders about the importance of visiting teaching, and met with each visiting teacher to determine the needs of the sisters in the ward. When a new Relief Society presidency was called, the foundation for their work of sisterhood and service was in place. A simple offering to the Lord prepared the way for future Relief Society leaders to accomplish great things.

Our contributions of time and talents to serve our Heavenly Father help build the kingdom of God. My friends Stan and Mavis Steadman accepted a call with another couple to go to Hanoi, Vietnam. Their mission was not to preach the gospel. That was not allowed. In fact, they were strongly cautioned to be alert to prohibitions and not to do anything that the government did not approve. When they were called to this tightly controlled Communist land, they were told, "This is not a call for sissies." Their mission, with no training in spoken Vietnamese, was to teach English to the leaders of the country and to children.

Let me share part of a letter I received from them: "It is early Saturday morning in Hanoi. It is 108 degrees with 90 percent humidity. The streets are lined with Vietnamese families squatting on low four-inch stools eating their breakfasts—chicken soup from big steaming pots. . . . The Lord is leading us in unbelievable paths. Each day is an amazing adventure. We are overwhelmed, overjoyed, and overworked.

"The big excitement is the *Messiah!* It will be magnificent when it is performed for two nights in October. We are in full rehearsal with the National Vietnamese Symphony and Chorus—100 professional musicians. We don't speak Vietnamese and they don't speak English, but the message of Christ [is] in the music. . . . We have taught the words of the text in English. Can you imagine the thrill of hearing these non-Christian, Buddhist friends sing: 'For unto us a child is born, and His name shall be called Wonderful, Counselor, the Mighty God, the Everlasting Father, the Prince of Peace'? . . .

69

"We rehearse in a dungeon-like room with no air conditioning. When it rains, it is usually flooded and we wade in barefoot. The conductor is a small, dynamic man who sits on a high chair with his feet dangling in the air. When we finished the 'Hallelujah Chorus,' which he takes at breakneck pace, he took out his handkerchief, wiped his brow, looked at us, smiled, and said the only two English words he knows which he has heard us use, 'very good.' We agreed.

"The concert has suddenly taken on a whole new meaning. It is the first time the *Messiah* has ever been done in Vietnam and probably in Asia, and it is the first time the U.S. and Vietnam have ever worked together on any musical venture. The government officials have seized upon this and want the title to be 'A Bridge of Harmony and Friendship.' There is no word in Vietnamese that means 'Messiah.' Also we cannot use the word 'God' or anything pertaining to government (like 'king') printed on the program. This is a reminder of the very thin line we are treading. . . . The hand of the Lord is in everything that is happening here. He has opened doors that are impossible. We see it every day. And every day I try to repent to be worthy of His trust in me. I have never worked so hard!"[8]

These dear missionaries are powerful examples of using talents and inherent abilities to build the kingdom. Of course, the Good Shepherd knows their names and will welcome them back home to him. I think of my favorite hymn, "Our Savior's Love," written by Edward L. Hart.[9] Consider the first verse:

> Our Savior's love
> Shines like the sun with perfect light,
> As from above
> It breaks through clouds of strife.
> Lighting our way,
> It leads us back into his sight,
> Where we may stay
> To share eternal life.

Yes, he knows your name. He knows your heart. When you are broken, he will tenderly pick you up and soothe you, as the good shepherd did. He will lead you when you wander in the wilderness, as he did Moses. If you will ask, he will be your strength and instruct you as he did the boy prophet. He will draw forth your abilities and accept your every offering in service. His love does shine like the sun with perfect light. It does break through clouds of strife. His love will light our way back into his sight.

NOTES

1. Bruce R. McConkie, *The Promised Messiah: The First Coming of Christ* (Salt Lake City: Deseret Book, 1978), 177.

2. John R. Lasater, "Shepherds of Israel," *Ensign,* May 1988, 74.

3. McConkie, *Promised Messiah,* 179.

4. Family genealogical records in the possession of the author, compiled and published by Kenneth R. Stevens.

5. Family genealogical records.

6. Mark E. Peterson, *Moses, Man of Miracles* (Salt Lake City: Deseret Book, 1977), 39.

7. See Thomas S. Monson, "Duty Calls," *Ensign,* May 1969, 44.

8. Mavis Steadman, letter in possession of author, 29 August 1993.

9. "Our Savior's Love," *Hymns* (Salt Lake City: The Church of Jesus Christ of Latter-day Saints, 1985), no. 113.

PRACTICE MAKES PERFECT

SHERI L. DEW

One year while I was attending BYU I invited a friend to make the eight-hundred-mile drive home with me to Kansas for Thanksgiving. As we prepared to leave, the weather was threatening through Colorado and over the Rockies. The night before we left, my father called and told me to buy some snow chains—just in case. I resisted at first—there wasn't a prayer that I'd know how to put them on should I need them—but ultimately I did as Dad instructed. As it turned out, we didn't need them. The roads were treacherous in spots, but we arrived home without incident.

While we were home, Dad insisted on showing my friend and me how to install the snow chains—again, just in case. My mechanical aptitude is pathetic, so I left it to my friend to pay attention to the snow-chain lesson. Frankly, I was a bit smug about the whole thing. I *knew* we wouldn't need them. I had made that trip at least fifty times, *sans* chains, and I couldn't imagine that we'd need them this time.

The trip back to Provo, Utah, proved to be unlike any other, however. We were barely into the Rockies when we came upon the iciest roads I had ever seen. For an hour or so we inched along, the speedometer scarcely registering

Sheri L. Dew is the second counselor in the Relief Society General Presidency. She grew up in Ulysses, Kansas, and graduated from Brigham Young University with a degree in history. A popular speaker and writer, she is vice-president of publishing at Deseret Book Company.

movement. Finally my friend wondered out loud if we shouldn't put the chains on. I resisted. Surely the icy conditions wouldn't stretch much farther.

Not five minutes later we crept around a hairpin curve just in time to see a car slide off the road ahead of us and plummet into the Colorado River below. I admitted it was time to pull out the chains, and we began the ordeal of attempting to install them. The process was, to say the least, an adventure. No sit-com duo has done a skit any funnier. For one thing, having paid little attention to my father's instructions, I was absolutely no help. Thank heavens, my friend patiently led us step-by-step through the process. An hour later and frozen through to the bone, we finally had the "easy-install" chains in place. Even then, we hadn't done something correctly, for as we headed down the road the chains clanked against the chassis with every revolution of the tires.

By now, I was not in the best mood. And the banging chains didn't help. You can imagine my reaction when, just fifteen minutes later, we drove out of the ice and onto bare roads. Muttering and complaining, I pulled over, removed the chains, and threw them into the trunk. Obviously, they had proven an enormous waste of time.

For several hours we drove on, attempting to make up time as we went. The poor roads through the Rockies had delayed us so severely, however, that late that night, when we should already have been in Provo, we ran into a horrible blizzard halfway up the last mountain pass between us and home. The snow came with blinding intensity. We couldn't even see the sides of the road, yet we couldn't stop, because there was no place to pull over. Frankly, we were both terrified.

We inched along until we arrived at the summit, where a turnout area allowed us to pull over, along with dozens of other motorists. The wind was blowing so hard that the snow was coming down sideways, and it was bitter cold. Though conditions were ten times worse than they had been when we put the chains on the first time, we had no choice but to do it again. Bracing ourselves, we hopped out, pulled the chains from the trunk, and began the unpleasant task. Because we had been through the process just a few hours earlier, however, we had the routine down. In fact, a truck driver approached us and said, "Well, I was coming over to help, but it looks as though you girls know what you're doing," and walked off. *Chivalry IS dead,* I thought.

Thankfully, we got the chains on—in under fifteen minutes. And as we headed down the mountain, there wasn't that telltale clanking. The second time around we had done a better job. Though the remainder of our drive was a slow one, we arrived home tired but safe.

I have thought about the parable of the snow chains many times. There is absolutely no way we could have installed those chains at midnight in a blinding blizzard with three feet of snow already on the ground if we hadn't had a practice run earlier that day.

Practice is a wonderful concept. To do *anything* well— whether it's perfecting a turnaround jump shot, performing a Rachmaninoff concerto, or excelling at open-heart surgery— we've got to practice.

The same is true of our spiritual sensitivity and our ability to hear the voice of the Lord—in other words, our spiritual skills. The scriptures are replete with examples of individuals who have enhanced their spiritual skills through practice. Consider the account of David and Goliath. Have you pondered the improbability of that story? An adolescent boy, dwarfed by the mature warrior Goliath, pledges to go up against him in one-on-one combat. But David revealed the source of his confidence when he said, "The Lord that delivered me out of the paw of the lion, and out of the paw of the bear, he will deliver me out of the hand of this Philistine" (1 Samuel 17:37).

David had already done the improbable at least twice.

Because of those experiences, he had faith that the Lord would magnify him and enable him to subdue Goliath. He had the spiritual know-how. He had been practicing.

The brother of Jared had a transcendent experience in which he actually beheld the Lord (see Ether 3). Prior to that remarkable event, Jared had asked his brother to plead with the Lord on their behalf: "Cry unto the Lord, that he will not confound us that we may not understand our words" (Ether 1:34). Clearly, Jared's brother was a man of faith; he knew how to hear the voice of the Lord. Yet, later, the brother of Jared was chastened because he had failed to call upon the Lord (see Ether 2:14). Even a man with tremendous spiritual knowledge had an occasion when the Lord had to remind him to continue in prayer. The brother of Jared repented and practiced—and as a result was prepared to have an absolutely magnificent, transcendent spiritual experience.

Do we really believe that when Moses arrived at the shores of the Red Sea, leading the entire congregation of the children of Israel with Pharaoh and his armies in hot pursuit, he waved his arms and the waters magically parted? He already knew how to exercise the power of the priesthood to control the elements. He had drawn upon that power in other situations and knew what to do in the very moment when circumstances demanded such know-how. He had been practicing.

The Lord, through our individually tailored spiritual tutoring, gives us opportunities to practice, refine, and develop our spiritual skills. With that principle in mind, consider this statement by President Gordon B. Hinckley: "Of all our needs, I think the greatest is an increase in faith."[1] President Spencer W. Kimball said it this way: "We need a storage of faith that can carry [us] over the dull, the difficult, the terrifying moments, disappointments, disillusionments, and years of adversity, want, confusion, and frustration."[2]

How do we increase our faith and stockpile a spiritual reserve? Among other things, we practice. Like anything else, developing the spiritual skills that may be ours takes practice, repetition, experience, and sustained effort. Alma taught it this way: "Behold, if ye will awake and arouse your faculties, even to an experiment upon my words, and exercise a particle of faith, yea, even if ye can no more than desire to believe, let this desire work in you" (Alma 32:27). Perhaps your faith in the Lord wavers from time to time, or you don't feel completely certain that the Lord will do for *you* what he has promised he will do for all of us. But in this verse we are counseled that if we only *want* to believe, we should experiment upon his words. In other words, practice.

When you face seemingly insurmountable problems, when you plead with the Lord for help with something that you can't possibly manage on your own, when circumstances clearly call for direction and strength from a Source greater than anything mortal, have you found yourself wondering, as I have, *Will God help ME?*

I love these two verses in the Doctrine and Covenants: "Verily, verily, I say unto you, ye are little children"—and aren't we all children spiritually?—"and ye have not as yet understood how great blessings the Father hath in his own hands and prepared for you; and ye cannot bear all things now; nevertheless, be of good cheer, for I will lead you along. The kingdom is yours and the blessings thereof are yours, and the riches of eternity are yours" (D&C 78:17–18).

We *are* little children, and we have no concept of the vast store of riches, spiritual riches, the Lord has available for us. But he has promised that if we will let him, he will lead us along. He will no doubt lead us along by providing opportunities for us to experiment upon his word—opportunities for us to practice. We can practice having faith in him as our Savior, our Redeemer, our Rescuer.

What exactly has the Lord promised he will do for us? How far-reaching is the scope and power of the Atonement?

In Alma we learn that he will take upon him our pains,

sicknesses, and infirmities. His bowels will be filled with mercy such that he will succor us—he will *run to us* (see Alma 7:11–12). He came to heal the brokenhearted, to deliver those who are captive. How many ways are there to be held captive—a captive of circumstances, of bad habits, of weaknesses? And he will "set at liberty them that are bruised" (Luke 4:18). How many of us are bruised emotionally, mentally, spiritually? It was Jacob who taught that the "pleasing word of God . . . healeth the wounded soul" (Jacob 2:8).

Ether recorded these transcendent words of the Lord: "My grace is sufficient for all men that humble themselves before me; for if they humble themselves before me, and have faith in me, then will I make weak things become strong unto them" (Ether 12:27). Consider the ramifications of such a promise! If you are like me, you regularly conduct the inventory that reveals all of the ways in which you are weak and lacking. You are painfully aware of your mortal weaknesses. Have you found yourself wondering, *Can the Savior really make those weak things become strong?* This is a doctrine more profound than any behavior-modification course, more penetrating than any resurgent attempts at willpower. Helaman added the promise that if we will build upon the rock of Christ, the devil will have no power over us (see Helaman 5:12).

Finally, consider these verses from the Doctrine and Covenants: "Look unto me in every thought; doubt not, fear not. Behold the wounds which pierced my side, and also the prints of the nails in my hands and feet; be faithful, keep my commandments" (D&C 6:36–37). The sequence of these verses is revealing. Might the Savior be saying, Because the nails pierced my hands and my feet, you have no need to doubt or to fear. In other words, because of the power and scope of the Atonement, we have somewhere we can go to deal with our mortal weakness, our fears, and our anxieties, Someone who can and will make up the difference between where we are and where we want to be—if we will come unto him.

Remember the American Express campaign that "membership has its privileges"? This company enticed new customers by appealing to the desire to become a member of an elite group entitled to special privileges. It was a clever tactic. Who doesn't appreciate privileges?

Have you paused lately to ponder the privileges that all of us have by virtue of our membership in The Church of Jesus Christ of Latter-day Saints? Have you stopped to think about the blessings that come from knowing who you are and whose you are, from believing that a prophet walks the earth, from understanding the priesthood ordinances that bind us to each other? Consider the magnificent blessings associated with the gift of the Holy Ghost and with an endowment of power from on high in the house of the Lord—all of which make you eligible for remarkable spiritual privileges. President Brigham Young taught, "If the Latter-day Saints will walk up to their privileges, and exercise faith in the name of Jesus Christ, and live in the enjoyment of the fulness of the Holy Ghost constantly day by day, there is nothing on the face of the earth that they could ask for, that would not be given to them."[3] And yet, on another occasion, he taught the sobering doctrine that, too often, "we live far beneath our [spiritual] privileges."[4]

I, like you, have been blessed with many opportunities to exercise faith in Jesus Christ, experiment upon his word, and practice what I believe. Through those experiences I have come to know that because of the phenomenal act of atonement begun in the Garden of Gethsemane and completed on the cross at Calvary, there is power, peace, comfort, healing, and strength available to help us as we attempt to negotiate life's challenges.

Thank heavens—literally—for the magnificent gift of the Lord Jesus Christ. We all encounter obstacles in life—they seem to be part of the journey. A greeting card from a close friend sums up my feelings when life seems overpunctuated with problems. The front reads, "Mother told me there would be days like this." Inside: "She failed to mention that they could go on for months at a time."

Very simply, things don't always turn out as we hoped or thought they would. Children don't always obey, despite our best parenting efforts. Our health sometimes lets us down, even if we are careful about diet and exercise and live the Word of Wisdom with precision. Money doesn't always magically appear at the end of the month, even for full-tithe payers.

Life circumstances don't always develop as we hope and even pray for. But sometimes the resultant disappointment and even heartache lead us to unlock the strength and power that can be found through fasting and prayer, earnest scripture study, and temple worship—in other words, the privileges associated with sincere spiritual endeavor.

At one point I believed I was within days of announcing my engagement. I was already into my thirties, so the prospects of marriage were particularly sweet. Instead, a few weeks later my intended married a close friend. Loneliness, anger, deep discouragement, and other poignant emotions surged within me. My initial remedy for the pain was to exercise such phenomenal faith, and to enlist all my family and friends to exercise their faith, that the Lord could not deny our combined and repeated petitions for my marriage. I launched an intensive effort to learn everything I could about the Savior and what it meant to truly believe in and trust him. I fasted and prayed, searched the scriptures, and sought solace and direction in the temple as never before. In my mind, it was an earnest search for something that was noble and good. After all, was it good for man—or woman—to be alone? As far as I was concerned, absolutely not! Without realizing it, I was essentially attempting to force the Lord's hand with my brilliant display of faith. After all, I could never be happy until and unless I was married. Right?

The Lord did not respond by giving me a husband. What he did give me, however, was new understanding, more strength, and a deep sense of comfort and peace that I'd never had before. It was a terrible experience; it was a wonderful experience. Through it, I learned that the Savior not only paid the price for sin but compensated for *all* of the difficulty, the heartache, the betrayal, the disillusionment and disappointment and pain that we feel and face. I learned that, in a very tangible way, he would be my companion. And I learned that he would never let me down or leave me alone.

President George Q. Cannon said: "No matter how serious the trial, how deep the distress, how great the affliction, [God] will never desert us. He never has, and He never will. He cannot do it. It is not His character. He is an unchangeable being; the same yesterday, the same today, and He will be the same throughout the eternal ages to come. . . . We may pass through the fiery furnace; we may pass through deep waters; but we shall not be consumed nor overwhelmed. We shall emerge from all these trials and difficulties the better and purer for them, if we only trust in our God and keep His commandments."[5]

With each new challenge, each new opportunity to increase our faith, comes the privilege of practicing what we believe and increasing our spiritual skills while adding to the "storage of faith" President Kimball spoke of. Just as school requirements become more challenging from grade to grade, so do the Lord's spiritual requirements of us increase as we progress, grow, and develop. My experiences have taught me that each new challenge results in a deeper faith in the Lord and greater confidence in the spiritual privileges that are ours. Dealing with difficult circumstances seems to prepare us to handle even more complicated opportunities for growth. As difficult as the time was when I dealt with the disappointment of not getting married, other challenges followed that required even more faith.

When I was asked to be involved in preparing President Gordon B. Hinckley's biography, I was both honored and overwhelmed. I had a more-than-full-time job, was serving as a stake Relief Society president, and now was responsible for a project that was filled with enough pressure, stress, and workload to itself deserve full-time attention.

I reorganized my life to be as efficient as possible and then began working on the book, usually scheduling time in the evening—after a long day at the office—to do research and to write. After a few weeks it became clear that this system would not work. There were too many interruptions in the evenings, and I was attempting to do the hardest work of my day—filling a blank computer screen with coherent sentences—after I'd already put in a full day on the job.

About this time, my stake president informed me that both of my counselors were wanted back in their respective wards and that I needed to select two new counselors. I was heartsick. Our presidency had been together for more than three years and worked seamlessly together. I couldn't imagine breaking in two new counselors when I was busier and under more pressure than I had ever been. But through prayer, I recognized that the stake president was right, and I went about the process of selecting new counselors. They were called, and I was with them in the stake president's office when they were set apart. Before we began, the first counselor in the stake presidency, who knew nothing of the extra load I was carrying, said that though there was no need to set me apart again, he wondered if it might be appropriate to give me a blessing.

I was grateful for the suggestion and was subsequently amazed when the stake president acknowledged, during the blessing, the heavy responsibilities that had fallen upon my shoulders. Then he added these words: "I bless you that your body will require less sleep, insomuch that you will not fall asleep in the many meetings you have to attend."

For several days thereafter I pondered the implications of that promise. Finally, I began to calculate just how early I would have to get up to do my writing *before* I left for work. The advantages were that there would be fewer interruptions and I would be doing the hardest work of the day when I was mentally the freshest. No matter how I figured the time, however, I would have to arise at 3:00 A.M. I am an early riser anyway, but that seemed absurd. Yet, I could not get the words of that priesthood blessing out of my mind. I kept thinking about some of the difficult challenges I had faced in the past and the way the Lord had shored me up, strengthened me, made me able to do things I could never have handled or accomplished on my own. Did I really believe he would support and sustain me? My experience told me that he would. I had been promised, by the power of the priesthood, that my body would be able to get along on less sleep. Did I have enough confidence in him to proceed, assured that he would honor the words of that blessing?

A week after the blessing I decided to take the Lord at his word. And for twenty-three months, six days a week, I arose at 3:00 A.M. Did I have the physical or mental stamina, in and of myself, to do such a thing? Absolutely not. My role in this process was simply to act on my belief that the Lord was able *and* willing to do something for me that I could not do myself.

I testify that the Lord will do for us exactly what he has said he will do—if we will believe in him and seek his divine direction and intervention in our lives. Strength and power, insight and wisdom far greater than our own are available to us. The key to unlocking those powers is to ask, see, knock, and believe (see D&C 88:63). In other words, to practice by experimenting upon the word.

I cannot describe how overwhelmed I have felt since being called to serve in the Relief Society General Presidency. The nature of the call itself is sobering; the demands on my faith and my time are incredible. I look back longingly at those twenty-three months of early risings and realize that wasn't all that difficult. But as it turns out, that experience provided me with more opportunity to practice, to experiment, and to draw upon the grace of the Lord. I know that if we will seek the Lord first and foremost in our lives, that he will never let us down. He will bolster us. He will do for us as he did for Joseph when he promised: "I will go before your face. I will be on your right hand and on your left, and my Spirit shall be in your hearts, and mine angels round about you, to bear you up" (D&C 84:88).

The Lord Jesus Christ will never leave us alone. He is who he says he is, and he will do for us what he has said he will do. Therefore, "let us cheerfully do all things that lie in our power; and then may we stand still, with the utmost assurance, to see the salvation of God, and for his arm to be revealed" (D&C 123:17).

NOTES

1. Gordon B. Hinckley, in Conference Report, October 1987, 68; or *Ensign,* November 1987, 54.

2. Spencer W. Kimball, *Faith Precedes the Miracle* (Salt Lake City: Deseret Book, 1973), 110–11.

3. Brigham Young, *Discourses of Brigham Young,* sel. John A. Widtsoe (Salt Lake City: Deseret Book, 1954), 156.

4. Young, *Discourses,* 32.

5. George Q. Cannon, "Freedom of the Saints," in *Collected Discourses Delivered by President Wilford Woodruff, His Two Counselors, the Twelve Apostles, and Others,* comp. Brian H. Stuy, 5 vols. (Burbank, Calif.: B. H. S. Publishing, 1988), 2:185.

STEAK AND SPAM SERVICE

LINDA BENTLEY JOHNSON

When I hear the phrase "community service," I feel an immediate clutch in my stomach, probably because it has long been on my "things-to-do-later-but-feel-guilty-about-now" list. It's hard to think about feeding the homeless when the thought of feeding the hungry in my own house overwhelms me. It seems like a group of Latter-day Saint women is the last crowd who needs to hear about how to give more of ourselves to more good causes when some of us are struggling to maintain a self at all. Even so, I'm grateful I was born to parents who live lives of service and generosity and married into a family that also offers wonderful examples of how serving others makes life rich and happy.

For the past twenty-three summers, I have been swimming in a glacial lake in northwest Montana. On each visit, I face the same moment of truth: jumping off the dock into the clear, frigid water. My skin is warm and comfortable from the heat of the sun. I know I will like the water once I'm in and have been swimming around for a while. Yet, I find myself hanging back, maybe dipping in a toe or dangling my feet off the end of the dock. It is hard to take the plunge.

Venturing into the world of community service felt something like that. I was a little uncomfortable, and the fear of

Linda Bentley Johnson is a part-time graduate student in psychology and a full-time mom to four lively sons. She and her husband, Mark Johnson, live in Ann Arbor, Michigan, where she enjoys teaching Primary in her ward.

drowning in yet another worthwhile demand held me back. Nevertheless, I wanted to test the waters because in a church setting, I sometimes felt lacking. On two different occasions, women I visit taught expressed suicidal thoughts to me, and I did not know how to respond. I wanted to learn more about the resources available in our community for those who needed housing, counseling, or services for the elderly and disabled. All my life I had been praying for God to bless the poor, but now it seemed that, in words I recalled being a catch phrase for the anti-slavery Underground Railroad, "It is always good to pray with your mouth, but sometimes you have to pray with your feet." Eventually I was ready to get my feet wet, especially since I felt I had a steamroller behind me ready to push me off the dock.

I was led to the SOS Community Crisis Center during a season of my life when I had the resources to swim in uncharted waters. My work there has been uncomfortable at times, sometimes a bit shocking, but on the whole exhilarating and refreshing. The SOS Community Crisis Center was established twenty-five years ago. Individuals can call the hotline number or walk into the agency twenty-four hours a day, 365 days a year, to receive a variety of services, including counseling, suicide intervention, financial assistance, showers, diapers, food, bus tokens, and housing. A computer database contains information about all the agencies and services available in our county. If someone calls needing a washer, or a domestic violence shelter, or a pet bereavement support group, we can give them information about the services available. The group's mission statement says: "Our programs and services will support families and individuals in developing the strengths and competencies necessary to move toward self-reliance and personal change." This organization appealed to me because it offered help for immediate problems and guidance to those beginning to address the systemic issues in their lives.

Volunteers at the center go through a fifty-hour training

85

period in which trainers review in depth a variety of relevant topics. Experts from the community educate volunteers in such areas as domestic violence, substance abuse, mental illness, racism, homelessness, and grief and loss. In addition, the training experience itself was a rare and enlightening opportunity to sit in a room and listen for an extended time to fellow volunteers share their perspectives on their experiences struggling, as members of minority groups, against the myths and stereotypes of our society. I became more aware of my previously unnoticed privilege of being white and middle class. Prejudices and defensiveness did surface, and we had awkward moments, but we felt bonded after discussing issues that are rarely even raised. These experiences were jarring but renewing and part of the risk of jumping off the dock. Such conversations can help us come closer to President Gordon B. Hinckley's vision of creating environments of growth and peace in our diverse communities: "Those who love Him will seek to do that which will encourage and uphold community standards which will create and maintain an environment of culture, of growth, and of peaceful relationships."[2]

Elder H. Burke Peterson taught that our capacity to love is directly related to our capacity to listen.[3] At the crisis center, we are taught that 75 percent of what we do for people is simply to listen. The other 25 percent of our time is spent resolving problems or providing services. This ratio is a good one for me to keep in mind in my nonvolunteer life. Reducing my urges to fix, rescue, and give advice to those who are struggling has helped me practice more empathic listening. I know I am trying to listen with empathy when I'm not preparing my perceptive response while the speaker is speaking. I try to resist the urge to immediately exclaim (usually while interrupting), "I know just what you mean. I had the same problem, only mine was worse. Let me tell you what I did. It worked for me, so it will work for you." In effect I am trying to hand someone a pair of glasses just like mine and with my prescription. Because each of us has a unique view of the world, empathic listening requires that I take off my glasses with my own view and try on my friend's glasses—not try to give her mine. With empathy, I can see for a few minutes with my friend's vision and sometimes even recognize how different her world looks.

Our need to be listened to, to be taken seriously, to be understood, and to have a sense of belonging is as powerful as our need for air. When we listen, we help others breathe. Listening without judgment doesn't mean that we condone what is being said. After we have done the work of listening, we can clarify values, solve problems, share similar experiences, and give challenges and suggestions. But people have to be heard before they can hear. In fact, I have learned at the crisis center that if I start the problem-solving process and the client comes up with all the reasons why my suggestions aren't going to work, I haven't listened long enough. This has been helpful in dealing with my children when they persistently reject my brilliant solutions. I start to "get it" that they sometimes just need to vent and share their feelings. Mom doesn't always have to make it better.

At the crisis center I have heard such statements as, "There is no one in my life I can talk to," "This is the first time I've told anyone how I feel," "I just need to talk," and "What a relief. Thank you for listening." Do not underestimate the power of the rare and sweet gift of listening. It can be just as warm and nourishing as a hot meal. But it is hard to resist the quick fix and instead accept the complexities of others' lives. When we listen, we give another person a chance to hear her own voice, sometimes for the first time, and arrive at her own path of action at her own pace. When I listen this way, I don't feel as overwhelmed by the many problems of others that I cannot possibly fix. I feel more available to do what I can, even when it may be "just to listen." I know now that listening counts.

Recently, I shared some of these ideas about listening with the women in my ward when I was a counselor in a Relief

Society presidency. After the meeting, I conducted a visiting teaching interview with an honest sister who informed me that she disagreed. "You can't tell me that when I visit Kathy and listen to her go on and on about her problems that I am doing her any favors. She has so many needs that it's overwhelming, and I feel I'm doing so little to help." I decided not to get defensive that she had rejected my astute power-of-listening theory, and I decided to try and, well, . . . listen. I listened a long time while she explained why she felt visiting teaching was useless to her and to others. At the end of the interview, I loved her more and could genuinely thank her for the things I had learned from her. Ironically, she turned to me and said, "Thank you for listening to me. Somehow I feel much better."

Many powerful verses in the Book of Mormon describe our urgent responsibility to the poor and the sad consequences of inequality in our communities. As many of us live our privileged lives of ease surrounded by well-fed children and numerous possessions, we are isolated from much of the suffering and destitution in the world. We often give valuable service in the school zone and show concern for the ozone. But in a lifetime, I feel it is important at some time to leave our comfort zones and risk serving the most impoverished and destitute. It can be uncomfortable, but Jesus taught, "The works which ye have seen me do that shall ye also do" (3 Nephi 27:21). When we literally feed those who have no meat, give drink to the thirsty, interact with strangers, clothe the naked, visit the sick or those in prison, we have the opportunity to see Christ in the faces of those we serve.

Mother Teresa taught: "If you pick up a man hungry for bread and you give him bread, you have already satisfied his hunger. But if you find a man terribly lonely, this is much greater poverty. You can find Calcutta all over the world, if you have eyes to see."[3] Indeed, we each experience hunger and poverty on some level. King Benjamin reminds us that we are all beggars. We all depend on the Great Provider for our substance, whether it be steak or Spam. He does not turn away from us, telling us that we brought this misery upon ourselves and that our punishment is just. If we put up our petitions to him, he has promised that our begging is not in vain. He pours out his mercy and grace until our hearts and mouths are full of his substance and his joy.

One of the first things Jesus did in the New World was to reveal his wounds to the people one by one. That is a powerful image for me. It feels sacred to hear others sharing their wounds at the crisis center. They do not expose their scars inappropriately, like an exploitive talk-show exposé. They take responsibility for their lives, saying, "I'm lonely. I'm hurting. I need to talk." These are souls asking for help and taking the steps to get it instead of blaming others or giving up.

I received a call one day from a young mother. In the background, I could hear two children crying as she described the agony of her infant, who was suffering from a medical condition that he might not survive. The three-year-old was acting out because of all the stress, and the father was not interested in participating in the parenting. Sleep-deprived and exhausted, this mother called because she had no one who would listen to her say, "This is hard." She broke down sobbing and said she felt like such a failure. Blinking back my own tears, I had the privilege of telling this daughter of God, "You are doing the best you can. You care about your children. You are not a failure." I felt like Heavenly Father let me carry her burden for a while.

It is holy work to hear people tell the truth about their lives. In a world of small talk and shallow conversations, it is refreshing to listen to others get below the surface and speak about what is real in their lives. I feel more connected to the human family and privileged to say to strangers, "You don't deserve this. It's not your fault. You're feeling scared. We can help you. You can talk to me." I hear back from them, "I feel better. You made me laugh. I can breathe now. Thank you for listening." These are small and simple things, but Mother Teresa reminds us, "We can do no great thing—only little things with great love."[4]

Lest you think that all is warmth and light, let me remind you of the cold, gray days at the lake when the water isn't clear and inviting and swimming isn't much fun. Community projects, like everything else worthwhile, have a shadow side as well. Some days are boring. It's not much fun to work with clients who are drunk, rude, ungrateful, or demanding. Sometimes I get explicit or upsetting phone calls. When I don't receive that warm glow of service, I try to remember that I don't give service so I can feel like a good person. I try to do good because it is the right thing to do and because Jesus has asked us to help each other.

As we stick in a toe or dive right in to opportunities in the community, what would the lifeguard suggest? How do we guard our lives when we add community service to our already full plate? Community service should not be like eating brussel sprouts—"It's supposed to be good for me, but I have to hold my nose." We can choose something that satisfies and nourishes like sweet fruit. What we have to give is who we are. We can give what feeds us, so we don't experience the malnourishment of burnout or dread. My advice is: Honor your diverse roles and the demands of your season of life. You may need to think about service in completely new ways to find the opportunity to serve while doing something you enjoy. Many of the things we are already doing in the schools, with sports teams, fund-raisers, and cultural arts, all "count" as community service. It's helpful to remember these guidelines from humanitarian Mirabai Bush: "Be brave, start small, use what you've got, do something you enjoy, don't overcommit."[5]

In my journal I copied these words that I refer to often: "I don't want to drive up to the pearly gates in a shiny sports car wearing fancy clothes, my hair perfectly coiffed, and with long manicured nails. I want to drive up in a station wagon that has mud on the wheels from taking kids to Scout camp. I want there to be grass stains on my shoes from mowing Sister Schenck's lawn. I want there to be a smudge of peanut butter on my shirt from making sandwiches for a sick neighbor's children. I want there to be a little dirt under my fingernails from helping to weed someone's garden. I want there to be children's sticky kisses on my cheeks and the tears of a friend on my shoulder. I want the Lord to know that I was really here and that I really loved."

I pray I will have evidence to show my creator that I have loved and cared and perhaps be a little wet behind the ears from trying to experience living water in my life.

NOTES

1. Gordon B. Hinckley, "To Please Our Heavenly Father," *Ensign,* May 1985, 50.

2. H. Burke Peterson, "Preparing the Heart," *Ensign,* May 1990, 84.

3. *Mother Teresa,* directed by Jeanette and Ann Petrie, Time Inc., 1975, PBS videocassette.

4. Mother Teresa, *Love: A Fruit Always in Season: Daily Meditations from the Words of Mother Teresa,* ed. Dorothy S. Hunt (San Francisco: Ignatius Press, 1987), 121; also in *Aloha!* by Chieko N. Okazaki (Salt Lake City: Deseret Book, 1995), 199.

5. Mirabai Bush and Ram Dass, *Compassion in Action* (New York: Bell Tower, 1992), 174.

DOING GOOD AND BEING GOOD

HAROLD C. BROWN

The Church has a long history of humanitarian service work. In 1842, Joseph Smith organized the Relief Society to, among other things, "provoke the brethren to good works in looking to the wants of the poor."[1] Brigham Young appointed "farmers to the Indians," men who were called to help Native Americans improve their agricultural skills. During and after World Wars I and II, the Church sent food, medical supplies, and clothing to victims throughout the world. Efforts much like these continue in the present day, though you may be surprised and certainly impressed with the extent of Church humanitarian work. Few people understand the breadth and the depth of the work of the Church in caring for people of all denominations throughout the world. Joseph Smith said that Church members should strive to "feed the hungry, to clothe the naked, . . . to comfort the afflicted, whether in this church or in any other, or in no church at all, wherever he finds them."[2] Let me touch briefly on the doctrinal basis for humanitarian work and then provide an overview of what the Church is doing and what you can do if you become interested in humanitarian service.

Why are Latter-day Saints involved in humanitarian work?

Harold C. Brown, an area authority seventy in the Utah North Area, is managing director of Welfare Services for The Church of Jesus Christ of Latter-day Saints. He previously served for nine years as commissioner of LDS Social Services. He and his wife, Penny Dalton, are the parents of ten children.

Four doctrinal principles point to its necessity in our lives. The first principle is from James 1:27: "Pure religion and undefiled before God and the Father is this, To visit the fatherless and widows in their affliction, and to keep [yourself] unspotted from the world." In short, pure religion is "doing good" and "being good." Mormonism may be summarized in those four words. When we do good, it is easier to be good. And when we are good, our hearts are turned to those in need.

Second, our happiness and joy are rooted in sacrifice and service to others. As we unselfishly give of our means and our hearts to others and discipline ourselves to sacrifice, we experience lasting joy. Giving blesses both giver and receiver. My son is on a mission in Oaxaca, Mexico, where the Saints are very, very poor. Nevertheless, they feed the missionaries. Our son is six foot seven, and our food bill was cut in half when he left. It was cheaper to send him than to keep him home. He seemed to eat everything and anything. He and his companion were invited into the home of a woman he referred to as the poorest woman in the ward in Oaxaca. They sat down to a dinner of beans and tortillas. He wrote to us, "We ate it all." She asked if they would like more. As I was reading his letter, I thought, *Please, Troy, say no.* But he said, "Yes, please." So she served him the rest of the beans. Then she said, "I have one very small egg left. Would you like that?" Again, as a father, I thought, *Please, say no.* But he said, "Yes, please." She fried the small egg and cut it in half for those two missionaries and fed them. Then they started to read the scriptures to express their gratitude for what she had done. She broke down in tears and said, "Thank you, thank you. I have felt that others who have come to my home did not like my food. Thank you for letting me give to you." That is the spirit of the gospel of Jesus Christ, the spirit of giving that can bless even the poorest widow in Oaxaca, Mexico.

In my work in LDS Social Services, I have visited with very unhappy people. Sometimes life is challenging. We are all unhappy once in a while. But when we become downhearted or most in need of spiritual strength, we sometimes neglect serving others, which is the very thing that could bring us the greatest joy and happiness.

Third, we have a covenant obligation to care for the needy. There are those today who worry about the world running out of food. But the Lord has said, "there is enough and to spare" (D&C 104:17). Proper distribution, rather than inadequate food, is the problem. We have been blessed with an abundance, especially compared to most of those who reside in other parts of the world, and the Lord asks that we give our portion to the poor and needy.

"What is our portion?" we might ask. I was thinking recently about the cost of automobiles. A friend purchased an expensive car, and I thought to myself, *You could have bought a car for less and given the difference to the poor and needy.* And then I thought, *Well, I don't have that kind of car, but I have a nice car. Why didn't I buy a car for less and give the difference to the poor and needy?* Someone who had purchased a new Ford could have purchased a used Ford or perhaps ridden the bus and then given the money saved to the poor and needy. The point is this: you must determine your "portion" in your own heart and soul. No one can decide for you or for me what our portion is. But we should think and pray about this regularly, realizing that we have a covenant obligation to care for the poor and the needy.

Fourth, both our temporal and our spiritual well-being are connected to our caring for others in need. The Lord's promises to us are marvelous. Listen to the prophet Isaiah speaking to those who fast and give to the poor: "Then shall thy light break forth as the morning, and thine health shall spring forth speedily: and thy righteousness shall go before thee. . . . Then shalt thou call, and the Lord shall answer; thou shalt cry, and he shall say, Here I am" (Isaiah 58:8–9). Our giving and caring for others is tied directly to our spiritual strength. I find that I receive more inspiration from heaven when I do my home teaching or volunteer hours at the cannery or at the Deseret Industries Sort Center than I can by spending long hours on my knees without serving.

Prayer is most effective when it is accompanied by service. Revelation comes to people who are on the Lord's errand. We read of the Lord's command to pray: "Cry unto him in your houses, yea, over all your household, both morning, mid-day, and evening . . . pour out your souls in your closets, and your secret places, and in your wilderness" (Alma 34:21–26). But listen to the sobering words that follow: "And now behold, . . . do not suppose that this [praying] is all; for after ye have done all these things, if ye turn away the needy, and the naked, and visit not the sick and afflicted, and impart of your substance, if ye have, to those who stand in need . . . , behold, your prayer is vain, . . . and ye are as hypocrites" (Alma 34:28). That is unequivocal. Yes, we are to pray, and pray constantly, but if we want God's blessings and presence in our lives, we must also care for others.

During the last decade or so, the Church has been involved in a significant way in assisting those in need in every part of the world. Why, other than for doctrinal reasons, do we do this? We do it simply for the good it does. It is wonderful to bless the lives of people, to care for and help them in some way. Humanitarian service also demonstrates the blessings of the gospel and shows through us, his servants, that God is a caring God. Service also promotes long-term, spiritual well-being, both in the giver and the receiver, and opens doors that may have, in the past, been closed to the Church and its message. Some countries do not officially recognize the Church, but they are willing to cooperate in humanitarian projects. Such efforts may, at some future time, lead to improved relations.

The Church has participated, often linking hands with other service organizations, in more than twenty-three hundred humanitarian projects worldwide during the last decade. At the end of 1995, the General Welfare Committee approved and established an organization known as Latter-day Saint Charities. Latter-day Saint Charities is a nongovernmental organization similar to the Red Cross, Catholic Charities, AfriCare, or Mercy Corps International. Such organizations register in various countries of the world to provide humanitarian aid.

Latter-day Saint Charities acts to relieve suffering during times of emergency when natural disasters occur throughout the world. Church humanitarian aid also addresses the needs of the chronically poor. For example, some African villages are without a water supply—water must be carried for miles. The Church's goal is to help these people help themselves. We help dig wells and organize other efforts to provide some of the goods and expertise that bring about self-reliance. We strengthen individuals and families to be productive and self-reliant and teach them welfare principles. We teach job search skills to help people find meaningful employment. We have sent missionary couples with medical and nursing expertise to train hospital personnel in underdeveloped areas. We help enlarge the capacity of communities and local institutions to teach and serve others.

Some of the money for this assistance comes from donations to the Church. During the last twelve years, $26 million in cash went to these countries. The value of donated products distributed over the same period equaled nearly $163 million, and 137 countries have received humanitarian aid from the Church. More than one thousand volunteers serve as full-time welfare missionaries in thirty-three countries. We have distributed twenty million pounds of food, forty-one million pounds of clothing, and two million pounds of medical equipment and supplies worldwide. One woman from St. Petersburg, Russia, wrote: "We are very pleased to receive this clothing. Last year's winter coats for an adult cost 4,000 rubles; today it is more than 40,000 rubles, an increase of tenfold. This is more than a month's salary for a teacher or an engineer to buy one coat.

When we receive these things, it inspires us to reach out to others."[3]

The Church has also been involved in several hundred projects working with communities to better themselves and more than a hundred individual productivity projects in the past twelve years. For instance, in Kenya, Africa, the Church, in cooperation with other relief agencies, donated 271 tons of food and medical supplies to save the lives of an estimated three thousand malnourished, refugee Somalian children. In Russia, a physician-training exchange significantly reduced infant mortality. Four Utah physicians trained staff members in Russia, and eight Russian neonatologists received training in Utah. The Church also donated equipment valued at $1 million to a Russian hospital. In Cambodia, the Church instituted a food-processing training program and sent experts—couples—to set up equipment and machinery. Cambodia has its first-ever cannery, and, at a local university, Cambodians are learning how to can various types of produce. In Guatemala, people with modest skills and certification can get jobs. But without the means to go to school, they have difficulty finding desirable employment. With a small amount of humanitarian money donated by the Church, Latter-day Saint Charities contracted with an electrician to train and certify more than two dozen Guatemalans in electrical work. All twenty-five or so of the young men who took the course got jobs.

Through the Thrasher Foundation, the Church is also sponsoring a project to help destroy the worms children pick up when they walk barefoot on fecal material. Mothers and fathers often refuse to rub salt on their children's feet to kill the worms because of the pain it causes the children. Once the infection is advanced, the children cannot walk, so they crawl on their hands and knees, and the worms then go into the palms of their hands and into their knees. Donated shoes and other clothing from Deseret Industries also helps address this problem.

Hundreds of thousands of lives have been touched by

humanitarian service. Joseph Smith said, "A man filled with the love of God, is not content with helping his family alone, but ranges through the whole world, anxious to bless the whole human race."[4] In our day, President Gordon B. Hinckley echoes those sentiments: "Where there is stark hunger, regardless of the cause, I will not let political considerations dull my sense of mercy or thwart my responsibility to the sons and daughters of God, wherever they may be or whatever their circumstances."[5]

What can we do to help? On the donation slip for tithing and fast offerings, a line has been added for donations to humanitarian aid. When we donate tithing and fast offerings to the Church, we may also donate for humanitarian aid that will go directly to care for the needy throughout the world. No administrative costs for overhead or salaries come out of that money. Every penny we donate goes to the care of the poor and the needy. We must not, of course, slight our covenant responsibility to pay our tithes and offerings. Above and beyond that critical responsibility, we are encouraged to donate as we individually are willing and able.

Another easy way to contribute is to donate clothing to Deseret Industries. Some of it will end up for sale in the stores, but yearly, nine to ten million pounds of clothing donated to Deseret Industries will be distributed to the needy worldwide. Income received at Deseret Industries stores is also used to bless the poor and needy who work there.

Consider serving as a Church-service or welfare missionary at some point. Raymond and Jo Reed served in India. He was a professor of physical education at Weber State. Their mission involved teaching basketball workshops at local schools and coaching both the girls' basketball team at a Catholic school and Special Olympics teams. George and Yvonne Hilton taught advanced eye-care techniques at fifteen ophthalmology conferences to specialists throughout India. Garth and Isabell Nelson supervised the installation and maintenance of the cannery in

Cambodia. And Doug Christensen helped distribute donations totaling over one million pounds of clothing, food, and medical equipment to the poor and needy in India.

At the Sort Center (where we may also volunteer), books, clothing, and medical equipment are gathered to be sent throughout the world. Some women knit bandages for the Sort Center. While waiting in the foyer for her temple recommend interview, a woman was asked by her stake president what she was knitting. "It's for the Sort Center," she replied. "It's a leper bandage. It's made out of special cotton material that stretches and can be washed." She said that she did not believe she would ever be a Relief Society president or other leader, "but I can knit leper bandages for people whom I will never meet." She has knitted dozens of them. She takes her knitting on the plane or wherever she goes and knits every spare minute for the care of someone she will never know. Just a simple project. You can do similar projects in your home as a family, as an individual, or as a youth or Relief Society project. Start small; a huge project may be overwhelming. Susan Webb, stake homemaking counselor in the Relief Society of the Smithfield Utah North Stake, has described how small projects, begun by the stake Relief Society, sprang up in the families throughout their stake like runners from ivy.[6]

Many possible projects can benefit our neighborhoods or cities. We do not have to wait to be told what to do. We don't have to work through Deseret Industries Sort Center or Latter-day Saint Charities. There is opportunity everywhere—to do good and be good.

NOTES

1. Jill Mulvay Derr, Janath Russell Cannon, Maureen Ursenbach Beecher, *Women of Covenant: The Story of Relief Society* (Salt Lake City: Deseret Book, 1992), 30.

2. Joseph Smith, *Times and Seasons,* 15 March 1842, 732.

3. Letter in the Welfare Services files, Church Office Building, Salt Lake City, Utah.

4. Joseph Smith, *Teachings of the Prophet Joseph Smith,* sel. Joseph Fielding Smith (Salt Lake City: Deseret Book, 1938), 174.

5 Gordon B. Hinckley, "The Victory over Death," *Ensign,* May 1985, 54.

6. See Susan Webb, "Afghans for Africa," in this volume, pages 101–5.

AFGHANS FOR AFRICA

SUSAN WEBB

As part of a stake Relief Society women's conference, we invited Brother Ron Garrison, director of Church Human Resources, to speak about the humanitarian work of the Church. As he walked through the building, he saw the items that had been donated, the quilts to be tied set up in the cultural hall, and the many other work projects that were planned for that day. He turned to us with tears in his eyes, "You do not comprehend what you are doing here today," he said. "You are literally saving thousands of lives." Because it was such a simple thing we were doing, we truly did not comprehend. We had merely chosen the high priority items suggested by the Deseret Industries Sort Center. We did not realize that a self-sealing plastic bag filled with items such as soap could save a person's life. In a country ravaged by cholera, that bar of soap means the difference between life and death. After he spoke, the Spirit of the Lord filled that building as we worked, quilted, assembled kits, and completed other projects. We knew that the Lord knew what we were doing. The sisters went home thrilled to have been part of humanitarian service work. These sisters enthusiastically spread the word, and before long everyone in our stake wanted to participate.

Susan Riley Webb, a graduate of Utah State University, taught speech and English in high school but has been privileged to spend her married life as a wife and mother. She and her husband, Alan K. Webb, are the parents of five children. She serves in her stake Relief Society presidency.

When we began, we did not have a budget for the humanitarian project. But this wonderful work does not take a lot of money. Everything you need is in someone's garage, in someone's closet, in someone's basement, in someone's attic. All you have to do is say, "This is what we want to do," and the Lord will provide the way.

Following the Sort Center's guidelines, Primary children made small toys that were simple and easily painted. The priesthood quorums donated the wood and all the other materials, and the brethren cut out the toys. What a sweet experience it was to watch four- and five-year-old children sanding wooden blocks. Our children could scarcely understand that those toys would be going to children who had never had a toy of their own.

When we wanted yarn for knitted and crocheted items, we asked for donations. We filled large plastic garbage bags full of donated yarn. The sisters in our stake made hats. They made scarves. They made mittens and booties and all sorts of other knitted and crocheted items. Sisters thirteen years old, sisters in their late eighties and nineties, and even men knitted and crocheted leper bandages. What a blessing this activity has been for our stake.

Women in their later years who felt they were not needed anymore, that there was no purpose for them, came to us and said, "We can do this. We can do this in our homes. We know we can make a difference." They now feel wanted and needed, and they tell us: "This is what Relief Society is all about." Those older sisters have taught the younger sisters skills they had not wanted to learn before: how to sew, how to knit, how to crochet. Our attendance at homemaking meeting has increased, and this work has brought the Spirit of the Lord into our wards.

One sister made three baby afghans and then began a full-sized one. She has made a lot of afghans, and she knew exactly what she was doing. When she was about a third of the way finished, she held up the afghan and found it was taller than she was. She thought to herself, *Well, there are a lot of tall people in the world; I'll just finish this.* She continued to work on it. One day her son-in-law visited her. He is six foot four. She held it up to him, and it was taller than he was. Now this sister thought to herself, *I am doing this for the Savior. It has to be perfect. I will do it over.* (Anyone who has made an afghan knows how much effort that is!) She sat down to take it out, but as she did, in her mind's eye she saw a tall, dark man standing in desolate surroundings. There was a child beside him, and the afghan was wrapped around them both. She decided to finish the afghan as it was because she had such strong feelings for this man. But as she continued to work, she began to doubt herself. She thought, *I just imagined that man, but I'll finish it anyway and send it as it is.* She took the finished afghan to our women's conference as her donation. She was especially interested when Brother Garrison began speaking about Africa and the need for blankets there, where you wouldn't think there would be a need. "But when people are starving, they must maintain their body heat or die," he explained. Blankets are needed in Africa. As he spoke, she again saw the tall, dark-skinned man in her mind's eye. And she knew that by fall he would have his afghan. What an incredible spirit this work brings with it.

The work has also blessed our youth, mostly through a variety of Laurel and Eagle projects, from gathering first-aid supplies and constructing shipping crates to handcrafting sock dolls. We have seen young people in our wards and in our stake change. Four of my five children are in their teenage years—a very selfish, me-oriented time of life, and a necessary stage in growing up and learning independence. But this project has widened their focus as they have made items for other people, such as leper bandages, quilts, sock dolls and stuffed animals, and, most important to the Laurels, wall hangings for orphanages. The need for brightly colored wall hangings touched their hearts. Many newborn babies in third-world countries end up in orphanages. There they are placed on their backs in cribs. They stare up at white ceilings, white lights, white walls; and they go blind because they never have to use their eye muscles. These cheerful splashes of color in their white world add interest and require them to exercise their optic muscles as they shift focus.

Several families decided to make school kits as a family project. The parents gave their children chores to earn money and then, on a family expedition, they bought the school items for the kits, put them together as a family, and donated them. What a blessing and what a spirit such united effort has brought into those homes.

At our request, the Sort Center gave our stake a special project: to mend clothing that would be sent to Africa and Russia in huge, four-foot-by-four-foot wooden shipping crates. My son decided his Eagle project would be to build shipping crates to contain the items that we mended. To emphasize the plight of people in these third-world countries, I explained to the Scouts at work in our garage why the Sort Center always needed more crates. The Sort Center representative had told us that often when they send shipping crates to Africa, they don't get them back because the people keep them to live in.

One day I went out into the garage where they were working on the crates and noticed a young man, down on his hands and knees on a board drilling holes right in the middle where there shouldn't be holes. I asked him what he was doing. Words can't describe the look on his face as he looked up at me and said, "I didn't want to do that, but something told me to mark this board. I didn't do it—but it came to me again: 'Mark your board.' So I am drilling three holes in the middle of this board. I hope they call me on a mission to Africa. And if they do, I'm going to find this board and preach the gospel of Jesus Christ to the family living beneath it." A fourteen-year-old boy had a spiritual experience with the humanitarian work of the Church in my garage.

I testify to you that this is the Lord's work. It does not matter how old we are or how young we are, blessings will come into our personal lives, into our homes, our wards, and our stakes as we participate in this incredible work. May you feel the joy of humanitarian service that we have felt.

SUCCEEDING WITH LITERACY

CARMEN PRATT SHUMWAY

I am from Taylor, a small northern Arizona town that is 75 percent Latter-day Saint. We began a literacy program in our stake in October 1995, and implementing it has been a marvelous experience. We not only teach people how to read and write but we teach faith and testimony. As we read the scriptures and bear testimony, the faith of our students increases. As their testimonies increase, so does their ability to master the reading materials.

Because literacy specialists are navigating in uncharted waters, two people should be called to work together. Developing your own program according to the needs of your members takes two. Sister Evon Rogers and I were called about eighteen months ago by the stake president. When I was discouraged, she was enthusiastic—and vice versa. We telephoned each other every day to confer because we each needed a sounding board for our ideas.

Priesthood support has been very important to us. Getting priesthood support is part of the calling. It's important to remember that priesthood leaders have many things to worry about and direct. We have been very specific in our requests and have explained the program carefully. It's our responsibility to teach them. Our stake president lets us use the high

---

Carmen Pratt Shumway, a graduate of Brigham Young University, taught grade school for seventeen years and served two missions. She and her husband, Lenn M. Shumway, are the parents of six children. She serves as the literacy specialist for her stake.

council room as a classroom on Tuesdays and Thursday nights for an hour. He announced the first meeting in stake conference; I had written out the announcement for him. He suggested that I accompany my husband, who is on the high council, to explain the program in all the wards when he did not have an assigned partner. All these things helped. The stake president also gave the education counselor in our stake Relief Society presidency the opportunity to present our literacy program in bishops' council. Bishops must understand this program for it to work. Next, the education counselor trained the Relief Society presidencies. As bishops and Relief Society presidents counsel with members, they are the ones who sense individual needs. A man said to his bishop, "I've gone as far as I can in my profession because I can't pass the test to go higher." "We have a program for you," the bishop was able to tell him. "Let me refer you to the literacy program."

At our first meeting, however, only one person attended, so we knew we had to go back to the drawing board and find a new way to draw interest. Our message of hope became: "If you have gaps in your learning, or if you feel uncomfortable when someone asks you to read or to write, we invite you into our homes. We will teach you, one-on-one, to fill those gaps and weave your vast experience together with literature and language. Our work will be completely confidential."

This approach gave people hope. They had had bad experiences with reading and were reluctant to put themselves at risk. We began to get calls—a timid voice on the other end of the phone saying, "Can I take the literacy class?" We have taught fifteen people in the last fifteen months, one-on-one, in our homes.

How rewarding it is to work in this program! We spend about forty minutes together using the Church's literacy manual, *Ye Shall Have My Words*. Sometimes we give three lessons at a sitting; sometimes we spend three sittings on a lesson. We're not teaching a program; we're filling individual needs.

After that forty minutes, they read to us from the Book of Mormon or short articles from the *Ensign* (the "Mormon Journal" at the back of the *Ensign* has articles that are just about the right length). If they are beginning readers, articles in the *Friend* have language that is appropriate for their level. They also read to us from their journals. Every lesson has a writing component: They write in their journals and start to write their life story. This shared reading and discussion time is precious. Although we caution students not to share anything private, the reading of their journal entries is a touching experience. The same Spirit that accompanies a good missionary lesson accompanies a good literacy lesson.

After about two months of work, I asked the stake president for some parameters concerning growth. He referred us to Mosiah 4:26: "I would that ye should impart of your substance to the poor, every man according to that which he hath, such as feeding the hungry, clothing the naked, visiting the sick and administering to their relief, both spiritually and temporally, according to their wants." This scripture has guided our program. We try to help people according to their wants.

Our area has Spanish-speaking people who are not fluent in English but are trying to fit into English-speaking wards. We announced a class time in our Spanish Sunday School, and twenty people—not all of them Latter-day Saints—came to the first meeting. In response to their needs and wants, we developed our own program of English as a second language (ESL). Because we try to help these people with the life skills they need to prosper here in the United States, we devised lessons using language needed for work at a pig farm, in a doctor's or dentist's office, in cleaning a home, or in communicating with teachers at school. As the students become more advanced, they begin to study our Church literacy books, though we have to help them with some vocabulary.

We have only English-speaking missionaries in our area, so our more advanced LDS Spanish-speaking students go on splits with the elders to translate and fellowship. Everyone who has taken an ESL class with us has ended up taking the missionary lessons. Eleven members of our ESL class have been baptized. We hold a weekly family home evening with about thirty in attendance, only ten being LDS. On Sunday afternoons we have a Spanish-speaking Sunday School, and sometimes half the Relief Society room is full. A year or two ago only five or six attended.

Another wonderful thing has happened. As we have begun teaching the Spanish-speaking people, other members of our stake have begun to recognize these neighbors' needs. A woman called me last Christmas and said, "I have a half a beef. Would you distribute it among some of the sisters that need it, members and nonmembers alike?" One interesting phone call brought seven girls and their dates to my house before a school dance. We took them to seven homes, and they left a turkey on each doorstep, knocked on the door, and ran. I can't imagine a better activity before a dance.

One nonmember man wanted to take the literacy lessons. When he called, I said, "You need to understand that part of our reading will be from the Book of Mormon." He said, "I will read from your Book of Mormon if I can take the lessons." He was a businessman who had hired secretaries to do what he couldn't do. Now his work has moved him to a town about eighty miles away, but he drives back twice a week to continue the literacy program.

Right now we're teaching six people one-on-one in our homes, and we're teaching about twenty in the Spanish program. The work hasn't all been easy, but our goal has been to proceed with faith. Look at your ward or your stake as if it were a small town, and then pray to determine what you need. Your situation will not be exactly like ours. Your need may be to improve the gospel scholarship of those who can read well. You may want to help members truly understand the scriptures as they seek understanding and comfort. You may need to provide listening ears for children whose single parents don't have time to listen to them read at home. You surely want to help members gain an in-depth testimony of the gospel of Jesus Christ, to truly know his words and to be able to live by his words. Ask Heavenly Father to bless your efforts, and he will direct you in what you need in your areas. He will open up a way.

Let me relate one example. We have found it very hard to change students from one teacher to another. I had two or three new students, but I didn't have any more teachers. I already had three students myself plus the Spanish class, so I knelt and told Heavenly Father, "I have to have a new teacher, and sometimes callings come slowly." The next day at noon, a sister came up to me and said, "How can I get involved in the literacy program?" I said, "The Lord surely sent you. When can you start?" She was called, and someone else was empowered with new knowledge.

I know the literacy program works. When we work under priesthood and Relief Society leadership, we work under an umbrella of faith and inspiration. The underlying success and strength of our literacy program stems from the fact that not only is it educationally sound but it is an inspired program. Heavenly Father will help you direct its implementation.

CONFLICT RESOLUTION: COME LET US REASON TOGETHER

SUSAN BRADSHAW, CHERYL B. PRESTON, AND KATHY PULLINS

Conflict is a fact of life. Lehi instructs his son Jacob, "For it must needs be, that there is an opposition in all things" (2 Nephi 2:11). Opposition is the source of all growth and an absolute necessity if one is to be alive, interacting with others. The goal and eternal principle is that the complementary joining of ideas and approaches leads to the best and most creative solutions.

The idea of conflict, a state of opposition, is often equated with contention, a negative and unrighteous attitude, something to avoid. How do we prevent conflict, which is useful, from escalating to contention, which we want to avoid? What are the skills to manage conflict in respectful, peaceable ways? How do we become peacemakers?

Susan Bradshaw is the mother of three children and serves as a Laurel advisor in her ward. She is the director of Utah Dispute Resolution, a community mediation service.

Cheryl Bailey Preston, a professor of law at Brigham Young University, is a researcher and published author on gender topics. She and her husband, Stanley J. Preston, are the parents of three children. She serves as the activities committee chair in her ward.

Kathy Pullins, chair of the 1997 Brigham Young University Women's Conference committee, is the assistant dean of the J. Reuben Clark Law School at BYU. She is a trained mediator and teaches alternative dispute resolution. Kathy and her husband, Gary, are the parents of four sons. Her interests include teaching aerobics, gardening, and appreciating people.

Imagine this scenario in a church kitchen. Sister S., the ward Relief Society president, is discussing with one of her counselors, Sister E., a problem the ward is having.

SISTER S.: I've been thinking about the parking problem at the chapel. Last week after we set up homemaking meeting, I walked around the parking lot and considered the problem from several angles. Based on my measurements, we could have another row of parking if traffic moved consistently in the same direction. If everyone entered the lot from Parkview and exited on 89th, the process of one ward emptying while the next is arriving would be smoother. If we painted the curb red in front of the church along Parkview, we could use that extra lane for making the right hand turn into the parking lot. Sure, some families will have to go an extra block to enter on the Parkview side, but the result would be well worth any inconvenience. Here, let me draw you a diagram to show you how it could work . . .

[*The scene changes to welfare meeting. Sister S. and Sister E. are sitting together in the bishop's office as members of the council.*]

BISHOP: Welcome to welfare meeting this morning. We have several items on the agenda, but first I want to talk about the parking situation. I am increasingly concerned about this. More and more members are late to sacrament meeting because of the confusion when one ward exits and the next arrives. And last Sunday, we had another "fender bender." By the time everyone gets parked and into the meeting, members are so frustrated it is hard to feel the Spirit. I also know there are really strong and somewhat bitter feelings about the situation with four wards in the building. But there is just no way the stake can take a ward to another building or give us more time between meeting blocks. Any ideas?

[*Various council members whisper to their neighbors with some undertones of disagreement. No one offers a specific response to the bishop's question. Sister E. looks meaningfully at Sister S., who just shrugs.*]

Was Sister S. right to stay out of the conflict? Every situation is different, of course, but it seems unfortunate to waste Sister S.'s contribution to resolving this problem. We suspect she is practicing avoidance—avoiding contention. Yet, the scriptures warn us about hiding our light under a bushel (see Matthew 5:14–17). In addition, we have all made a commitment to sustain our leaders. Sister S.'s idea could have resolved the controversy, or at least opened a discussion, but instead the problem will continue to fuel bad feelings among the members meeting in this building. Jesus did not shy away from teaching when he had an audience that might learn, even if some people might have been offended by his teachings. In Matthew 5:2, the scripture says that "he opened his mouth," and in Matthew 13:57, we are told that some people "were offended in him."

Perhaps we should give Sister S. another chance. Imagine that same welfare meeting. The bishop has just said, "Any ideas?"

SISTER S.: Well, I'm really no expert or anything, and you don't have to take my suggestion—I mean it is just an idea—but I was thinking we could have the traffic go one way . . .

BROTHER O. (interrupting): We've tried everything already. Remember last summer when we told everyone to walk to church or shuttle from the grocery store parking? [*Silence for a moment.*]

SISTER S.: Well yes, but I was thinking we could paint arrows to indicate one way and the priests could help direct traffic for a few weeks until everyone gets accustomed to the routine . . .

Sister S. volunteered her idea, but how effective was she in conveying it? Her manner of delivery sabotaged her content. *Sabot* is the French root of the word *sabotage*. A sabot is a heavy, wooden-soled shoe. During the French Revolution, factory workers who wore them, when being watched, ran the machinery as trained. But, unobserved, they slipped their shoes into the works of the machinery, jamming it so nothing was accomplished. That seems to be exactly what Sister S. is doing. Although she is now expressing her idea on one hand, she is discounting it on the other. We doubt she intends this result, but she has fallen into several language traps that diminish her chances of being taken seriously.

Research shows that women are perceived as less credible and less effective in influencing mixed group decisions when they use culturally trained "self-trivializing messages."[1] These include an unnecessarily high voice pitch; a rising intonation (a swing upward in tone at the end of phrases or sentences) that conveys hesitancy, uncertainty, and incompleteness of thought; qualifiers; disclaimers; tag questions; and compound requests. In addition, Sister S. allows herself to be easily interrupted and drawn off her point.

Although women in many cultures learn to communicate with each other this way, they can relearn their communication style to talk in more powerful ways when the occasion calls for it. This is not to say that one type of communication style is better than another. Many of us have a closet full of shoes: boots, sandals, dress shoes, athletic shoes, and maybe a sabot or two. What you select to wear for the day depends on where you are going, what the occasion will be, and what you are trying to accomplish. We all have learned how to make appropriate choices in most aspects of our lives. Boots may be the best choice for shoveling snow off the driveway, but sandals are the best choice for a hot day at the beach. Athletic shoes may be the most comfortable, but we don't recommend them for weddings or for wearing with graduation robes. Similarly, we are more effective in our communication if we make style choices based on the best information we can get about the context, audience, and objectives of a discussion.

To avoid being misunderstood, we have to learn the dialect

of others with whom we hope to communicate, just as missionaries learn the languages of the people they are sent to teach. And just as there are cultural differences, so there are generational and gender differences in language. In fact, linguists have identified a "genderlect," a kind of dialect that differs by gender.[2]

Sister S. has a good idea, and she knows it. Yet, she weakens her message in the mind of her audience before it is fully explained. She appears less knowledgeable and prepared than she really is. Moreover, her style suggests that she lacks conviction about the feasibility of her own idea. If she doesn't believe in it, why should anyone else? Although there are audiences, especially in other cultures, to which Sister S.'s style would appear more polite and therefore be more respected, we need to learn the positive elements of a variety of approaches and use each as appropriate to our objectives and audience.

With this suggestion in mind, let's go to Sister S.'s presentation at next month's welfare meeting.

Sister S. (showing a chart): So, to sum up, we could increase parking stalls by fifteen and reduce accidents by directing traffic in the same direction.

Brother O.: It just isn't practical to have everyone turning off Parkview into the lot. That would cause serious backup on one of the city's busiest streets. Just painting the curb red does not make it a turn lane. The city would need to restripe the road, and they will never do that for us. It just isn't workable!

Sister S. (looking hurt and defeated): You're probably right.

[*Later, between meetings, Brother O. passes Sister S. in the hallway. He smiles affably at Sister S., who turns away, still offended. She walks out to her car and complains to her family about Brother O. being arrogant.*]

It's obvious that Sister S.'s feelings have been hurt by Brother O., but instead of working through their disagreements about the feasibility of a turn lane, Sister S. has become personal and defensive. This interferes with her ability to contribute effectively to the dialogue. In addition, Sister S.'s reaction could poison her relationship with Brother O. Although he probably should have been more sensitive in how he commented on her idea, he most likely didn't mean to offend or to suggest any disrespect for Sister S.

Even in situations where a comment is meant to be hurtful or demeaning, Sister S.'s response is counterproductive. Elder Neal A. Maxwell warns us that "we have an obligation to work out impasses as well as trespasses in interpersonal relationships." He quotes scripture in support of that idea: "Moreover if thy brother shall trespass against thee, go and tell him his fault between thee and him alone: if he shall hear thee, thou hast gained thy brother" (Matthew 18:15). As Elder Maxwell explains: "To take the initiative in repairing or strengthening a relationship takes both love and courage. Others don't always respond to such initiatives: some peacemakers are spurned. Absent such initiatives, however, the impasses remain or deepen."[3]

Let's give Sister S. another try in this situation. Back to the welfare meeting.

BROTHER O. (interrupting again): Just painting the curb red does not make it a turn lane. The city would need to restripe the road, and they will never do that for us. It just isn't workable!

SISTER S.: If we do need to restripe the road, I believe the city will cooperate. I looked in the public records, and the city has restriped or changed traffic patterns in more drastic ways at the request of citizen groups seven times in the last two years. We shouldn't have any problem convincing the city engineer that restriping Parkview is in the city's interest as much as ours.

[*Later Sister S. approaches Brother O. in the hall.*]

SISTER S.: You seemed quite unhappy with my proposal this morning. I am concerned that you may have a problem with me, as well as with my idea. Have I done something to offend you? I have always considered you a good friend and will do whatever it takes to clear up any difficulties in our relationship.

BROTHER O.: I'm sorry I was abrupt, Sister S. It definitely isn't you. My father has been staying with us, and he is very ill. I have a lot of things on my mind, and I realize I've been irritable with everyone the last few days. You certainly have done your homework. I didn't realize that the city had cooperated with other groups. The more I think about your plan, the more I see it makes sense. It could work.

Our fictitious character Sister S. has come a long way in resolving conflict. She has learned to take the risk of contributing, she can express her ideas with confidence, and she has learned to respond to criticism without becoming defensive or developing hurt feelings. But Sister S. has been in fairly supportive and friendly environments. What happens if she runs into some real hostility? Let's see Sister S. at the city engineer's office.

SISTER S. (explaining her idea across the desk from the city engineer): With this minor change in the layout of Parkview, the traffic will flow much smoother and we can avoid the congestion that is common on those days activities are held at our church building.

ENGINEER (hostile): That isn't the point. I just can't go around moving city streets at the whim of every organization in the city.

SISTER S.: I understand your concern. We acknowledge that this will require some expense and time on your part. The nearly twelve hundred citizens of this city who attend church meetings and weekday activities in that building, though, will appreciate your cooperation. And making a right turn lane on Parkview for the length of the church property will ease traffic for everyone who uses that street.

ENGINEER: You people are so pushy! "Twelve hundred citizens"! Is that a threat? The snobs in that part of town think they have a right to demand all kinds of special treatment. Can't you see I'm just too busy for this nonsense?

Sister S. is in a tight spot now. She may be sorry she ever brought up the idea, but there is bound to be some discomfort when we take risks and seek changes. If we want to make a difference, we can't just avoid discussion. On the other hand, we don't need to become part of the contention in a negative way. The scriptures warn us not to revile against revilers (D&C 19:30) nor respond in kind when we are attacked (Matthew 13:55–57).

When dealing with conflict, it helps to understand on what level the conflict is occurring. At the first level, there is simply a problem to solve. The second level involves problem solving but includes the difficult element of relationship mixed into the problem to be solved. The third level escalates the conflict to a point where one side must "win" or "be right." On this third level, both sides enlist others to agree with them. The fourth and fifth levels represent conflict that has grown out of control and shifted beyond a desire to win to a desire to hurt, banish, or destroy the other.

When determining how to manage conflict, first try to determine the level on which the conflict is occurring. Then think about how to resolve the conflict and also how to avoid having the conflict escalate to the next level.

Most of our conflicts exist at level two. When we have a disagreement with another person, it is difficult to separate the problem from the feelings. The desire to protect ourselves becomes as important as solving the problem.

A primary goal in resolving conflict at level two is to recognize what is making us afraid and what might be creating fear in the other party. It is interesting to note that heavenly messengers often begin by saying, "Fear not." The angel Gabriel said to Mary, "Fear not, Mary: for thou hast found favour with God" (Luke 1:30). An angel appearing to the shepherds said, "Fear not: for, behold, I bring you good tidings of great joy" (Luke 2:10). Christ also used the phrase many times in his teachings. For instance, "And Jesus said unto Simon, Fear not; from henceforth thou shalt catch men" (Luke 5:10).

To resolve a conflict at level two without letting it escalate into contention, we must first take a step back and look at our fears. Consider Susan's experience: "I am one of three Laurel advisors in my ward. I was assigned to prepare the lesson on Easter Sunday. I worked hard and late into the night to prepare, but when I arrived early on Sunday morning, no Laurels were there. The new Young Women president had decided to have them attend Relief Society where one of the other Laurel advisors was giving the lesson for Easter. At first I was very angry. In fact, for a few days I mumbled to myself about how much the new Young Women president had to learn. I soon grew tired of these bothersome thoughts, however, and I took a step back and asked myself, 'What is your fear?' I realized that I was afraid the new Young Women president or others who might have notified me of the change did not value me. I feared not being valued. Once I realized this, my anger dissolved. After recognizing these feelings, the next week I approached the Young Women president to resolve my concerns. Ironically, before I could say a word, she turned to me in tears and said, 'I feel so incompetent. I am making so many mistakes. I am so afraid I cannot do this job. I just don't have what it takes.' When I understood my fears and knew her fears, future conflicts were easy to resolve. I felt nothing but warmth and a desire to support her."

Christ declares, "Blessed are the peacemakers: for they shall be called the children of God" (Matthew 5:9; see also 3 Nephi 12:9). If we are peacemakers, we will indeed be as God would have us be. We will resemble him because we act as he acts, contributing peace to a world of strife. With the covenants we have made comes responsibility to change our own hearts and to assist others in their change and growth. Such "heart changing" leads us to view conflict, which is an inevitable occurrence in human interaction, in the way Christ, the bearer of peace everlasting, would—to promote growth and progress toward perfection. Such is the approach of a peacemaker.

NOTES

1. See Deborah Borishoff and Lisa Merrill, *The Power to Communicate: Gender Differences as Barriers,* 2d ed. (Prospect Heights, Ill.: Waveland Press, 1992), 27–31.

2. For more information on "genderlect," see Deborah Tannen, *You Just Don't Understand: Women and Men in Conversation* (New York: Ballantine Books, 1990); Janet E. Ainsworth, "In a Different Register: The Pragmatics of Powerlessness in Police Interrogation," *Yale Law Journal* 103 (1993): 275–86; Roger Fisher and William Ury, *Getting to Yes: Negotiating Agreement without Giving In* (New York: Penguin Books, 1991); Tom Peters, "The Best Managers Will Listen, Motivate, Support: Isn't That Just Like a Woman?" *Working Woman,* Sept. 1990, 142; Lee A. Susardi, "When a Woman Speaks, Does Anybody Listen?" *Working Woman,* July 1990, 92.

3. Neal A. Maxwell, *Wherefore, Ye Must Press Forward* (Salt Lake City: Deseret Book, 1977), 88–89.

THE GRIEVING PROCESS

IONE J. SIMPSON

I became a widow when I was fifty years old. My husband died in a drowning accident. One day we had been planning what we would do for the rest of our lives; the next day he was gone. All except one of our children were married, in college, or on a mission. Our youngest daughter was a senior in high school, but she also would soon be off on her own. We figured we had about five more years, and then we could make definite plans.

How did I react when my husband was suddenly taken from me? I reacted in a normal way, but I didn't know it was normal. I wish I had known at the time some of the things that I learned later when I went back to school and became a social worker. I wish I had known about grief and its stages. Grieving is so important to our mental health and to our eventual recovery. It's good to understand the grieving process before you are in the midst of it. The steps of grief may not be the same for every individual, but the stages of denial, anger, depression, and acceptance are recognizable and present in almost every kind of trauma.[1]

Briefly, this was my experience. My husband and I went

Ione J. Simpson is the mother of six children, grandmother of thirty-two, and great-grandmother of thirteen. Widowed at age fifty, she earned her master's degree in social work and worked for ten years at LDS Social Services in adoptions. Now retired, she volunteers on a help line for unwed mothers. She has served on the Relief Society General Board and presently serves in her ward Relief Society.

with some other couples—stake presidents and their wives—on an outing. As we were canoeing down what looked like a quiet river, our canoe tipped over. I got out of the water, but Del drowned. As we drove home that evening—there were five of us in the car—I could hear others crying softly, but I couldn't cry. I was numb. I felt embarrassed, wondering what was wrong with me. I was totally numb. Mentally, I knew what had happened, but I had absolutely no feeling. It hurt me that I didn't. We drove home, and my daughters met me at the door. I told them that their father was gone—that he had drowned. I didn't even think about it at the time, but they didn't cry either. They just looked at me quizzically. I later learned that I was in shock, the first stage of grieving, as were they. But it was a blessing. Had I fully realized at the time what had happened, the shock could have been too difficult to handle. As it was, I temporarily had no feeling or real comprehension of what had occurred. I was in denial.

The next few days seemed unreal. I stoically made plans for the funeral—made decisions about details; spent hours writing a talk to be read by my daughter-in-law about his life; talked with his sisters, gathering information about their early years together—all with little emotion. Even at the funeral and afterward as the family gathered for a meal, I felt nothing.

I don't recall just how long this went on, but I do remember several instances in the next few months of unexpectedly breaking into tears in public with no apparent cause and then feeling embarrassed because by now I was supposed to have "recovered." I later learned that when least expected, something happens that triggers a memory or a feeling, and the tears come. In one instance, I ran into some dear friends of my parents. My parents had been on a mission in Sweden for a year, and I had not seen them since Del's death. Meeting these friends was like seeing my parents, and it brought a flood of uncontrollable tears, which to them must have been most disturbing.

The next stage is usually anger. It can be a totally unreasonable emotion and at times very inappropriate. I recall stamping my foot in front of my husband's picture and saying, "Why did you do this to me?" I felt hurt and angry that Heavenly Father would let this happen, and I recall in my prayers reminding him that we had planned to go on a mission and asking him, "Why? Why did you let this happen? Why?" I even bargained with the Lord, pleading with him to help me handle what seemed like an impossible situation: "I will read my scriptures more faithfully; I'll be more thoughtful of others." And at times I directed the anger at myself: I felt guilty because my husband hadn't particularly wanted to go on that trip that day, but he thought he probably should and he knew I wanted to, so he went. I blamed myself. I cycled through all these irrational thoughts and feelings. I felt anger, and I felt guilt. It's normal to have these feelings. At such times, it is good to have someone to talk to—someone who will listen and not be critical even when you are unreasonable. I was fortunate to have my sister-in-law, who let me call her night or day. Many times I poured out my heart to her. She listened.

The stage of anger may be followed by depression. A woman left suddenly alone may feel lost, wondering what she is going to do for the rest of her life. Often her entire adult life has been centered around her husband's comings and goings, his responsibilities at work, his church callings. Children may also have been a great part of her life, but in a different way; she has been responsible for them. Who is going to be responsible for her? Who will she talk to at night when it's quiet? Who can she tell her problems to? How can she manage without him?

Although the stages of grief are almost universal in times of serious personal disaster, not everyone who has tragedy in their lives reacts the same way. In the case of the widow, the reaction may depend on how death comes. When I went back to school, I read a study of two groups of widows. Half of them had gone through a long period of illness with their mate, knowing that the illness was terminal. The other half had lost their husbands in accidents or by sudden, harsh, unexpected illnesses. The study, continuing over a follow-up period of twenty years, found that those who had time to get used to the idea of the death of their mate before it happened seemed to adjust more readily afterwards. They more often remarried and resumed their normal activities sooner. Those who experienced the sudden trauma of a mate's death had more difficulty adjusting, and more of them did not remarry. Both experienced the grieving, but the first group resumed a normal life more easily.

For me, perhaps the lowest point came after about six months. One evening when I was at MIA, someone, without realizing it, said something that hurt me. I drove home that night in despair. "If Del was home," I reasoned, "I could tell him what happened, and everything would be all right." That thought hurt, but a deep depression swallowed me after I got home when it hit me that *never* again in this life would I be able to talk about little things like this with my husband. I believe that was when I finally realized what Del's death meant. For days the hurt was so deep and painful I could hardly endure it. Problems that ordinarily would have been small became large; there were no solutions. The depression deepened.

Days later an incident occurred that made me realize I was not alone, and I knew I never would be if I did my part. From then on I began to think more clearly and to accept the fact that Del was really gone and I must go on with my life. Reaching the stage of acceptance did not mean that I did not have feelings of denial, anger, and depression again, but gradually it got easier. The truth is that grief doesn't progress in an orderly fashion. It's messy, disruptive, and overwhelming. One day you'll think, *I'm well. I feel so good today. This is finally over now.* The next day you'll be right back down in the bottom. You simply have to work your way through it. Don't give up.

Grieving eventually leads to healing, and understanding the process can help.

Many wise people advised me correctly when they counseled, "Don't make any big changes in your life for at least a year." If you start making big changes when you're not thinking clearly—and I certainly wasn't thinking clearly that first year—you do things that are unwise. Widows sometimes invest money unwisely or sell their homes and move to another place to get away from memories. But it does not help to run away. Wherever you go, you will want to be in some other place. I had to start rebuilding my life, but I needed to do it when I was thinking clearly.

Another bit of advice that helped me concerned finances. If you receive a large sum of money, perhaps from an insurance policy at the death of your spouse, be careful. It may look like more than enough to live on the rest of your life. Your children with young families may be struggling or there may be others you would like to share with, but what if you live another fifty years? "Put it away until you can plan for what you are going to do with your life" was excellent advice.

Life is not easy. It was not meant to be. Though it is good to know and understand ways to help yourself through these times, the greatest source of strength will come from your faith in our Heavenly Father and the knowledge that he truly loves you and will always be there for you. Through prayer you can talk with him and tell him of your hurt. He may not take your trial away, but he will give you the strength to handle it. We are his children, and he loves us. Someday you will look back and see how he has helped you, and you will understand and be grateful.

NOTE

1. For further information on the stages of grief, see "From Grief to Solace," in *Follow Me* (Relief Society Personal Study Guide 4, 1992), 138–41; *Relief Society Handbook*, rev. ed. (1988), 38.

THE PEACE WHICH PASSETH UNDERSTANDING

BONNIE BALLIF-SPANVILL

Why me? Why this? Why now? What purpose does this serve? Is there no other way? These are some of the questions we ask about our disappointments and heartaches in this lone and dreary world. As we begin to look for answers to these questions, we must know our sorrows, turn them around and around in our minds, and find words to describe our tender feelings. Finding ways to talk about the things that hurt us helps us to weep, to grieve for our losses, and to mourn. Author Judy Tatlebaum, in her book *Courage to Grieve,* says: "Grief is a wound that needs attention in order to heal. To work through and complete grief means to face our feelings openly and honestly. . . . Many of us fear that, if allowed in, grief will bowl us over indefinitely. The truth is that grief experienced does dissolve. The only grief that does not end is grief that has not been fully faced."[1]

I often turn to poets, who have words I could never find to capture my feelings so that I can hold them in my mind. When my husband, Robert, died a few months ago, I found the English poet Pamela Gillilan. In a few lines from her poem "When You Died," I found my grief described:

Bonnie Ballif-Spanvill is a professor of psychology at Brigham Young University and director of the Women's Research Institute. She and her husband, the late Robert John Spanvill, are the parents of three daughters.

> My eyes melted
> Spilling the inexhaustible essence of sorrow.
> The soft flesh of the body
> Melted onto chairs and into beds
> Dragging its emptiness and pain.[2]

Your own troubles and sorrows may not deal with a loved one's death. If you are wounded in any way, perhaps you can borrow a few words from Meiling Jin, a woman in Ghana:

> My poems are all jagged at the edges
> because I am a woman
> who is jagged at the edges
> I speak only of what I know.[3]

Our sorrows must be given words and space within us, but we must also move on. As long as we hold on to the happenings of this world as though they are our only purpose for being here, we are like the monkey who sees a cherry in a narrow-necked bottle. Anxious to have the cherry, the monkey slips his hand through the narrow neck of the bottle and clutches it, but with his fist closed around the cherry, his hand is imprisoned. He is so determined to have it that he will never let it go and wanders significantly disabled without the use of his hand. If we fasten our minds onto the things that have gone wrong in mortality, we are similarly disabled, imprisoned by our preoccupation with this world. We must look beyond.

This world, as the Sufis[4] say, is an illusion. Many years ago I dreamed that my husband and I were walking down a long path. We first came to a small town where people were dressed in clothes of the 1800s. Someone needed help cleaning a fireplace. Immediately I got down on my hands and knees and started cleaning. I felt happy helping. After a few minutes, my husband gently took my arm and lifted me up, urging me to leave the job that I was doing and to walk on down the path. I did so reluctantly. We had not gone very far when we came to another group of people. This time they were dressed in western cowboy clothes. Someone was injured. Again, I immediately began helping another woman care for the wounded man. Hastily we stopped the bleeding and made clean bandages from an old shirt.

Once again my husband took my arm and gently pulled me away toward the path. I hesitated but eventually followed him. We continued down the path until we met a third, a fourth, and a fifth group of people, each with problems. I quickly began to help and felt I was involved and needed in each situation. And, each time, my husband nudged me to continue along the path we had started. After we left the last group of people, we walked up a small incline to the top of a hill. We turned and looked back across the valley where we had been. All the people were taking off costumes, breaking down cardboard sets, loading big trucks, and preparing to drive away. I was stunned. What I had seen as reality was fake, and the fact that I had been caught up in it frightened me. I realized that even though the experiences of this life seem compelling, they are but tiny moments along a path that goes on forever.

Christ teaches us that this world is temporary and that the sorrows of the world will pass. Time and time again he urges us to repent and to cry repentance to others. He does not want us to tell people they are doing everything wrong. He wants us to tell them there is another way to think about our experiences in this world. *Repentance* is translated from the Greek word *metanoia*.[5] In Greek *meta* means to transform, as in metamorphosis, and *-noia* means mind. *Metanoia,* then, means the transformation of the mind. Repentance suggests a whole new way of thinking, a change in the way we view this world, lifting our thoughts to a higher realm, thinking about our problems with Christlike minds.

Everything that Christ tries to tell us is about making this transformation happen in our own hearts. We have to move away from the way the world thinks and on to this new way.

Listen once more to some of Christ's teachings about this new way of thinking: When people have taken advantage of you, turn the other cheek; when sued for your coat, give your cloak as well; if compelled to go a mile, go two; love your enemies; bless them that curse you; do good to them that hate you; pray for them who despitefully use you. Do you think about your enemies in this way? What about the people next door who have been rude or judgmental? In your everyday interactions, do you use this pattern of thought that Christ tried so hard to teach us? Most of us do not, at least not all the time.

When I was fifteen, my father was called to be the mission president in New Zealand, a beautiful country of small rolling hills. New Zealand is also called Ate'aroa which means *land of the long white cloud.* As we traveled up and down the green hills, while moving around the islands, we often saw clouds in the valley and sunlight on the hilltops. It seemed strange to me that we could go down in the valley, slow almost to a stop, unable to see our way, and then climb up to the top of a hill and see perfectly in the bright sunlight. Soon we would drive over the hill and down into a valley where we were again blinded by fog. In a similar manner, we travel through our lives, climbing up to moments of illumination and then sinking down again into habits of thinking about things in a worldly way.

In the last few years, I have lost five of those most dear to me: my eldest sister, my eldest brother, my mother, my father, and most recently my husband. Before his death, my husband was very ill and nearly died on several occasions. I often went to my Heavenly Father to try to understand how to stay up on the hill, to keep my vision clear, to keep from sinking back into the valleys of fog. Let me share one of the many experiences I had that helped me to see my situation more clearly. About seven years ago, my husband went into the hospital for a transfusion. While he was receiving the second unit of blood, he went into a coma. My father and my bishop came to the hospital to give him a blessing; they also blessed me, promising that the righteous desires of my heart would be granted unto me. I sat in the intensive care unit waiting for my husband to come out of the coma. I had lots of time to think. I prayed constantly. I talked to the Lord about Robert. I wanted so much for him to be well. Each time I began to pray, the words of the blessing I had received came strongly into my mind—the righteous desires of my heart would be granted. I wondered what could be more righteous than to have my husband live? My young children needed him! I was confident that my desire was righteous.

The long days passed. I continued to ponder and struggled to understand the righteous desires of my own heart. I finally realized that what I really wanted more than anything else was the greatest possible spiritual development for my husband, my three children, and for me. After that, if God could consider the cries of my heart and let my beloved live a little longer, that was what I wanted. I came to understand that the spiritual well-being of those I love was more important than his living or dying. A rush of the Spirit flowed through me and over me, assuring me that my righteous desires were also God's desires for me; we wanted the same thing. My thinking had been transformed. I went into that week wanting my husband to live at all costs, believing I had the faith for him to be healed. By the end of the week, I was humbled and grateful for the knowledge that whatever was needed to bring about the greatest spiritual well-being in my family was what I desired and God would do. I was beginning to learn how to see my personal struggles from God's point of view.

How do the patterns of thought Christ has outlined in the gospel help us to deal with our own heartaches, losses, and disappointments? I have found a few ideas that help me.

First, manage with grace. Notice that I did not say gracefully manage. Most of us are hanging on by our fingernails. But you can manage *with* grace. You must realize that of course you cannot handle illness and divorce and difficult children and a host of other problems by yourself, and that you are not alone. The Holy Ghost and God's grace will help. Get up in the mornings, get dressed, and work on one thing. The next day, work on something else. Keep holding on to God's hand. He has promised to lead us through our trials. Hold on. Manage with his grace.

Second, do not be surprised that you have problems. Pain is inevitable in this lone and dreary world. Do not feel that you are being picked on; problems are the fare of this existence. You cannot escape them. When you get through one, others will be waiting to come your way. Problems hurt, but they also teach wisdom, patience, and an understanding of the good and evil.

Third, let suffering go. You cannot avoid pain, but to hold onto pain is to wallow in it. Christ suffered for us. If you have faith in his suffering, then you can let it go and rest upon the Lord.

Fourth, nothing lasts forever. Life continues. Storms come and go within as well as without. Problems challenge and subside. When pain gets unbearable, just hold on; it, too, will pass. Life will get better . . . before it gets worse again.

Fifth, hold on to hope. Keep moving toward righteousness. Keep seeking after good things, after beauty and truth. The American poet Langston Hughes said:

> Hold fast to dreams.
> For if dreams die
> Life is a broken-winged bird
> That cannot fly.[6]

We have the assurance that we will never be kept from seeking after what is most important in this life. We are guaranteed that opportunity.

After we grieve for our disappointments and losses, we must move on. The gospel of Jesus Christ gives us the pattern for thinking about our problems in different ways that will free us from suffering and allow us to keep growing. In the world you and I will have tribulations, but Christ has overcome the world. His ways are not the ways of the world. If we truly seek to understand, our trials open the way for Christ to teach us. Had my husband not been in that coma, I probably never would have learned an important lesson. Trials bring sorrow, which urges us to seek answers, which in turn bring understanding and peace. This is the peace which passeth the world's understanding.

NOTES

1. Judy Tatlebaum, *Courage to Grieve: Creative Living, Recovery and Growth through Grief* (New York: Lippincott and Crowell, 1980), 9.

2. Pamela Gillilan, "When You Died," in *Poetry with an Edge*, ed. Niel Astley (Newcastle-upon-Tyne: Bloodaxe Books, 1988), 63.

3. Meiling Jin, "Judgement," in *Sisters of Caliban*, ed. M. J. Fenwick (Falls Church, Virginia: Azul Editions, 1996), 165.

4. Sufism is a mystical movement of Islam that originated in the eighth century. Sufis believe that deep intuition is the only real guide to knowledge.

5. Maurice Nicoll, *The Mark* (New York: Thomas Nelson and Sons, [1956]), 89–99.

6. Langston Hughes, *The Dream Keeper* (New York: Alfred A. Knopf, 1932), 82.

DAUGHTERS OF THE MILLSTONE

SHARI S. CRALL

Like a tickler file embedded deeply in my mind, my eldest son's eleventh birthday set off an alarm. Years later, a therapy discussion about "triggers" sent me to my journal to find the date the memories began. Previously my mother had checked her meticulously kept Christmas card file, complete with children's birthdays, and told me my first abuser would have been eleven the year he molested me. I was five. Dismayed by the connection, I wondered what other tangled paths I walked, which, from an aerial view, were charted roads.

According to my journal, that birthday morning of 20 February 1993 brought the first flash of insight into scary and evil dreams, which had startled me awake for a month. That morning, as if I were flipping through a photo album, static images swam up before my eyes. Half-awake, I strained to see them, trying to make sense, but they went quickly, and the snippets I caught made me gasp.

For days this continued in the moments between sleep and waking. I began to dread sleep. I prayed deeply to understand what was happening. Was I caught in some warp of evil imagination? What was true? What was real? What had suddenly

Shari S. Crall received her B.A. degree in political science from Brigham Young University. A homemaker, she and her husband, Christopher D. Crall, have four children. She has written a weekly column for her local newspaper and won awards for essays and articles. She cofacilitates a SOTA (Survivors of Traumatic Abuse) group.

knocked me from my roles as housewife, PTA mom, and stake Young Women counselor to this insanity?

Soon, the pictures ran together, and the shock of what I saw overwhelmed me. With my teeth clenched to hold back the cascade of more scenes, I desperately called my bishop. Miraculously, he said he could be over later that morning. Feeling pressure like that of a delivering womb when told not to push, I waited.

Finally he arrived, and as we sat in my living room, the story unfolded. In the process, the self-hatred and confusion that had defined my life fell away like old skin. Washing my face later, I looked in the mirror. Startled by what I saw, I realized I had not looked myself in the eye in two decades.

A stillness enveloped me. I was in the eye of a storm—the fury of self-hatred, confusion, and rage was behind me, and the fury of self-knowledge, understanding, and healing was in front of me. The surge of sweet peace I felt then had to carry me through the years of pain ahead. Although a spontaneous healing was not to be, I consider the healing process no less a miracle.

I never knew before that when people spoke of emotional pain, they were talking about the very physical sensations that curled me in a ball, slumped me in a heap, or slammed me to the ground. Searching diligently in the only realm I knew, the light of Christ, I learned to seek priesthood leaders for spiritual assistance, receive help from professionals for my mental distress, and build a network of friends and family to support my crumbled emotional structure.

For my spiritual progression and strength to bear this cross, my bishop was key. I was fortunate to act quickly on the prompting to speak with him and to be met with kindness and sincerity. This step is often very difficult for survivors of sexual abuse, as barriers of distrust for both men and authority loom tall.

During times when rage and bitterness engulfed me, when

even the scriptures mocked me as irrelevant, it was my bishop's extended arm that brought the Savior to me with clarity. Although he did not say everything perfectly and at times I felt hurt and misunderstood, I knew he was straining to hear the directions of the Lord to help me. When he gave voice to those whisperings, I felt sweet confirmation of the Spirit.

He gave me blessings when my husband, struggling with his own feelings about events, delayed and didn't. He gently helped me remember the basic essentials of my covenants, which marked the pathway out. He confirmed for me, through the witness of the Spirit to him, that these happenings were true and were no fault of my own. He prayed for me; he checked on me—most of the time by simply catching my eye during sacrament meeting; he encouraged me, initiating meetings and conversations I was too weak to seek.

The time for me to seek professional help came when my daily routine was regularly disrupted by the intensity of feeling, whether sadness, shame, confusion, rage, or fear. I chose LDS Social Services because they gave me a comfort zone of shared faith and values. Although the events were in the past, indeed twenty years earlier, my confusion, self-destructive behavior, and rage were very much in the present. Entering therapy felt like emerging from a jungle—like finally finding treatment after walking crippled for decades.

What seemed a miracle to me, although as common as a doctor setting a broken bone in a cast, the therapist asked me questions and gave information that went right to my symptoms.

"Do you live your life in fear?" I remember him asking one session.

I had never articulated that feeling before. Given thought, the answer was certainly yes.

"Okay, next session I'll take you through an exercise that will help with that."

I left exhilarated. There were exercises for fear? Exercises that, like physical therapy on a broken leg, could help me regain full movement?

After individual therapy, I entered a group organized through LDS Social Services. Survivors of Traumatic Abuse (SOTA) was composed of five women dealing with past sexual abuse, a therapist, and a cofacilitator who was also a fellow survivor.

The group particularly helped me deal with blaming myself for the abuse. As I heard others tell their stories with the usual self-blaming remarks, it was obvious to me they were not responsible. The idea, which had been cultivated in my head, finally took root in my heart. Now I could move even further. I could think, despite a molester's words to the contrary, that maybe his perversion wasn't my fault either.

During this time I also made progress toward understanding the Lord's plan, learning to trust God, and rebuilding my personality to accommodate both the innocent person who existed before the abuse and the wild, frightened, yet still innocent person who remained afterward.

Finally, I purposely built a network of family and friends to rely on. I looked to therapy as a process for my mental health akin to chemotherapy for physical health—and I prepared for sessions the same way. I had three young children in school (one in half-day kindergarten) and one preschooler at home. I told a few close neighbors I was embarking on this process and enlisted their help for regular baby-sitting on the day of therapy, including time to decompress afterward. I asked a friend with no children at home if she would be willing to drive the hour distance with me to Social Services if I found myself too drained to do it myself. Although I never needed the favor, her gracious willingness was an insurance policy with the premium paid.

I felt guided to rely on the direction of my husband. Enduring a marriage when abuse is a factor is heroic. He faced kissing me, even when I turned to stone or started crying because a smell or touch flashed me to scenes of terror. He braved rolling over to pull me close as I slept, only to have me startle and scream. Despite his dismay at what was happening, my husband continually drew boundaries for me, creating space to survive. "I need you to do the dishes today and get some laundry done," he would say. Just as anyone who helps another recuperate, he respected my need to heal without allowing me to just roll over and die.

Finally, I withdrew from what for me were unnecessary activities. When I first remembered the abuse, I was writing the Relief Society birthday program. It was cute, it was fun, but it was not finished, and I could find no strength to finish it. A friend gently told me it was time to call for help and to turn the program over to someone else.

The bishop changed my calling, and I did not substitute teach or volunteer for any extra assignments. I gave myself permission to do what I could, drawing strong limits. For instance, because one of the incidents of abuse happened in the breezeway of my childhood ward building, for months it took all my courage and literal physical effort to keep my body sitting in a pew for sacrament meeting. I weekly fought the urge to run screaming from that familiar chapel scene. During those months, I did nothing more at church than just that.

My son's birthday four years ago gave me knowledge. The ensuing years have challenged me to find ways to use it to progress. As the puzzle of my life came together in the Master's hand, I stepped up to take my turn. I could choose rage, or I could choose peace. I could choose hate, or I could choose love. I could remain crippled, or I could try to move forward.

Because I loved God, all things worked together for my good (see Romans 8:28). When I regained my strength and returned to my former commitments and activities, I realized the years of struggle had been but a small moment. I am amazed I can say that. I hope it in no way trivializes the depth of anyone's struggle with this devastating trial, including my own.

God loves us, and though the mountains depart and the hills be removed, his kindness shall not depart from us, neither shall the covenant of his peace be removed. Indeed he does protect and care for us, continuing mercifully, "O thou afflicted, tossed with tempest, and not comforted, behold, I will lay thy stones with fair colours, and lay thy foundations with sapphires. And I will make thy windows of agates, and thy gates of carbuncles, and all thy borders of pleasant stones . . . and great shall be the peace of thy children" (Isaiah 54:10–13).

Searching diligently in the light of Christ, I was able to find refuge in his healing wings. I have strength to walk again.

THE OTHER SIDE OF SERVICE

CATHERINE STEFFEN THOMPSON

Like many Latter-day Saint women, I tend to be independent, self-reliant, and at times a bit prideful. I don't like to ask for help. Yet, I realize that I am on the receiving end daily of multiple blessings—not only from the Lord, but from friends, sister Saints, and family members whom I love and who love me.

The apostle Paul in 1 Corinthians teaches us that we all have different gifts, and yet we are to come together in one whole unto Christ. "And the eye cannot say unto the hand, I have no need of thee: nor again the head to the feet, I have no need of you. Nay, much more those members of the body, which seem to be more feeble, are necessary: . . . That there should be no schism in the body; but that the members should have the same care one for another" (1 Corinthians 12:21–25). The Lord's plan was to have us be interdependent. That interdependence, which often does not come easily, fosters love and growth. We learn to appreciate one another.

The Lord taught us powerfully on this subject when he served the Twelve at the Last Supper. He rose from the table, took off his outer garment, and tied a towel around himself. Then he poured water into a basin and began to "wash the disciples' feet, and to wipe them with the towel wherewith he was girded. Then cometh he to Simon Peter: and Peter saith

Catherine Steffen Thompson is a homemaker and a senior in history at Western Kentucky University. She and her husband, Tod D. Thompson, are the parents of three children. She has served as the education counselor in her stake's Relief Society.

unto him, Lord, dost thou wash my feet? . . . Thou shalt never wash my feet" (John 13:5–8). Peter's distress is evident. This is his Lord and his King, his Savior. He is embarrassed by the Master's lowering himself to wash the apostles' feet. And yet, the Savior's act was symbolic: he gives to us daily. We are all in need. Sometimes we are in more visible need—unemployed, seriously ill, or emotionally devastated. Even then, it is hard for us to ask for or accept help from our brothers and sisters. But why? Is it our pride? Do we feel unworthy? Do we feel that we *should* be able to take care of ourselves? If we are having those feelings when we need help, then we don't understand the blueprint for life that Heavenly Father in all of his wisdom set up for us.

Again, Paul says, "Nay, much more those members of the body, which seem to be more feeble, are necessary" (1 Corinthians 12:22). Necessary for whom? Just as one of the purposes of coming to this earth is to experience the bitter so we can appreciate the sweet, so we have to be on the receiving end, the needy end, or we will never fully understand the whole range of experiences that make us whole, like our Father in Heaven. The more I learn of the gospel, the more I realize that all of God's commandments are twofold. Yes, we are commanded to help, forgive, love, and serve others for their sakes; but the commandments are just as much, if not more, for our sakes—for in forgiving, loving, and serving, we learn and mature.

Realizing that this give-and-take process is the cycle of life, we need to recognize that we will at times be on the receiving end as well as on the giving. And we should learn to receive in a way that will help the giver grow as much as possible. That is the other side of service.

Returning to the scriptures, Jesus answered Peter, "If I wash thee not, thou hast no part with me. Simon Peter saith unto him, Lord, not my feet only, but also my hands and my head" (John 13:8–9). After we, like Peter, recognize our rightful place

THE OTHER SIDE OF SERVICE

on the receiving end of service and blessings from the Lord and from our fellow brothers and sisters, the next most important step is to feel gratitude for all that we are given.

Elder James E. Faust, in his April 1990 general conference address, taught that gratitude is more than a social courtesy; it is a binding commandment (see D&C 59:7). He quoted from Doctrine and Covenants 59: The Lord said that "in nothing doth man offend God, or against none is his wrath kindled, save those who confess not his hand in all things" (v. 21).

Corrie Ten Boom was a Dutch Christian woman who tried valiantly to help Dutch Jews during World War II. She and her sister, Betsie, became prisoners of war when their efforts with the Jews were discovered. The last prison they were transferred to was Ravensbruck—a women's extermination camp. It seemed impossible, but the camp was even grimmer than the other places they'd been. Women were packed into barracks like cattle and expected to sleep in three-tier rickety beds, nine per tier, on straw that was foul from human excrement, lice, and fleas.

As Betsie pleaded aloud to the Lord to show them how they could endure their new circumstances, it occurred to her that the Lord *had* provided the answer. It was in their Bible reading that morning. "Read that part again!" she urged Corrie. Corrie "glanced down the long dim aisle to make sure that a guard wasn't in sight, then drew the Bible from its pouch." Trying to understand, she read, "Comfort the frightened, help the weak, be patient with everyone. See that none of you repays evil for evil, but always seek to do good to one another and to all."[1] Those words did seem to be "written expressly for Ravensbruck," Corrie agreed. But then Betsie said, "Go on . . . that wasn't all." So Corrie read on: "Rejoice always, pray constantly, give thanks in all circumstances; for this is the will of God in Christ Jesus."

Betsie interrupted, "That's it, Corrie! That's His answer! Give thanks in all circumstances!"

"That's what we can do?" Corrie was skeptical, but Betsie led her on to express gratitude—for still being together, for no inspection of their belongings. She even found something to be grateful for in the crowding, but when Betsie suggested they should be grateful for fleas, Corrie revolted.

"Thank You," Betsie went on serenely, "for the fleas and for—"

"'The fleas!' This was too much for Corrie. 'Betsie, there is no way even God can make me grateful for a flea.'

"'Give thanks in *all* circumstances,' she quoted. "It doesn't say in 'pleasant circumstances.' Fleas are part of this place where God has put us."[2]

Corrie and Betsie found out later that the fleas truly were a blessing, for it was the fleas that prevented thorough and frequent inspections, which allowed them to keep their Bible, read from it, share it, and feel the love and peace of their Savior, Jesus Christ.

Elder Faust also taught: "A grateful heart is a beginning of greatness. . . . It is a foundation for the development of such virtues as prayer, faith, courage, contentment, happiness, love, and well-being."[3] I believe that, and I also believe that being grateful when we are facing adversity in our lives magnifies greatly the influence for good we can have on others.

My daughter, Lauren, died five years ago at the tender age of eleven from an unknown lung disease. Even in the face of extremely difficult trials in her young life, Lauren counted her blessings daily; and a day never passed without her telling us how much she loved each of us. She also reached out to *everyone* in her world and let each one know of her appreciation.

In the mailbox one day, I noticed a note for Lauren from the mailman. It wasn't enclosed in an envelope, so I snooped. Reading the note, I realized that Lauren had previously thanked him for the joy his daily mail deliveries brought to her and others. "You must be a very special girl," he wrote in reply, mentioning that no one had ever thanked him before.

Once she had to fill out a questionnaire for a class that she attended when her health permitted. This questionnaire, which asked about hobbies, goals, and aspirations, was designed for the teacher to get to know her students better. One question asked, If you could be any person in the whole world, either past or present, who would you choose? Lauren thought long and hard about that and finally said, "Mom, is it okay if I just put myself? I wouldn't want to be anyone else. I'm happy being who I am." Here was my little daughter, hooked up to an oxygen tank, whom I knew would have loved to have healthy lungs, to enjoy school and sports and outings with friends as she had before her illness. In spite of that, she felt so blessed to be who she was and part of her own family that she didn't wish to trade places with anyone.

We have her last Christmas on video. That morning, instead of tearing into her pile of presents, as most children her age would have done, she took forever just emptying her stocking because she was so interested in watching all of our reactions to our gifts. At one point, her little three-year-old brother started to fuss over a particular gift. Lauren turned to him and lightly scolded, "Adam, that's not being grateful." That sums up Lauren's attitude toward life—she was grateful. She could have been bitter and withdrawn. She could have complained, "Why me, Lord? What did I do to deserve this?" Instead she learned to cope with her limitations, and she reached out to others—family and friends became precious to her. She counted her blessings often and appreciated each big and little thing done for her.

We had only a short eleven years here on earth with Lauren; yet I watched her grow in compassion, gratitude, and even humor as if she had led a long and rewarding life. Yes, she was needy. Yes, she had to have much done for her. But who do you think benefited most from exchanges with Lauren?

At her funeral, I was overwhelmed. I realized that the large crowd of people there to honor her—Church members, neighbors, doctors, and nurses who had worked with her, even deliverymen who had brought oxygen tanks to her every couple of weeks—had been deeply touched by her. These people had all served her diligently.

A wonderful ninety-four-year-old lady lives in my ward. She still lives at home by herself, and though she is frail, her spirit is feisty and independent. When I ask her how she's doing, more often than not she replies, "Oh, I'm still kicking—not too high, but still kicking!" As Relief Society president, I accompany her visiting teacher to deliver a food order from the bishop's storehouse to her every month, which she eagerly and gratefully accepts. She tells us, if we find her dead tomorrow, not to worry because she didn't die hungry! And then, before we leave, we always join hands and pray together for peace and comfort. Her cheeks wet with tears, she then takes our faces, one by one, into her soft, wrinkled hands, kisses our cheeks, and tells us that she knows we are angels from the Lord because she didn't know us, but she had been praying earnestly to the Lord for help. At the end of each visit, she tells us that she loves us and prays for us daily and asks if we will always remember her in our prayers, too.

Who gains the most from that exchange?

I know of one dear woman who was abused in just about every way imaginable during her childhood and consequently struggles with both anorexia and alcoholism. Her life has painful ups and downs as she tries to cope with the past and the present, and her friends are not always sure she is going to be okay. She struggles daily with low self-esteem. But her heart is not bitter or cold. In fact, she is loving and kind and is always serving others. As friends try to help meet her emotional needs, they gain strength from her love and courage as she tries to keep moving forward, to hold on.

Who gains the most in these exchanges?

Every experience, no matter how difficult, can have a purpose and be a time for growth. We all have twofold missions here on earth—to gain our own salvation and to help others along their path. In our most needy times, if we remember with clarity who we truly are and the blessings we still possess, we have the power to bless others, perhaps more than at any other time in our lives. We are in a position to inspire others in our times of need. Our courage can teach others how to deal with their own problems.

A heart completely filled with love and gratitude has no room for bitterness, pride, shame, despondency, self-centeredness, or self-pity. These emotions stunt our growth. Gratitude spurs us on to better things. The commandment from the Lord to be thankful in all things isn't only for the recipient but also for the giver. The Lord is wise and knows what we need—even if it's not what we would ever choose for ourselves.

Gratitude sustained me through my darkest time, the death of my daughter. I am grateful that the Lord honored me to be the mother of such a magnificent spirit. I am grateful for the example that Lauren has left me to ponder and pattern my life after. I am grateful that my testimony of the gospel of Jesus Christ tells me this life is not the end. Gratitude heals my pain and motivates and inspires me.

When we find purpose in our burdens and receive from others with gratitude, then not only do we benefit and grow from our trials—which is one of the purposes of mortality—but the love and inspiration that we generate can allow others to grow from our trials.

What legacy do we leave? Who will benefit from exchanges with us? The last paragraph in *The Hiding Place* tells what happened in the final years of Corrie Ten Boom's life. She spent them in a pleasant home provided by friends in California. There, a series of strokes curtailed first her physical movement, then her writing schedule, and finally even her power of speech. But her ministry continued. Those who came to cheer the bedridden, speechless old lady marveled that when they left, they were the ones cheered, uplifted, strengthened.

NOTES

1. Corrie Ten Boom, *The Hiding Place* (New York: Bantam Books, 1971), 198.

2. Ten Boom, *Hiding Place,* 198–99.

3. James E. Faust, "Gratitude as a Saving Principle," *Ensign,* May 1990, 85–86.

AND ACQUAINTED WITH GRIEF

WIN L. MARSH

In writing this essay, I have hesitated over many things. For one thing, someone reading these words is thinking, *She doesn't know what I feel—she can't possibly know.* And that's true. My experience does not make me an expert on anyone's pain or grief except my own. I can write what I found helpful, though it may or may not be what you need. But I write because perhaps an aspect of my experience may help you deal with your own experience of loss and grief.

When I was young, I would listen at church to talks about the glories of motherhood. I would shake my head and tell myself that I wasn't ever going to have that role. I was a tree climber, a fort builder, and a girl who would do absolutely anything to spend time with horses. As a young woman, I became a fairly good mechanic and a fiercely independent person who truly never expected to marry until late in life. How life can change! I met a wonderful young attorney during my last year of college. Steve quickly became my best friend, my confidant, my everything. He was in the process of moving to Texas. Right away I knew that I wanted to spend my whole life and eternity with him. We felt prompted to marry immediately . . . and so we did. I know that the Lord guided that choice.

Win L. Wallace Marsh, a registered nurse, holds degrees from Brigham Young University and Midwestern State University. She and her husband, Stephen R. Marsh, are involved in a variety of organizations in their North Texas community and serve on several local and state boards. Their primary focus has always been their children.

We planned to wait to have children—I hoped to pursue a career and a graduate degree—but we had such an overwhelming feeling that there was a little girl just waiting to be born to us. Again, we felt that we had followed the Lord's promptings. We prayed and decided to start a family. Thirteen months after our wedding, our first child, Jessica, was born. We had two more daughters over the next six years, and I felt that our lives were going the way the Lord wanted them to. We hoped for another child and talked of my returning to school when the youngest started kindergarten. We had a young law practice, a young healthy family, and dreams for the future.

When our oldest daughter, Jessica, developed the flu, we never imagined she would get so sick. During long days of waiting and praying, I had lots of time to reflect. Why was the Lord allowing this to happen? It was so odd. First graders just get better when they come down with the flu. She had always been healthy; we used seatbelts; her vaccinations were current; we followed the Lord's teachings. What had we done wrong? Why was this happening?

The first inkling I had that something horrible was going on was when Jessica had a blessing. I had always associated priesthood blessings with a warm, peaceful feeling of comfort and reassurance. When Jessica received a blessing, however, I felt an awful sickening in the pit of my stomach. But what did such an indescribably horrible feeling mean? Did it mean that her illness was going to be lengthy? That she would have long-lasting problems? That she would die? We did not know. I prayed for her to be healed if it was the Lord's will.

Jessica died on our wedding anniversary. I do not know how my little family survived that time in our lives. Jessica's medical bills were over $614,000. We found that our medical insurance was not as good as we had thought. That next November I miscarried. It was a very difficult time. Language lacks words to describe such times adequately. The one thing that kept me going was my toddler, Courtney, who needed my constant attention. She was the reason I got up in the morning and tried to function. After bundling my kindergartner, Heather, off to school, Courtney kept me functioning as a mom and as a person for the rest of the day.

As Christmas approached, we wanted to be anywhere but home. We wanted to go someplace without memories of Jessica to tear at our souls. Finances were still a serious concern, so we drove to California to stay with my husband's family. Courtney started displaying flulike symptoms—and not wanting to take any chances with her health, we left presents unopened and spent Christmas morning in the emergency room. Courtney—at twenty-two months of age—was diagnosed as a new diabetic. We were beside ourselves. Jessica had seen her first doctor on Christmas Eve the year before, and now—a year and a day later—our youngest was being admitted to an intensive care unit as the doctors tried to stabilize her. Late that night she had a seizure, which herniated her brain stem. She was pronounced brain dead.

We were far from home, and all our savings were gone—we had been through too much too soon. I shook my fist at God and felt that I really did not want him in my life any more. If this was going to be the way he ran my life, by golly, I would just run it myself.

Back at home, I continued to attend all my church meetings, but I was angry at God. I looked at my life and couldn't find anything I had done to deserve this burden on my soul. I felt that I had given up worldly ambitions to concentrate on being a mom. And I was a good mom. So why had the Lord taken away my identity as a mother? Our middle child, Heather, came to me repeatedly and asked when she was going to die. She just assumed that she would be next. All I could do was hold onto her and pray that the three of us would survive.

A few months went by, and Steve and I desperately wanted another child. We knew that we could not replace what we lost, but our arms ached with emptiness. I became pregnant again, and that pregnancy ended in another miscarriage. Again, I shook my fist at God. I tried to pray, but feelings of betrayal made my efforts painful.

I needed to fill the void in my life. I needed to find something I could excel at. I felt that God had declared me a failure as a mother when he took two of my children. On a rational level, I knew that was not true, but on an emotional level, that was what I felt. I threw myself into volunteer work until I had no time left to think or feel. The void remained. I went back to school, this time in nursing, to take up even more of my time. Gradually I began to be able to handle issues. I began to heal more and more as the months went by. I limited my commitments and took time to feel emotions and reflect. When I was ready to take an active role in the healing process, my anger subsided. My angry question "Why me and why my children?" expanded to "Why anyone?"

I thought back to the month I had spent with Jessica in intensive care. Children arrived at that hospital from all over the world to be treated for various ailments. A large board in the waiting room listed the room number and name of each patient in the intensive care unit. Family and friends left notes and messages there about phone calls to return. When a child became well enough to be moved to a regular floor, the bed was wheeled past the waiting room, and everyone in the room cheered. All too often the names on the board were just quietly erased. I started to ask, "Why would the Lord allow so many children to die before they really had a chance to live?"

I started working part time on a medical-surgical floor. I have seen families grieve as diseases take their course. Why? Why is a young family left without a father? Why is a man taken just before his fiftieth wedding anniversary celebration? Why does a vibrant woman die just weeks before her daughter's wedding? Why do we have to feel such pain?

My questions became more complex:

How can a God who loves me allow such horrible things to happen to me?

How can I trust a God who did not protect me from this disaster?

How can I live through this?

Can I live through this?

Can I be healed?

How can I be strengthened?

The first two questions are really one—Why? Why me? Why this? Why?

The easy answer is the one the world gives. We are either loved by God and saved, or we are hated by God and suffer adversity. That is the message John Calvin gave his followers. Calvin was not alone. Job's friends told him that all adversity comes from sin and any adversity is merely the just and immediate punishment for our sins.

But God reproved Job's friends. It is such an easy thing to hope that all adversity comes from sin. If all adversity comes from sin, then it is a simple matter to avoid at least all major adversity and to quell our fears that we might suffer the same afflictions that others have suffered.

To find real answers to my questions I had to understand, first, why there is adversity and, second, knowing this, learn how I can still trust God. We find answers by hearing the messages God has given over and over again.

The scriptures tell us repeatedly that we are here to gain experience. Our experiences will vary in type, intensity, and duration. We are given opportunities to help ourselves and others. Experience gives us perspective and balance. Adversity offers no simple "either-or" answers, but instead, a balance. We do not either suffer or move on, feel grief or heal, experience pain or grow. Balance allows us to both suffer and move on, feel grief and heal, experience pain and grow, pick up our burdens and keep moving forward—learning the good from the evil and the bitter from the sweet.

When I asked the next questions, "How can I live through this?" and "Can I live through this?" I was really asking, "What can I do when faced with adversity?"

The message of the world is that you either understand or you suffer pain. Television teaches us that in half an hour or less we can escape any pain through understanding. The reality is that it takes longer than thirty or forty or sixty minutes to overcome the pain of adversity. I was surprised at the number of people who asked me, "Why are you grieving? Don't you realize that your children are with God?" They assumed that understanding and a strong testimony of the gospel would protect me from feeling the pain of loss.

The truth is that understanding may actually make pain more intense. The truth is that what makes adversity adverse is that the pain and problems are as real as we are. They will not simply go away if we just look at things "in a more positive light." And the pain is as painful as it feels. We aren't imagining it.

I feel pain because I miss my children. I miss their laughter. I miss feeling them snuggle into my arms. I even miss cleaning up after them. Knowing how long it will be before I see them again just intensifies the pain. Although I know that this life is short, right now I am living it minute by minute, and the time seems to pass slowly.

The real answer to the question "What can I do?" is to keep living. Keep moving through this life and keep your faith. As Paul wrote in Hebrews, "Let us run with patience the race that is set before us" (12:1).

The final questions I began with, "Can I be healed?" and "How can I be made stronger?" really ask: "How can God keep his promises to heal us and turn all things to our good?" The conventional wisdom of the world is that we can either be "a man of sorrows" or we can be happy. The world tells us that joy is always lessened and ruined by any sorrow.

The truth is that we, like Christ, can gain strength through what we suffer (Isaiah 53:5; Mosiah 14:3) and we can know deep and abiding joy. We will find peace—in time—and a renewal of joy—in time—by coming to understand that this world is truly not "all there is." The celestial world of God is a deeper, more real and more present reality than is this world.

As I have grappled with pain and adversity in my life, I have learned much about living and dying, about priorities and what really matters.

I find myself thanking God for the new knowledge and insight I have gained. I admit that the price paid for knowledge has been very high. I would prefer to remain terribly ignorant of grief and have my children back. I find myself asking God: "Is there no other way?" and the answer is "There is no other way." It is only through earthly experience, which includes suffering and adversity, that we are able to learn the things that the Lord wants us to learn. The author of this poem states it well:

> Pain stayed so long I said to him today,
> "I will not have you with me anymore."
> I stamped my foot and said, "Be on your way,"
> And paused there, startled at the look he wore.
> "I, who have been your friend," he said to me,
> "I, who have been your teacher—all you know
> Of understanding love, of sympathy,
> And patience, I have taught you. Shall I go?"
> He spoke the truth, this strange unwelcome guest;
> I watched him leave, and knew that he was wise.
> He left a heart grown tender in my breast,
> He left a far, clear vision in my eyes.
> I dried my tears, and lifted up a song—
> Even for one who'd tortured me so long.[1]

I have realized that in this life, we all will either live long enough to experience the grief and despair that accompanies the loss of those we love most dearly, or we will die young enough that we will be the object of their grieving. That is part of the Lord's plan for all of us—to gain knowledge and experience.

God can keep his promises because he offers us infinitely more than we have lost—in tenderness, kindness, and patience. God waits to bring us home, to heal our losses, and fill us with his grace. He can keep his promises because he waits for us.

Each of us will face real pain, disappointment, and loss. Each of us will have real trials and real tests and "the fiery trial" of our faith (1 Peter 4:12). But from those pains, we can grow in love and hope and care for each other until that perfect day when God takes us home and gives us peace.

NOTE

1. Quoted by Spencer W. Kimball, *Faith Precedes the Miracle* (Salt Lake City: Deseret Book, 1972), 99.

Win Marsh was seven months pregnant when she wrote this essay. On 6 July 1997, Robin Elizabeth Marsh was born with a heart defect. Open-heart surgery was performed five days later. Two more surgeries were planned. Robin died in her sleep at eight weeks of age.

REARING GOOD PARENTS

JAMES M. HARPER

Parents worry a lot. Have you noticed that? "Why are you so serious? What are you so worried about?" our eager-to-be-independent children sometimes ask. The best answer I've found comes from *Families Who Laugh . . . Last,* by Janene Baadsgaard: "We worry that you won't wash your hands after using the bathroom unless we make you. . . . We worry that you'll go outside without your coat, get a cold, then get double pneumonia and die. We worry that you'll forget to look both ways when you cross the street, and a cement truck will run you down before we have a chance to get your braces paid off. . . . We worry that you really *do* need to go to the bathroom when we pretend that we can't hear you anymore because we told you to go before we left the house. . . . We worry that you will never quit eating, and we'll end up having to sell the house to keep you in milk. . . . We worry that your brain will rot from watching too much television and that your eardrums will burst from too much loud music. . . . We worry that you'll stuff *another* pea up your nose, and we won't know about it until it starts stinking. . . . We worry that we made a mess of you because we forgot to say 'I love you' enough

James M. Harper is chair of the Department of Family Sciences at Brigham Young University. He is a licensed marriage and family therapist and psychologist, and a fellow in the American Association for Marriage and Family Therapy. He and his wife, Colleen, have five children. He has served as a mission president in the Korea Pusan Mission and as first counselor in the presidency of the BYU Fifth Stake.

155

between all the 'Don'ts' . . . and that you won't forgive us. . . . [And] we worry that you'll grow up to be just like us."[1]

It's true. Our children, despite all we do or say, will more often than not turn out to be just like us. That's why rearing good children is really about rearing good parents.

Along those lines, I want to discuss three general parenting principles.

VISION

First, parents must recognize themselves and their children as eternal offspring of our heavenly parents. Moroni 7:24–25 gives us a key: "The children of men . . . began to exercise faith in Christ; and thus by faith, they did lay hold upon every good thing." Faith in Christ gives us a vision of our divine nature that allows us to "cleave unto every good thing" (v. 28).

Many years ago, my son received his patriarchal blessing. He was about sixteen years old and was well prepared for the experience. But I discovered that I was not. We arrived at the home of the patriarch, an older man who had once been our stake president. He began by asking my wife and me to describe our son. We answered thoughtfully, reflecting back on the sixteen years we had shared with our son. I felt certain that I knew him very well. He next asked our son to describe himself, an interesting way to lead into a patriarchal blessing. Then he began the blessing. During the blessing, I experienced a strange sensation. I felt as if I floated out of the room, and at a distance I saw my son in an entirely new light: as an eternal person, not mine, but simply given to me for a time, a child of our Heavenly Father. Up to that point, I had known intellectually that I did not own my son, but I know that at times I did not behave or feel that way. My experience during this patriarchal blessing changed me.

Why is vision a first principle of parenting? Because understanding our divine parentage directly affects how we handle the mistakes and sins in our lives. It determines whether we respond with guilt or with shame, a subject that I have researched carefully.[2] We feel guilt when we believe we have violated a standard of ours or of someone we respect. The way to get rid of guilt—the way to feel good about ourselves—is to change, to repent. Shame, on the other hand, is a feeling that something is wrong or bad about us as a person, that our very core is different from others. A guilty person feels "I made a mistake"; a shamed person feels "I am a mistake." Many people in our world respond to mistakes with shame. "I am a bad person, flawed. My actions prove that about me." Shamed people rarely repent. They feel bad a lot, but they rarely change their behavior because they feel nothing can change the badness at the core, anyway—who they really are. People who feel good about themselves repent and change their behavior to match who they are or who they aspire to be. Some shamed people eventually do change their behavior, but they often continue through life to feel faulty and inferior and try to prevent other people from discovering their shameful self.

Guilt can be healthy—it pushes us to change and repent—but it should never make us feel that we are bad people. Guilt should help us to do better, to continually restore us to the holiness, to the goodness, that we came to earth with. We must learn this aphorism: I made a mistake, but I am not a mistake. Then we must believe it.

Our children will feel less shame if they understand that it is all right to make mistakes. And we, as parents, need to understand that, too. In fact, our attitudes about our own mistakes convey more strongly than any words what we really believe. Our fourth child, our first daughter, is now seventeen. Much against her mother's counsel, she decided to register for four advanced placement (AP) courses in her junior year of high school. She's a bright young woman, but the teachers in AP courses assume theirs is the only course of any consequence their students are taking, and they pile on the homework. Even her advanced sculpture course was tremendously time consuming. As the third term ended, she was mega-stressed. I asked her one morning, "What can I do to help you? I know it's the end of term, and you're stressed with so much to do. How can I help?"

"Dad, it's my ceramics class. My sculpture is cracking in some places. If you'll just soak it in water, it will be malleable when I come home from school, and I can work with it."

"Okay, I think I can manage. How do I do it?"

"You just soak it in water for a few minutes," she tossed off as she hurried out the door. So before I left for work, I filled the sink full of water and immersed the sculpture, a marvelous candy bowl in the shape of a turtle. How long? Well, a few minutes—that must be about seven to ten, I reasoned. I'll go unload the dishwasher, gather things I need for work, and plan my day. When I returned, I carefully reached down into the sink and brought up the magnificent turtle—disintegrating, dripping through my fingers. I panicked. In that moment, I instantly lost faith in myself as a basically decent human being and adequate parent. I foresaw my daughter returning home, becoming even more stressed, and forming the message that she would remember for the rest of eternity: her father let her down. I've known supposed grown-ups who didn't speak to each other over less significant affronts.

Possible solutions flashed through my mind. I could stay home from work and shape the clay so that it looked like her candy bowl. But not having much experience in ceramics, I decided that was not a workable idea. Instead, I prepared myself for the speech I would give when she returned from school. I could have prepared a shame speech: "I'm a bad father and an idiot. I should have known that ten minutes was too long—that clay turtles disintegrate in water." Not only did I discover that clay turtles rapidly decompose in bathroom basins, I discovered later in the day that you can't scoop silty clay out of the water once the turtle has disintegrated. So I washed it down the drain. Not long afterward, I discovered that ceramic clay solidifies in drains.

By the time my daughter returned home from school, I had prepared several alternate speeches about the demise of the clay turtle and had called a plumber to clean out hardened clay from our drains. It had not been a good day. But, I said to myself, I arrived on this earth as a child of Heavenly Father. There was a time in my life when I was holy, though maybe it's not today. Nonetheless, knowing that shame is a bad thing, I will not assume that I am a bad person, but that I am a good person who has made a bad mistake. Therefore I can change. Never again will I leave a ceramic turtle in water for ten minutes; that's easy. I will do my best to make restitution; that will be more difficult.

I left work early so I would be at home when my daughter arrived. "I have made a big mistake," I told her when she walked in. Then I told her the story, expecting her to fall to pieces. She looked at me and smiled a slow, wide Cheshire cat smile. "Dad, you really owe me on this one," she said. We then worked together through most of the night to recreate the ceramic turtle.

In retrospect, this is a funny incident, but it loomed large in my emotions at the time, as I thought it would hers. My daughter could have decided not to trust me again. I could have felt shamed, tried to shift the blame to her for scanty instructions, or decided not to offer help in the future. Some people do judge each other and make decisions based on trivialities. That is not to say I have not made more serious mistakes as a parent or a person, ones I can't laugh about. But the principle still applies. Two good people, a father and a daughter, who sometimes make mistakes, stayed up till three or four in the morning to recreate a turtle. My daughter survived her third term. So did I.

So the first step in rearing parents with celestial vision is to admit to mistakes and then to repent. The second is to beware of criticizing. Not only does our criticizing our children negate the larger vision of them as offspring of God but it also may indicate that we're uncomfortable with something in ourselves. For example, adolescent children often force parents to deal with unresolved issues from their own childhood. That's one of the reasons adolescence can be so rocky for parents. I hassle my own children about school the most. I've concluded that it's an issue I didn't resolve in my own adolescence—not that I had poor school performance; in fact, just the opposite is true. I couldn't give myself a break as an adolescent. I was a high achiever, driven to perform. It's taken me a long time to be more flexible, to see others' ideas, to relax, to experience leisure. When I feel critical of my children, I let that signal me to look first at myself. Am I feeling something not quite right about me? Am I unconsciously thinking that if I can correct this in my children, they won't have to experience what I have or that somehow it will make me better? Life never works that way.

Sometimes we criticize simply because life is chaotic or too fast-paced. It's almost a given that when the pace of family life is in high gear, there will be more irritation, argument, and contention. Children respond with similar irritation and more petty squabbles to the anxiety that a fast-paced life creates in fathers and mothers. What's the solution? Be easier on ourselves, learn to manage our schedule better in the next few days or weeks—give ourselves a break. When we do that, we will be less critical of others.

The first general principle of parenting includes, then, the ability to develop a vision of ourselves as an essentially good person who is not perfect. Yes, we need to repent because we make mistakes, but our very being is from God. We are essentially holy, and the work we are about in rearing children is God's work. Sister Patricia Holland has said, "When the Lord created parents, he created something breathtakingly close to what he is."³ We need to pray for a clearer vision of ourselves and our purpose as well as that of our children.

HEARING

The second general principle in rearing good parents is to learn to listen and respond to feelings. It's very important for you and your children to know that it is normal to feel. It is the very process of living. The scriptures speak of beliefs of the heart, not of the head.⁴ For five years in a row, I was asked to give a talk on Easter in church. Moving made no difference; leaders still asked me to speak on Easter Sunday. I finally decided that Heavenly Father was trying to give me a message, but I hadn't gotten it yet. In preparing that fifth Easter talk, I finally discovered the message: there are many ways to die other than physical death. We can die emotionally. We stop feeling. There is just as much a need for resurrection from that state as there is from physical death. I've never been asked to give an Easter message since that talk. I guess I finally got it right.

This idea applies to children. At times they are angry or sad; they cry; they have fears. But we often aren't very patient with those feelings. We get impatient, angry, or correct their feelings with "Oh, there's no reason to feel sad. Buck up and go on." Or "You shouldn't be jealous. That's not nice." Or "Don't be silly. There's nothing to be afraid of." And so on. Over time, children assume that if so many feelings that emanate from inside and are part of them are wrong, then they themselves must be wrong inside—they themselves must be bad. Or they may learn to distrust or reject their feelings. After all, most feelings seem to be just wrong. You're not supposed to have them. If you do have them, it's not wise to share them with anybody.

Children whose feelings are often dismissed or corrected never learn the language of talking about feelings. The vocabulary isn't difficult. There are basically only seven categories of emotions: anger, fear, sadness, hurt, love, happiness, jealousy—although there are lots of synonyms and words full of nuances but close in meaning. Giving credibility to children's feelings helps them understand their emotions and feel good about themselves.

Listening accomplishes the same vital task; yet even in the family, people too seldom listen to each other. Unfortunately, when children want parents to listen to them, we tend to respond by giving advice. As one adolescent daughter wrote her mother: "When I ask you to listen to me and you start giving advice or telling me I shouldn't feel a certain way, or solving my problems, you aren't giving me what I've asked for. Please just listen to me. Don't talk or do." Do you suppose that one reason prayer is so effective in people's lives is that God listens? He seldom gives us quick fixes in prayer. He seldom tries to talk us out of the experience we have. He listens and from time to time gives subtle suggestions. Generally he lets us work to solve our concern ourselves. Perhaps the reason we have difficulty listening to children is that we lack faith in them or in the Lord's plan for them. We assume that they can't solve problems for themselves, so we've got to solve them for them. We've got to fix what's wrong, tell them to buck up, or give them advice. If we really had a vision of who they are, we would see them as capable of discovering their own solutions. Our role as parents is to trust and be a sounding board, dispensing advice only when requested.

Have you ever wondered how you might have responded if you'd been Joseph Smith Sr. when young Joseph came and told you about his experience? Would you have rushed him off to the local psychiatric ward for fear he was hallucinatory? Or would you have trusted him and had faith in who he was? To see our children clearly and support them through what Heavenly Father intends for them is an important task for parents. It involves turning our children to Christ, preparing their hearts for the Savior's touch. There's a subtle difference between forcing children to come to Christ—which we cannot really do—and facilitating their personal relationship with God.

Let me tell you a story to illustrate what I mean. Eighteen-year-old Latter-day Saint young men struggle to decide about missions, some more than others. My second son was no exception. We watched him go through this struggle, but when he turned nineteen, he filled out his papers, had his physical and dental exams, and made an appointment with our new bishop to turn in his mission papers. This was the bishop's first interview with a prospective missionary. My son returned from the interview with all his papers still in hand and announced: "I just told the bishop I am not going on a mission." I said nothing, at least knowing better than to be critical. I had learned that maybe I needed to look inside myself to find why this was so scary for me. His mother said something very interesting. "Son, we'll support whatever you choose to do," she said, "but far more important than how we feel about this as your parents is that you work out your relationship with Heavenly Father, with Christ as your mediator. So I ask only one thing of you. Make sure that you pray about this." I suppose my wife could have tried to convince our son that a mission was the best thing to do, reminding him of all the teachings in our family. Instead she chose to facilitate his own discovery and try to prepare his heart for the Spirit's touch in that prayer. A week later he went back to the bishop to turn in his papers.

This must have been quite a trial for our new bishop. He later shared with us what our son had told him: "You know, when I came in last week, I thought that the only reason I wanted to serve a mission was because my parents expected me to, but I've learned this week that my parents will support me no matter what I choose. Far more important, I've learned this week that the Lord expects me to serve a mission, and I need to do it to be of service to him." He served his mission and has been home for several years. It changed his life in all the ways that missions do.

Children of God come equipped with some natural and some God-given abilities to solve their problems. I am certain I have learned far more being a parent than my children have learned from having me as a parent.

BEING THERE

The third principle of parent rearing concerns sharing our lives with children: ideas, experiences, affection—the good in life. Develop a language of emotion and closeness—women are often better at this than men—and along with this, tell them stories rather than drowning them in do's and don'ts. Often we don't think to tell children the personal stories that contain the themes and values of our lives and our personal feelings. Tell your children stories of your spiritual experiences as they occur. Every Sunday I share with my children some spiritual experience I've had as a member of a stake presidency.

Share favorite books. From the time our children were little, we've enjoyed reading books together out loud, especially when we're riding in the car. We've shared *The Best Christmas Pageant Ever, A Swiftly Tilting Planet, Clarence's Last Chance,* and in recent years (because our children are now in high school), *The Scarlet Letter, Grapes of Wrath, Jane Eyre.* Our reading has provided a context to discuss and share. We also read individually and share the stories with one another.

Share music—maybe not everything, but enough. Music opens our hearts to each other. My children could tell you that my favorite music is from *Les Miserables.* I think it's easy to feel God in this music. It's about things that really matter—justice versus mercy, forgiveness, grace. But do you know who listens to that music almost as much as I do these days? My children. If you cultivate the music of the spirit that you love, it will rub off. Music can spring your spirit into instant empathy.

Share service and family work projects, even projects as simple as the daily work of washing and drying dishes. When we work together, we transmit values from one generation to the next. And don't hesitate to share physical affection. When Mormon says, "Lay hold upon every good thing" (Moroni 7:25), I take that literally—lay hold on your children. Give them hugs. Be affectionate. They learn, even with all the mistakes they make as children, even with all the mistakes we make as parents, that they—and we—are good inside.

Recognize that your children can share things with you. Too often we dismiss our children's thoughts as negligible—intrusions in our adult conversations. It's reported that when Joseph Smith met visitors, he first stooped down to look in the eyes of children and pay attention to them, and then he greeted the adults. We can learn something from the Prophet's behavior about valuing children and their contributions. At least ten sources in diaries from individuals who were children in Joseph Smith's time talk about their experiences with the Prophet. Once he simply held a little girl up to a mirror. They both looked in the mirror, and he smiled. As an old woman, she recorded in her diary that she never forgot the experience. Another time the Prophet was speaking in a meeting, and a small girl began fussing. He stopped, put her foot on his knee, and put his hand on her foot. She stopped fussing immediately, and he went on teaching. Another time he was talking while some boys were playing in the area. A man motioned for the Prophet to stop and called out, "Boys, you need to go home. You're being disruptive." But Joseph stopped him, "No. Let the boys stay. They may hear something today that they will never forget."[5]

Please allow for differences in your own style of parenting. What works for other parents may not work for you. Be flexible—different children need different styles of parenting. If you are blessed to be in a traditional household with a father and a mother, and your parenting styles are quite different, count your blessings: the two styles are often complementary for children. Even if you think your husband is too harsh and he thinks you are Marshmallow Woman, children compensate for those differences in style and benefit from them as long as parents don't pick at each other over those differences. There is no one model for good parenting. Read all the parenting literature—it can be fascinating and helpful—but only one Expert should guide your life. Prayer often gives me a whole different perspective, and it changes my heart and mind more quickly than all the literature aimed at doing just that.

Being a good parent is more about changing ourselves than about changing our children. If we learn to love ourselves, our children will benefit. We must learn to love our children, not their accomplishments. Joseph Smith once said that celestial people would create a celestial environment around them.[6] Have you ever considered that your very nature, the fact that you are holy by nature, by the endowment that comes with you as an offspring of our Heavenly Father, has potential in and of itself to create goodness for the people around you? Even if you are not on your best behavior, even if you are not directly serving them, just being in your presence can be a good thing for your children or for other people. If you have ever been with the First Presidency, members of the Twelve, or other people of exceptional quality, you have probably experienced this goodness of presence.

We often talk about children developing, but we tend to forget that parents are developing too. I'm a far better parent today than I was twenty years ago. I'll be a far better parent as a grandfather than I am today. The temple experience teaches us symbolically about progression, and that principle applies to both children and parents. We talk as though parents have all the knowledge and wisdom to impart to their children. In my experience, my children have imparted far more wisdom and information to me—when I have been willing to pay attention to them. We are all learning, precept by precept. From the perspective of our eternal progression as children of God, living and growing together, we are in a sense, rearing each other.

166

I pray that we will be blessed on this journey—this curriculum that the Lord has planned for parents—to learn about ourselves. When we focus more on our own need to learn and grow than on our children's, they will benefit. As we become better people, we become better parents.

NOTES

1. Janene Wolsey Baadsgaard, *Families Who Laugh . . . Last* (Salt Lake City: Deseret Book, 1992), 7–8.

2. James M. Harper, *Uncovering Shame: Integrating Individuals and Their Family Systems* (New York: W. W. Norton, 1990).

3. Patricia Holland, "Parenting: Everything to Do with the Heart," *Ensign,* June 1985, 12.

4. See, for example, Deuteronomy 6:6: "And these [commandments] . . . shall be in thine heart"; 2 Nephi 8:7: "Ye that know righteousness, the people in whose heart I have written my law"; Ecclesiastes 1:17: "I gave my heart to know wisdom."

5. Truman G. Madsen, *Joseph Smith,* vol. 2 (Salt Lake City: Bookcraft, 1997), audiocassette tape.

6. Madsen, *Joseph Smith,* audiocassette tape.

AS GOOD AS I WANNA BE

LISA O. FILLERUP

I was sitting at the kitchen table one Sunday digging in a bag of microwave popcorn with my teenage daughters when the phone rang. A member of the bishopric. Would my husband and I speak in church next Sunday on families? I hung up the phone and told the children, hoping for some positive response—like what wonderful parents we are, or a least what made being in our family fun. But instead our most dramatic daughter asked with a smear of sarcasm, "Oh, because we have the perfect family?"

That remark made me take an honest look at my family of six children, beginning with our youngest, James, who lives in the Paleozoic world of stegosaurus and is rarely interested or fully present in the real world; then Micky and Rebecca, elementary-age partners in crime, who can break anything you really like, free of charge; or Bo and Heidi, teenagers who would rather serve at a ward dinner for two and a half hours than take five minutes to empty the dishwasher at home; and, last, our oldest daughter, Sarah, whom we never worry about at college until she calls and tells another white-knuckle story of almost losing her life skiing, bungee jumping, or walking to the library. Speaking in church on the topic of families caused me to look at our family objectively. We're just a regular, slightly

Lisa O. Fillerup manages the art business Wild West Designs, Inc. She and her sculptor husband, Peter M. Fillerup, are the parents of six children. She serves in Young Women and as ward newsletter editor.

weird family, trying to do good but feeling far from perfect or even as good as we want to be. I wondered, *Could we create an environment where searching for the light of Christ meant more than looking for the family home evening manual?* I knew we needed "home improvements," but just where to begin I wasn't sure.

Then I remembered visiting with our stake patriarch, Jim Smedley, who shared with me how he prepared his home for giving a patriarchal blessing. He was specific: "Before each blessing, I make sure the room where we will be is vacuumed, dusted, and orderly. I usually ask my daughter Rachel to play hymns about an hour before each blessing—music makes such a difference. Conflicts and disagreements at work are something I try to avoid on 'blessing days,' or, if possible, I solve them quickly. All these things invite the Spirit—something I can't give blessings without." In his home, I *could* feel a spirit and a light that went beyond their smudge-less picture window.

The idea grew in my mind like July's zucchini. Could this same spirit and feeling happen in our rambunctious family? Not long after our speaking experience came the dedication of the Mount Timpanogos Utah Temple. My husband and I had never been involved in a temple dedication, and this was to be "our" temple. Could we build on this event to invite the light of Christ into a home like ours, and if it came, would it want to stay? I thought it worth the test.

Peter and I knew that we needed to lead out, to decide together our course of action. Like fearless Christians in the lions' den, this took some prayers not unlike Daniel's—prayers that our lions would begin by being kinder to each other. Not that we hit and scream, but we are big-time teasers—with a slight twist, that can turn combative in a flash. A couple of weeks before the dedication, I wrote down all the dedication activities on the kitchen calendar so everyone who was conscious and eating would know what was going on. This list included a ward project planting bushes on the temple grounds, distributing dedication tickets to ward members, and ushering for one of several dedication services. The two youngest, James and Becca, were not old enough to attend the dedication, but they participated when we sought the cooperation of all at family home evening and proceeded to make The List.

First, we knew that our family watched too much TV. Even though most of our time was spent with videos, we still wanted to cut that time. I decided the TV cables should mysteriously disappear. We also set aside rowdy popular music in favor of more reverent classical pieces.

As I mentioned, we have trouble with teasing at our house. It's something genetic that comes down from both sides, I'm afraid, but despite the odds, Peter and I really prayed for a miracle—that bickering and teasing would be kept to a minimum. And when conflicts did flare, we tried to resolve them immediately and not let anyone enjoy being mad.

I also tried having planned and organized meals. I'm not good at this. I actually know how to cook five things that "knock your socks off," but after that it's hit or miss. You might get liver nuggets or tofu brulee. I wanted to gather everyone to a fully set table, smiling as if they were on a Bisquick commercial, and not have any forks thrown from the dishwasher to the table after the prayer. I had to plan, but the peaceful meals seemed worth the effort.

Our scripture reading had at times deteriorated to yelling scriptures to the kids as they were running to the bus— "Remember: 'A soft word turneth away wrath!'" And to tell the truth, we had been discouraged by irreverence, so we hadn't been all that consistent. We decided being consistent was what we needed, and maybe the Spirit would follow. With the dedication only two weeks away, the children cooperated. We actually sat down for scripture study and read whole chapters in one sitting.

Last, we all tried to keep the house a little more orderly. Everyone was assigned a station, and when we cleaned, we referred to the phenomenon as the "white tornado." I could feel the Spirit begin to thrive in our new "house of order." Perfection was an impossibility, especially in only two weeks. "How good do we want to be?" was a question we asked ourselves when things got tough. But being better was something we really wanted—so we pressed on.

As the two weeks neared their end, the results were noticeable. There was a distinct difference in our home, an increased feeling of love, and amazingly, less teasing, more piano playing, more reading, more jokes without a jab attached. I even saw one of the children pet the dog. Feelings were shared without having to take a trip to the mall (shopping and sharing seemed to go together at our house), and the children were more willing to help. Mom was less critical, and Dad was more patient, even when he found his hammer out in the strawberry bed . . . again. By Sunday our home was a much better place. When we welcomed Sarah home from college, we watched in awe as she took an arm-in-arm walk with Bo, who last year considered herself Sarah's personal terrorist.

The Monday of the dedication finally came, and just the fact that the children got to miss school generated an intense degree of excitement. As everyone ate sandwiches in the car on the way down Provo Canyon, I read the dedicatory prayer used at the Kirtland Temple and prayed that this same feeling would extend to this dedication. The service was simple, the children even reverent, and after the beautiful dedicatory prayer, we walked out of the temple squinting in the sunshine. Bo put her arm around me, Micky was walking close by and I grabbed her hand, seconds later Heidi put her arm through Bo's, and Sarah latched onto Micky and Peter to Heidi. We walked in one linked chain, and in all that brightness we felt for a brief moment a taste of something celestial, something as real as the building we had just walked from, a link so alive it could not be mistaken.

This was no less a miracle than Moses parting the Red Sea, only this involved people, who are a lot harder to deal with than water. And for this average, macaroni-and-cheese-type family, an amazing transformation had taken place. We all knew it, but for fear recognition would make it disappear, we kept quiet about it. I felt like we were the group mentioned in Isaiah's prophecy—"the people that walked in darkness have seen a great light; they that dwell in the land of the shadow . . . upon them hath the light shined" (2 Nephi 19:2).

But as wonderful as this experience was, we found it difficult to maintain. Reality bites hard some days, and life's spiritual experiences ebb and flow. I know that there will be nights of frozen pizza and Monday night football, that eventually my children will find the TV cables, and that despite our reading scriptures daily, all our conflicts will not be resolved in an hour or a day or even a lifetime. And that is when I think of Peter's grandmother, a bright, intelligent woman who passed away at the age of ninety-six. After her death, we were given a book from her lifetime collection, and when we opened its pages, out fell a three-inch-by-five-inch card. In her familiar, shaky script were written the words: "Do better; be better," a reminder to herself that even at ninety-six she was still working on a few things and knew that searching for the light of Christ was a daily struggle. Those words haunt me as if they're being whispered from somewhere between heaven and creamed tuna over peas. Doing better is a journey. It's a lifetime of laundry for people you love, sweeping up popcorn every Sunday evening, loving the unlovable, doing beyond yourself, always reaching for the light.

STRENGTHENING OUR NURTURING NATURES

LADAWN JACOB

Women as caregivers—wives, mothers, grandmothers, teachers, friends—are at the center of the wheel of life and, as Anne Morrow Lindbergh wrote, must strive "to be the still axis within the revolving wheel of relationships, obligations, and activities."[1] How can we bless the lives of those intertwined with ours so that they can come to know, through our love, the love of the Savior—and their importance?

To be effective nurturers, we must look to the Savior who taught us to be gentle, meek, full of love, patient, and long-suffering. But how can we be like that when our two-year-old has just created a Picasso look-alike with his permanent markers on our new wallpaper, or when our delightful sixteen-year-old calls to tell us he has just had one more "well-I-was-just-changing-the-CD-and-didn't-notice" fender bender, doubling our car insurance.

At times, we all feel overwhelmed, our reservoirs of love nearly empty. Several years ago, I read a biography of Mother Teresa. As a young Albanian nun, she trained in medicine, nutrition, academics, and religion, and then donned the Indian

LaDawn A. Jacob received a B.A. from Brigham Young University in elementary education and music and has enjoyed teaching children in her home over the last twenty-seven years. She and her husband, James C. Jacob, are the parents of eleven children and the grandparents of eleven. She serves as her ward's newsletter editor.

sari worn by those she served and began her work among the poorest of the poor in Calcutta. The first few days she walked among the endless poor and saw disease, ignorance, malnourishment, and death everywhere she looked. She returned home each night exhausted with the magnitude of what she had undertaken. But she did not return to her peaceful, cloistered life among the Sisters of Loreto. "She was determined. She would not stop. Instead of thinking of the crowds, the thousands, she thought of the one—the one closest, the one she was helping."[2]

Mother Teresa's example leads me to ask myself, *How can I, in the most effective and Christlike way, minister to the one nearest me?* Several years ago, my cousin Donna was a Gospel Doctrine teacher. The course of study that year was the Doctrine and Covenants. One morning, her husband, dressed for work in his immaculate, pressed suit, mentioned that he had an appointment for lunch with the stake president. Donna had put on her old work clothes, gearing up to manage their seven boys at breakfast. "You know," she said to her husband, "the Doctrine and Covenants is such a wonderful priesthood manual for men. I'm wondering, Where is my mothers' manual for handling these spirits that the Lord has entrusted to me?" As she later worked in her garden, this question kept returning. Finally she prayed, "Heavenly Father, where is the manual, the instruction booklet for me, for all mothers?" And the Spirit whispered to her, "Donna, I wrote it in your hearts." Women have been blessed with the gift of inspired nurturing, entitling us to have his words written in our hearts to guide each of us in our individual stewardships.

All of us need his words written in our hearts, especially when we are called upon to offer strength, love, and care. Those words may direct us to cradle in our arms a child taller than we are, stroking her hair in silence while she sobs. Perhaps a loved son needs those words in a letter, a son struggling with larger-than-life problems. We need them to exercise gifts of the Spirit. I think of my husband's great-grandfather, Thales Haskell. He was a missionary to the Indians and spoke many Indian languages, but his greatest accomplishment was that he could remain silent in all of them. Knowing when to be silent is a gift of the Spirit.

Nurturing may mean being with a suffering, beloved, and broken friend, or holding up the hands that hang down, or strengthening the feeble knees of aging parents. Nurturing wears many faces. Charlene, a dear neighbor of mine, brought me, in a moment of need, a framed statement in calligraphy that reads, "A friend knows the song in my heart and sings it to me when my memory fails."[3] My Grandmother Andersen is an example of inspired nurturing. She could zero in on the needs of others and know how to lift them just by being around them. My aunt once told me of a man who came to her home and was visiting with my grandmother. This man had about thirty grandchildren. Glowing with joy, he told my grandmother about all the successes and wonderful accomplishments of these grandchildren, and my grandmother basked in his joy with him, saying how much the Lord must love him to fill his quiver so full of righteous posterity. After he left, my aunt said to my grandmother, "Mother, why didn't you tell him that you have eighty-plus grandchildren?" She replied, "You know, Donna, that wouldn't have increased his joy one bit." I think of those words often. One way we nurture is to increase joy. People need us to share their joys with them.

Many times my mothering has been far from inspired. In fact, my children say that when they were sick, if they got a glass of orange juice every other day and a quick check to see if they were still alive, they felt fortunate. Many times I have felt that the best thing I could have done for my children is to have put them up for adoption so they could be raised in a really good home.

As a mother I always feel it is unfair that every time I am mad, the whole family is mad. I used to say to my children,

"Can't I be grumpy without the whole household turning sour-puss?" For years, every New Year's I resolved to speak in a quiet voice. I have a very loud voice, and the decibels go higher and higher as my frustration mounts. I put beans in my shoe until I was practically crippled, trying to remember. I tied bandanas around my mouth and nose and everything else. My house was full of signs that said "Her voice was ever soft, gentle, and low—an excellent thing in woman."[4] One day when I was screaming at my kids, I tore that sign off the fridge, ripped it up, threw it in the garbage, and shouted, "I will yell without that thing looking at me!" We all struggle with weak-nesses when we try to develop charity within ourselves. Can we still nurture others, faults and all? Yes. My mother says I've forgotten a lot of things that she did wrong, and I keep hoping that maybe my children will be forgetful, too.

A major roadblock to nurturing that I have found in my own life is judging and criticizing others rather than feeding their souls. Several years ago I read a talk by Sister Patricia Holland entitled "The Fruits of Peace." She cautioned against expecting perfection from people and urged us to overlook faults in others. How? For one day, Sister Holland suggested, note every time you speak or even think critically of someone else. If you pass judgments on yourself, your children, hus-band, friends, the bus driver, the neighbor, or anyone, keep track of them. Then the next day, see if you can go an entire day cutting off each critical thought that comes into your mind. "This little exercise might surprise you," Sister Holland said. "My husband will verify that I conscientiously work at never speaking ill of anyone. It is a virtue I earnestly seek, and I see it as fundamental to true Christianity. When I undertook this little exercise, therefore, it amazed me to realize how often I did pass judgment, at least mentally. I was even more amazed to note how incredibly good I felt about myself when I was able to go through a whole day keeping that tendency in check." To explain why being uncritical of others feels good,

Sister Holland referred to Matthew 7:2: "For with what judgment ye judge, ye shall be judged: and with what measure ye mete, it shall be measured to you again." Our attitudes bounce back at us. "A critical, petty, or vicious remark is simply an attack on our own self-worth. On the other hand, if our minds are constantly seeing good in others, that, too, will return, and we will truly feel good about ourselves."[5]

I am trying hard to develop this ability. To nurture others is to love them rather than judge and criticize them. Some time ago in my mothering, I was struggling with particularly difficult and challenging problems with one of my children. The harder I tried to get through, the greater the chasm between us seemed to grow. I wrestled alternately with keeping my mouth closed to giving lengthy and emotional lectures. Was I being too hard, or not hard enough? Had I exacted enough justice, or was I being too merciful? On a relatively quiet day at home, I went to my room to pray and think and ask the Lord's direction as I had done so many times before. This time I felt desperate for his help. I knelt at the edge of my bed and tearfully entreated the Lord. After a time in prayer, I opened the scriptures. My eyes were drawn to these words: "Sufficient to such a man is this punishment, which was inflicted of many. So that contrariwise ye ought rather to forgive him, and comfort him, lest perhaps such a one should be swallowed up with overmuch sorrow. Wherefore I beseech you that ye would *confirm your love toward him*" (2 Corinthians 2:6–8; emphasis added). Through my tears, I read the words over and over again and felt the sweet, comforting voice of the Spirit instructing that what my child needed was not added reproach or directives but rather assurances of my unconditional love.

Judging and criticizing is a serious obstacle to nurturing. Another is neglecting our own needs. Do you ever feel overwhelmed and drained by the needs of others? Have you ever wondered, *How can I possibly be to everyone, give to everyone, what they need?* When a very busy father, physician, and church leader asked President Harold B. Lee, "How should I handle my time?" President Lee said to him, "A man's [or woman's] first responsibility is to himself, then to his family, then to the Church, realizing that we have responsibilities in our professions as well."[6] We need to bring our best selves to whatever tasks we are engaged in. That means that eating well, exercising, and sleeping—the basics—must not be sacrificed to our responsibilities to nurture others. We want to bring to our nurturing "our healthiest, happiest, heartiest self," explains Sister Holland. "When they ask for bread, let us not be so weary and unhealthy that we give them a stone."[7]

Many people in my life have nurtured me. There have been exceptional teachers, affectionate neighbors, and loving friends. My home was also a place of warmth and security. As a little girl, I thought that the greatest thing on earth was to have a new baby come to our home. In fact, every time we went under an overpass, we'd stick our finger on the car roof and wish for another baby. It seemed to work because my mother had twelve. My parents brought home my youngest brother, Dean, on Thanksgiving Day. We all had our noses pressed against the front window, waiting for the car to drive down "washboard lane" and pull into our driveway. When it did, we rushed out, opened the doors, and ushered in my mother and father and our new little brother. Carefully we unfolded the blankets, looked in, and wondered at the beautiful baby inside. He looked a lot like me, I thought. Then my father laid this little boy on our front room table, and as a family we knelt down. It seemed unusual because it was in the middle of the day, not in the morning or night when we usually had family prayer. Then my father acted as voice for our family and expressed his gratitude for this little child that the Lord had sent to our home. That day as he prayed, I felt a warmth covering me. I realized that I had been loved and wanted in just that same way. I'm so grateful to have been reared in such a home. Once while my mother and father were on a mission in

Mexico, my father wrote to me, "LaDawn, what a transcendent privilege it is to have the association of little children." I kidded him that it was only because he was three thousand miles away from us that he was able to say that.

I realize that many have not been reared in a nurturing home. Perhaps you are one whose parents, or father, or mother, didn't treat you as if you were their most cherished possession. If so, I want you to know that the Lord can fill those vacancies in your heart and teach you how to nurture even if you have been denied nurturing in your own childhood or youth. The Lord can mend and fill broken hearts and teach us all things if we will but be prayerful and humble and submissive to his will.

Several years ago, a dear friend I will call Pam went through some tremendous trials. Her husband developed chemical allergies and was unable even to go out of the house. He stayed in a tiled room, and Pamela put his food outside the door and then told him on the intercom that it was ready. They had four sons and a baby daughter. Hoping for improvement, they decided to move from California to Arizona, which had fewer air pollutants. Finding a home and caring for her sick husband and her children was incredibly stressful. Pam also suffered a physical illness that caused all her hair to fall out. She had no eyelashes, no eyebrows, and was completely bald. One day she was driving between the home where her husband was staying and the one where she was staying with their children (he couldn't be around anyone who had been contaminated with chemical pollutants). As she drove, she said, "I thought of all of the dreams of my life and how many had not come true as I thought that they would. A lot of those dreams had shattered and fallen down around me. I also thought as I drove along how ugly I was. Nobody could love me, I was so bald and thin and unattractive." As the tears began to flow, she felt a warmth around her and the words, "Do you think that I don't love you?" She remembered the love of the Savior for her. She knew she was precious to him. The warmth of that moment carried her through many, many weeks of difficult times.

God's nurturing can be felt in warm support as we learn to be nurturers, even when we are dealing with the pinpricks of daily life. A word or two of practical advice from my mother has helped me through the years to nurture my own companion. First, she said, clear a path in front of the door so that he can get in. That may sound kind of obvious, but it's so nice to come home to your "palace" and find some semblance of order. Second, identify where your children are. It's embarrassing for a husband to drive up to his home and see little Johnny running down the street naked. Third, have some evidence of dinner in the making. You may just set the table—that would make him believe that food is coming—or throw an onion in a pot of boiling water—the smell promises sustenance to come. And fourth, meet him with a smile, not a snarl. My husband was a rancher, and he always came home later than he said he was going to. I'd give him a kind of snarling look that said "Where have you been?" He would sometimes remind me with a sheepish grin, "Honey, it is better to dwell in the wilderness than in a wide house with an angry and contentious woman" (see Proverbs 25:24).

Though few of us will have the good fortune to be full-time, stay-at-home wives and mothers all our married lives, these principles from my mother's era can be adapted to make home feel like home. Establishing order and planning to be affectionate is worth the effort. My daughter-in-law Jennifer impresses me. Every night when my son comes home and she is there before him, Jennifer runs from wherever she is in the house and almost knocks him off his feet with her exuberant welcoming hug, she is so excited to see him. She told me, after they were married, that several months before they were engaged she felt she would probably marry him, and each night after she had been with him, she would go home and write in a little booklet something about him that she had learned that day or some act that she loved and appreciated. On their honeymoon, she gave that booklet to him. He told me, "You know, if we ever had a fire, I'd grab Jennifer and then that book. To think someone thinks all those things about me!" Just think how much happier so many homes would be if a husband or wife, coming in from work, could expect a hug and a smile, and if they each were thinking, I'm going to find something that I love and appreciate to write about my sweetheart tonight.

Several years ago I read a narrative called "Eve's Diary" by Mark Twain. Twain gives a humorous account of the struggles, challenges, and experiences of our first parents. At the end of the play, Eve dies. Adam, who had learned to love this complicated, talkative woman, stands by her grave at her death. His words are simple, yet profound: "Wheresoever she was, *there* was Eden."[8] I have often thought the same of my mother. It is said that God could not be everywhere, so he gave us mothers. I am grateful for a loving mother in heaven who nurtured me; though the veil is drawn, I know she is there with my Heavenly Father. I am grateful for a mother on earth who is precious to me and who has given me love undauntedly through the years. May we have a clearer vision of the great, profound influence that we have as nurturers, and rejoice and be glad in that Christlike service.

NOTES

1. Anne Morrow Lindbergh, *Gift from the Sea* (New York: Random House, 1955), 51.

2. Patricia Reilly Giff, *Mother Teresa: Sister to the Poor* (New York: Viking Kestrel, 1986), 31.

3. Attributed to Kathy Davis. Framed quotation in possession of author.

4. William Shakespeare, *King Lear,* act 5, scene 3, lines 273–74.

5. Jeffrey R. and Patricia T. Holland, *On Earth As It Is in Heaven* (Salt Lake City: Deseret Book, 1989), 29.

6. Holland and Holland, *On Earth As It Is in Heaven,* 65.

7. Holland and Holland, *On Earth As It Is in Heaven,* 66.

8. Mark Twain, "Eve's Diary," in *The Bible According to Mark Twain,* ed. Howard G. Baetzhold and Joseph B. McCullough (Athens: University of Georgia Press, 1995), 33.

WHAT'S RIGHT WITH ME: ADHD

SAM GOLDSTEIN

Not long ago, a mother told me about her child's plight. He was bringing unfinished work home from school nightly. For a time, this schoolwork masqueraded as assigned homework, but she soon realized that the rest of the class completed this work at school. This family, which—like most of us—had only a few hours each evening to enjoy each other, was now embroiled in fighting over homework that was in actuality schoolwork, unfinished by a child with Attention-deficit Hyperactivity Disorder (ADHD). The frustrated mom wrote a catharsis letter to vent her feelings. (Catharsis letters are for journals, not to be sent.) She wrote to his teacher: "Since it appears that I am going to be doing at least two hours of your job each evening, I'm going to start sending Jake's laundry on Mondays and Thursdays. Please don't mix the colors with the whites."

Children with ADHD are a unique group of individuals. They require unique strategies for parenting. Remember what life was like before you started to have children? At the Neurology, Learning, and Behavior Center, we call that period B.C., which doesn't stand for Before Children; it stands for

Sam Goldstein holds a Ph.D. in psychology and chairs the national professional advisory board for Children with Attention-deficit Disorder (CHADD). The author of numerous articles, textbooks, and videos, Dr. Goldstein is an instructor at the University of Utah, serves on the staff at both University Hospital and Primary Children's Hospital, and has a private practice. He and his wife, Janet, are the parents of two children.

Before Chaos. The children who come to see us are having trouble meeting the expectations of adults. According to the adults, they don't behave right, or feel right, or think right, or learn right. Because they don't fit the system that we adults have designed for them, life has become chaotic for everyone.

When you envisioned the kind of parent you were going to be—patient and calm, never angry, doing things democratically, and so forth—and compare that to what has happened along the way, especially if you've had a child who differs a bit from the norm, I predict that you have learned a lot. For one thing, you may have discovered that children with ADHD have more power to control you than vice versa. For another, you will have discovered that mental illness is inherited—we get it from our children! My purpose is to provide some helpful suggestions for parents of children with ADHD. I'll begin with a general framework for understanding ADHD.

In taking client histories, I ask parents to bring me pictures of their children. One mom showed me a family photo she had just taken at her daughter's preschool graduation. It was mid-August. These children would be in kindergarten in a few days. They were outside singing a song, lined up in straight rows, teachers standing tall, parents watching. This mom's rather active little girl was not mean or nasty, just one of those children who get asked to leave preschools because they don't sit on their carpet squares the way they are supposed to. So I asked, "Which one of these little girls is yours?" She said, "Oops, she's not in this one." I thought, *Oh my, it's only preschool, and this child's in time-out already.* The mother produced a second picture, scrutinized it briefly, and said, "Oh, there she is. See her—way up on the hill?" She explained that her daughter had agreed never to get out of sight. As long as she was in sight, the teachers allowed her to wander; they had given up trying to get her to keep her body in one place. I thought, *Too bad. This behavior, which was labeled as acceptable in preschool, a week from now in kindergarten is going to be labeled as bad. The teacher is going to say, "This is bad. You can't do this."*

How we label a child's behavior powerfully influences our thoughts and behavior toward that child. If I call a child "careful," I like what he is doing. If I call him "slow," I have a very different response to the same behavior. If I decide that a child is creative and energetic, I deal very differently with her than if I regard the child as hyperactive and difficult. So, we have not only to think about what we want for our children and how to help them get there, but we have to think about what we think about our children and why we label some behaviors good or bad.

Children with ADHD commonly display multiple and varied problems, but the core problem is impulsivity. Impulsivity leads to difficulty in three other skill areas: an impulsive child has difficulty paying attention and is easily distracted; an impulsive child has difficulty delaying rewards; an impulsive child tends to be excessively active and emotional.

Let's consider the emotional factor in more depth. Children with ADHD express the extremes of their emotions faster and with greater intensity than is normal for their age. They also become frustrated quickly, often over minor events. Everyone around a child with ADHD is well aware of the child's presence and current feelings. Another problem with impulsivity is threshold. Little things get big reactions, but ten minutes after a major blowout over some minor event, children with ADHD can't understand why you are so upset—they've moved on to something else. Think about what life is like for these children. Imagine yourself with their extremes of emotion. When you are happy, you are *so* happy people tell you to calm down. When you're unhappy, you're *so* unhappy people tell you to calm down. Think about what they learn about emotions and feelings. Too often their feelings are what get them into trouble rather than being qualities to cherish in human interaction.

So impulsivity can lead to problems, but is being impulsive

185

bad? Why isn't it good? Children who exemplify, as educator Rick Lavoie has said, the OTM-OTM syndrome—"on the mind, out the mouth"—take higher risks, act without thinking, and have difficulty separating thought from feeling. These children learn from their experiences but have trouble acting on that knowledge because immediate needs overwhelm their limited capacity for self-control. But is this behavior, the tendency to act without thinking, bad in a moral sense? No. It is a morally neutral quality, a normal variant of human behavior. Some people are very reflective; some are not. Children with ADHD are not. Some people are typically calm; some are volatile and exuberant. Children with ADHD are not among the calm.

In our modern, competitive society, we tend to look at everything, including children's behavior, on a scale from the best to the worst. If your child is in the top 5 percent for how fast he runs, the soccer coach wants him on the team. If she is in the bottom 5 percent, the soccer coach says, "Go play with dolls." If she is in the top 5 percent for how well she reads, she's in the gifted readers class that puts on a play at the end of the year; if he is in the bottom 5 percent, he gets to do remedial phonics exercises and maybe watch the play—if he's not in time-out. Which activity will teach a child that learning to read is fun and worthwhile? In our society, children and adults in the bottom 5 percent for how well they manage their impulses—how well they control their emotions, stop and think, do the right thing, or learn from experiences—are in trouble.

What I want to suggest is that we look at ADHD and identify the core deficit. Children with ADHD don't have any trouble paying attention when the task is something they have chosen to do. Give the child with ADHD a roll of quarters. Send him to the noisiest, loudest, most distracting video arcade you can find. Offer him a favorite machine. He's not inattentive. He pays attention just fine. He has trouble paying attention when tasks are repetitive, uninteresting, effortful, and not

186

of his choosing. Now I've just defined half of what children have to do in school. If we identify what ADHD children have trouble with, those four factors will determine their level of difficulty. The more these qualities come into play, the more trouble these kids will have.

It's important to see the world through the eyes of these children if you are going to be effective advocates for them in school or enjoy them at home. When a child with ADHD is doing something he likes, he pays attention as well as everybody else's kid. When he doesn't like it, doesn't choose to do it, or it is repetitive, he has trouble. The way I stick to something that I don't like is with guilt—I was raised by a Jewish mother, so I know how to wield guilt. I think, *People are counting on me to do this.* An adult with ADHD, however, faced with a task she doesn't like, simply finds something else to do. When I say to an adult with ADHD, "But, Nina, that had to get done," she will reply, "Oh, I know, but it wasn't interesting. It didn't hold my attention." And that's that. Guilt doesn't kick in.

When most children make a mistake, a parent asks, "What were you *thinking* when you did that?" We want to understand their motives or correct their thinking. When children with ADHD make a mistake, a parent must ask, "What *weren't* you thinking when you did that?" Their problems occur not because they don't know better, have a mean streak, or are inherently bad, but because they don't think before they act. They often know what to do, but they don't do what they know. A child with ADHD becomes distracted by his own thoughts and desire for immediate reward. In these instances, the child acts impulsively.

Although the child may have been punished numerous times for similar misbehavior—"Don't run out in the street without looking first!"—and is able to clearly explain the rule, when the moment arises, she acts impulsively and does not follow the rule. The problem isn't in acquiring knowledge but in

187

the follow-through. Children with ADHD are not clueless but cueless. Let me explain. When a pedestrian gets to a street corner, the corner curbing is a cue to look both ways. If the pedestrian forgets to act on the cue, understanding that traffic is dangerous doesn't help.

Impulsive children often don't pick up on cues. Punishment for yesterday's trouble seems to be enough for most children, faced with the same choice, to trigger the thought, "Oh, I'm not going to do that again." But a child with ADHD doesn't recall what happened yesterday without a reminder cue. These children have trouble learning to do repetitive things because they don't pick up on cues. After a month of practicing tooth brushing, Norman doesn't have to be rewarded anymore. He goes into the bathroom, and the bathroom is a cue: *Oh, brush my teeth*. After a month of practicing brushing teeth, Jed, a child with ADHD, the day I don't remind him or give him a reward, goes in the bathroom, looks around, thinks, *Why am I here?*— and out he goes. Now, does he know what to do? Yes. Does he do what he knows? No. If you assume this is deliberately obstinate or "bad" behavior, you're buying into trouble, because it is not. Jed simply needs more repetition, more practice, to adequately reinforce those cues. As a parent, you can adjust your expectation and say, "This kid needs more practice."

If it takes most children thirty days to learn to remember to brush their teeth, the ADHD child may need three hundred. Now, that's not three hundred days of trying. That's three hundred days of establishing the habit, of developing an internal cueing system. All children eventually learn to look both ways when they reach traffic and to brush their teeth. So it is not hopeless. These children are not morally, emotionally, or psychologically diseased. They do not have some terrible problem as human beings. They're simply at the bottom for certain qualities that our society increasingly values: Hurry up. Move quickly. Do it fast. Catch on quick. Don't waste time. Let's go.

The first lesson, as we talk about what to do, is to make the task more interesting because if the task is more interesting for these kids, they stick with it better. The second lesson is to make the payoff more rewarding. This group of children, because they need more practice, seem to need more immediate, frequent, predictable, and meaningful payoffs than other kids. They don't like punishment; they like rewards just like anybody else. But they seem to need more rewards. If I am going to continue asking my child to practice brushing his teeth five times as long as his brother, I'd better make that task five times more interesting. And I'd better make the payoff five times as enticing. So make the task interesting, make the payoff enticing, adjust your expectations, and allow more practices. Or if that's more energy and creativity than you can devote to this particular task, expect it to take longer and be more patient. Eventually everybody learns to brush his teeth.

As for speeding up the learning process using appropriate medications, let me clear up a couple of misunderstandings. First, stimulants are performance enhancers. Divide any group of ordinary people and give one half a stimulant and the other half nothing. The half receiving a stimulant will make fewer mistakes on boring, repetitive tasks than the half without a stimulant. In one study some years ago, entire classrooms of children were given low-dose stimulants. These were not children who had significant problems—nor does the study say that the teacher was given a stimulant. But every teacher reported after the trial that all the children paid attention better and did better work. That's not a reason to add low-dose stimulants to school lunch. It's a reason to recognize that the brains of children with ADHD, in fact, operate in basically the same way as the brains of the rest of us. Stimulants work the same way for everyone. Some individuals, however, have a lot more room for improvement in attending to boring, repetitive tasks than others.

About medicine, my second point is that pills won't substitute for skills. We shouldn't overstate the benefits or understate the liabilities. Not a single study indicates that if you take your Ritalin today, you'll turn out to be a better adult. About six hundred studies, however, suggest that if you take your Ritalin today, your mother and your teacher will be less likely to be angry with you today. So what the medicine provides is relief from symptoms. I want this message to thread through everything else I have to say about the benefits of medicine for behavior modification. Relief of symptoms is not enough. We can do a lot of things to relieve the symptoms of children with ADHD and give them survival tools, but giving them life skills requires something more than treatments for ADHD. If a child's mother is an untreated depressive who cycles in and out and his father is an antisocial alcoholic or a never-home workaholic, then with or without medicine, behavior modification, or school intervention, that child's chances for a happy, successful future are slim. That will be true for any child, with ADHD or without.

For any child, the best predictor of what therapists call "life outcome" is the quality of family life. That is true for any child, including those with ADHD. The good news, then, is that biology is not destiny. It affects probability. A family's genetic risk factors—or lack of them—do not guarantee that every child in that family is going to turn out a certain way, good or bad. How you rear your children and the quality of your relationships with them determine on what field the risk factors are played out.

For me, medicine is a tool. If parents say, "I don't want it," I say, "Well, here's the information. You make that decision. I'll support you." If parents say, "This is great. This will help us. I want it," that's fine, too. I want parents to be experts, to make informed choices, because they have to be the advocates. If parents harbor unrealistic expectations about what medications can do, they run the risk of attempting to treat nonmedication problems with medications and believing that more and more medication is needed to solve the child's problems.

Medications will not cure learning problems, resolve a deficit in social skills, nor remedy an emotional disturbance.

Also, at some point, at a certain age, the child has to be in charge. The child must tell the parent if the medicine makes a difference. What I tell children is, "The medicine is a tool. It doesn't fix you. And it doesn't fix the world to make it go better for you. If you pick up the tool and use it effectively, life will be better. If you choose not to use it, it's not going to make any difference for you." The child should be in control, not the medicine.

Now let me provide some general information about how children with ADHD fare in school settings. First, let's look at intelligence and achievement. It has been argued that children with ADHD are innately less intelligent than their peers who do not have ADHD. Careful research suggests that this is not the case; rather, we are observing the effect of impulsive, inattentive behavior on test performance. As a group, children with ADHD appear to be as intelligent as their peers without ADHD.

So why do report cards of elementary school children with ADHD, as a group, characteristically look worse than those of their peers without ADHD? Achievement testing suggests that most are learning adequately. They simply are not performing. Although there appears to be a greater incidence of specific learning disabilities among children with ADHD, most appear to have intact learning skills. Over time, however, the cumulative effect of lack of attention and completion of work takes its toll. By adolescence, a significant number of students with ADHD begin to lag behind their peers in at least one academic subject.

Two other traits trouble teachers of children with ADHD: (1) their uneven and unpredictable ability to perform a given academic task, and (2) daydreaming. Let's consider the first factor: performance. A third grader with ADHD may successfully rattle off the complete times tables in ninety seconds one day and find most of those facts have vanished the next day. A

191

mother drilling spelling words will breathe a sigh of relief to find the list already mastered by Tuesday only to be dumbfounded when the child can't spell those same words on Thursday. She feels sure the child "just isn't concentrating" or isn't "trying"—but that's not the problem. Uneven performance extends to skills as well as retention of facts. Teachers frequently reassure children with ADHD that they can do it "if they try" and "they did it yesterday so they should be able to do it today." This is somewhat analogous to telling a child he hit a home run the last time at bat, and, therefore, he should be able to hit a home run every time at bat. Frequently, completing work for the child with ADHD is equivalent to hitting a home run.

Children with ADHD are also frequently described as daydreamers. Studies suggest that they are not as much daydreaming as they are interested in something other than what the teacher is focusing on. Children with ADHD appear to engage in a significantly greater degree of nonproductive behavior than do their peers who do not have ADHD. Most elementary school age children find something productive to do during unstructured activities. Children with ADHD characteristically engage in unproductive activities, such as zipping and unzipping their coats or rearranging the clutter in their desks.

To be an advocate in the school system for your child with ADHD, be proud, patient, and persistent. That's Goldstein's rule. What special help should these children receive in school? How do they learn best? What settings are best suited? They do best in organized and structured classrooms with clear rules, a predictable schedule, and separate desks. Teacher feedback should be frequent, immediate, and positive. Minor disruptions are best ignored. Rewards should be consistent and frequent. Self-paced rather than teacher-paced tasks can be helpful, and expectations should be adjusted to meet the child's skill level—both behaviorally and academically. Keeping up isn't as important as keeping going. Although there is no way to predict which children or when, by adulthood at least one-third of children with ADHD have outgrown the core problems and do not experience serious difficulty. Another third continue to be bothered by some ADHD symptoms. The remaining one-third may have more significant difficulties in habits, jobs, and marriage.

What about teaching styles? The best teacher is one who can adjust and find the best in every child. Beyond that, I don't think any particular qualities are essential. Should kids with ADHD have teachers with ADHD? Probably not. Nobody would know what time it was, when to start or stop an activity, or what happened to the homework. But that might be better than an unreasonable teacher reared by authoritarian parents who shames and blames a child who loses homework.

What do teachers need to be able to teach? Put yourself in the shoes of the child with ADHD. What do your teachers want from you? Basically, they want you to stop, start, and think along with everybody else. They want you to think about what everybody else is thinking about. They don't want your mind on the beach in the Bahamas somewhere. They want you to start working when everybody else starts and to stop when everybody else stops. Don't start before; don't stop after. When everybody else comes in from recess, you come in.

Can children with ADHD do that, or do they need a special educational setting? If parents step in as advocates for their children, I think adaptations can be made. These children learn best when they talk and move and question and interact with their learning environment. Does that mean there is something wrong with them? When I ask a teacher to make an adjustment so a child can move a little bit or have his hands on the learning materials, teachers will sometimes say, "I just don't have the time." My response is, "You know, hands-on, interactive learning is good for everybody. You don't need to set up a separate curriculum for one child. Do it for the whole class." Again, the principle is: what's good for kids with ADHD is good for everyone, and what's bad for everyone is extra bad for kids with ADHD.

Above else, the child with ADHD needs compassionate understanding, both at home and at school. Parents and teachers should not pity, tease, attack, be frightened of, angered by, or overindulge this child. They must understand the condition is real; it involves critical skill deficits; it is primarily a disorder of competence, not defiance. In other words, the child did not cause or want the condition.

So in working with schools, identify your child's strengths. Be proud. What works best? Schools tend to quickly gloss over strengths: "Oh, he's a nice kid. He smiles," and then they spend all their time on what's wrong. No. I want to see his strengths. Tell me his academic strengths and how you are going to make them stronger, so he feels like he is really good at something academically. That's what will get him through life. As my friend and colleague Bob Brooks says, "If you've got a big sea of dysfunction, you'd better have big islands of competence to rest on."

Unfortunately, although some people may eventually learn to make ADHD an asset, in our society being given a diagnosis of ADHD at ten years of age has zero assets. I'm not talking about treasuring your child as a family member. I'm not discussing your relationship with your child. I'm referring to his or her ability to deal with the world we've designed for children, and ADHD is a liability, period. If the world would make some adjustments, these children would function better. The world is not about to do that, however, so we must focus on how we can adjust the child. What I ask children is, "What is it we don't understand about how you learn, about what you need?"

One last word about education and your role as parents in preparing your child for life. We tend with children to focus on what's wrong with them and then try to fix it. What we've discovered is that focusing on what's wrong with children and fixing it relieves symptoms but doesn't necessarily mean their future is going to be better. Remember that ADHD involves a set of behaviors and problems that are managed, not cured. You as a parent have to create a balance. Yes, the teacher is concerned with getting the spelling done. But your relationship with this child is more important to future happiness. So if you've got only ten minutes to spend with this child today, and you can either fight over spelling homework or take a walk, take a walk. I'm not saying the spelling is unimportant, but you have to create a balance.

One day a mother came in obviously upset. "Help me. I'm losing my child," she begged. At first I thought she was talking about divorce. She wasn't. She had a third-grader with not just ADHD but learning problems as well, and she devoted two hours of every afternoon to working with her child. She had overheard him tell his friend that he didn't care if he ever saw her again because if she left, he wouldn't have to spend his afternoons doing this work. That's not worth it. If you're going to spend an hour working on what's wrong with this child, you'd better spend an hour reinforcing what's right. Balance.

Most children with ADHD exhibit impulsivity, hyperactivity, and inattention. A smaller group, about 10 percent, are inattentive without hyperactivity. They respond to Ritalin but not quite as well. Theirs is a different problem. Those kids have different risks, different life outcome probabilities, and a low probability of substance abuse. Whenever I mention substance abuse, parents' alarm bells go off. Let me emphasize: these are not "bad kids." People will say, "Oh, ADHD? Substance abuse. ADHD? Criminal behavior." Not so. If you take a group of children with ADHD, and they do not develop beyond being just a pain in the neck (meaning plenty of irritation but no serious problems with delinquent behavior, depression, or anxiety), then they have no greater risks for substance abuse as teenagers or seriously dysfunctional futures than anybody else.

195

ADHD doesn't dispose a child to the disease of addiction. ADHD is a catalyst. A child with ADHD is more likely to try something on an impulse. Placed in a bad environment, impulsive children are more likely to get themselves into trouble, especially if they don't have parents willing or able to struggle with them during the teen years, setting limits and boundaries, hanging in there and loving children when they are hard to like.

My message to parents comes down to this: you can make the difference for your children, not just by giving them medicine and by understanding ADHD but in the way you live your lives. Children don't do what we say; they do what we do. You are the best model for your children. The way you go about living your life, day in day out, is the best insulator for children with ADHD.

AT HOME WITH ATTENTION-DEFICIT DISORDER

PAMELA BUSHMAN

INTRODUCTION BY NINA JOHNSTON, ADULT WITH ADD AND SESSION MODERATOR

Living with Attention-deficit Disorder (ADD) is diffi-cult but doable, and our families are a terrific resource. Older siblings can be very helpful to little children who struggle with trying to keep on task and be appropriate socially. Our older children thought their younger brother was truly wonderful with all his energy, creativ-ity, and joyous spontaneity. They included him in their assemblies in high school, creative asking-for-a-date preparations, and even on some dates. They helped build this child's self-esteem when lots of life's experiences were knocking it down.

I am an adult with ADD. I appreciate many parts of the personality, and I enjoy now much of what was a challenge to me to get control of when I was younger. It would have been helpful as I struggled as a child to have understood why I was so restless, why I had the impulse to run to whatever sounded more fun, why I talked out impulsively, and why I annoyed people without

---

Pamela Jeanne Bushman is an artist and the mother of seven children, three of whom she and her husband, Willard M. Bushman, have adopted. She serves in the community and in her ward Relief Society presidency.

intending to. Luckily, I was blessed to be born into a structured, loving home with high expectations. As an adult, I find that having ADD is more of a plus.

As a mission mother and the mother of missionaries, I am concerned that we focus on the positive abilities of these creative missionaries. When my son with ADD was sixteen, he said to me, "If you were going to be lost in a jungle, would you rather have a survivor's kit, or ME with a pocketknife?" It was a no brainer! If I were lost, I know that his creativity and ingenuity would get us out, and besides, we would have fun doing it. There is a long list of advantages to having ADD: high energy, creativity, intuitiveness, resourcefulness, tenacity, a hardworking, never-say-die approach, warmheartedness, a trusting attitude, a forgiving attitude, sensitivity, ability to take risks, flexibility, loyalty, and a good sense of humor.[1] These great characteristics could get us out of all kinds of jungles in life.

I would like to give you a synopsis of our family. We have seven children. Our three adopted children have Attention-deficit Disorder (ADD).[2] Our twenty-year-old son has ADD with anger disorder. The seventeen-year-old has ADD with oppositional disorder. The fifteen-year-old has ADD with hyperactivity (ADHD). (He was a drug baby, which accounts for a host of other brain disorders: Tourette's syndrome, manic-depression, obsessive-compulsive disorder, anxiety disorder, oppositional disorder, and excessive impulsivity.)

Neither the fact that they are adopted nor their ADD and other disorders has lessened our love and commitment to them. The very struggles that these time-consuming challenges require are part of what binds our family so strongly together. In addition, many of the parenting strategies that we have found to be effective for our children with ADD can benefit the whole family. As Sam Goldstein, a specialist in learning and behavior disorders, points out, "What's good for kids with ADHD is good for everyone, and what's bad for everyone is extra bad for kids with ADHD."[3]

HOME ADAPTATIONS

Three core principles guide our parenting. First, we provide our children with structure and a narrow range of choices. Our children with ADD functioned poorly when offered a wide range of choices. They functioned better within a structure of only two or three choices.

Second, we try to be consistent and persistent. Our children with ADD can be very annoying. We learned early to resist the temptations to indulge, to get angry, or to give up and turn our backs on them. *Indulgence* is not love. *Anger* is not love. *Indifference* is not love. Love is unconditional, but it does not tolerate the wasting of their lives. True parental love insists on the children obeying righteous rules. For my own peace of mind, I have prayed often to know when to insist and persist— and when to let something go. Many times, the Lord has inspired me. That gives me confidence and our boys security. I recommend the Lord's inspiration to you. It will be your best resource.

Third, love their eternal spirits. Knowing the restored gospel, we expect to find sterling qualities in our sons. We know they achieved brilliantly in premortality. We know they can achieve in the next life. Meanwhile, we want to make their mortality as productive and joyful as anyone else's. Outside the Church, I have met parents who have given up on their children with ADD. The stress and difficulties overwhelm them. But you and I understand that these are children of God whom we should love and help for their eternal sakes. We, and they, will be blessed for every honest effort we make.

Our honest efforts include becoming educated about ADD. We joined the local CHADD chapter, a support group for parents and friends of people with ADD. Along the way, we learned much from reading many useful books on the subject. We called local mental health agencies and private groups that work with ADD and learning disabilities. They sent information, much of it without charge. They were eager to offer help and leads to other resources. We were amazed at the resources made readily available to us.

Throughout the months and years, I prayed. These giant challenges with ADD motivated me to really listen for answers. Let me emphasize again how important prayer is. I knew that we couldn't handle these challenges on our own. We needed divine guidance. I needed the Spirit with me every minute of the day. So, I continually fine-tuned my relationship with my Father in Heaven. Several times each day, I still pray for help from the Holy Ghost. The Lord has blessed me many times with the knowledge I have needed.

Then, my husband, Bill, and I had to educate our parents and other relatives who would interact with our children with ADD. Of course, some of them blamed us as parents. "If you were stricter," they'd say or think. It took many sessions and much time, but the ones we converted became valuable allies. It was worth persevering.

Because most children with ADD misbehave much of the time, they hear few compliments about their behavior. Frequent criticisms—ours and others—undermined their self-esteem. We tried to counterbalance those messages. For example, we remind them often of their intelligence, talents, and spiritual nature. My husband gives them priesthood blessings. We speak of them lovingly and appreciatively in family prayer. We avoid calling them insulting names. Instead of criticizing, we try to say, "I like it better when you do such-and-such," giving an example of what the child can say or do.

We show confidence in them: "Knowing you, I'm sure you'll do fine," or "That's a good idea. Let's try it." We focus on their contributions: "That was thoughtful of you," or "I've really enjoyed being with you today." We recognize effort and improvement: "It looks as if you've really worked hard on that. I'm proud of you for persisting." "Look at the progress you've made!" We learned that highly structured martial arts, such as Karate or judo, taught them self-discipline and obedience. We put our sons with ADD into a martial arts class. They gained self-confidence.

Structure and high expectations go hand in hand. All children need to accept responsibility for their words and actions, including those with ADD. Our children will not function as adults if they grow up thinking that not they, but "the ogre," ADD, is responsible for their actions. Bill and I have tried to emphasize that the gift of agency involves consequences. We teach our children that they are free to choose their actions but not the consequences. They must accept responsibility for the results of their choices.

Even though we know children with ADD are highly impulsive, when our children speak or act impetuously and offensively, we hold them responsible. We don't let it slide. We must teach them to think and behave correctly, just as we teach any child.

MEDICAL APPROACHES

Not all children with ADD perform better on medications. Mine do; medications help them modify their behaviors. They can focus better and learn more. But medicine does not think or act for them. I think of medications as bringing them up from the basement to the main floor, where they can act for themselves, as children without ADD can. Medications don't take them up to the second floor; they have to do that themselves.

We involved our children in decisions, including medication, as much as their age, intelligence, and desire permitted. We educated them about the disorder and how to compensate for it. Sometimes parents forget that the disorder is the child's challenge more than theirs. A child with ADD has to learn how to live and cope with his or her own ADD.

If your doctor recommends medication, learn all you can from doctors and pharmacists about the effects and side-effects of available medications. Once incomplete information from a doctor about a medication caused one child a serious problem. Since then, I have been careful to stay well informed.

A doctor also depends on continuing feedback to determine the optimum level of medication for each individual child. I kept a daily log for the doctor to help track how the medications were affecting our sons. In that log, I wrote the highlights of the day. Then I asked the child, "What kind of day did you have?" Seeing me write down their answers involved my sons in solving the challenge of their having ADD, another benefit of record-keeping.

Two cautions: First, do not expect any prescription to be the right one forever. Some medications may work well for a year or two and then taper off in effectiveness. We found a few that worked only six weeks. We kept alert to changes, so the doctor might increase, decrease, or perhaps discontinue or change the medication. Second, be aware of "rebounds" from medication. Some children may act aggressive, angry, and insolent, or, in some cases, sad, weepy, and depressed when medications wear off. When a son becomes insolently aggressive at the end of the day, I tell him, "Son, you are in a rebound period. You are not a disrespectful person. You are kind. This is not how a respectful person speaks." We talk until he calms down. This isn't easy. I have had to learn, so he can learn from me, which emotional muscles to flex to get hold of himself.

Medication may be one part of helping children with ADD cope with their disorder. A structured environment in a loving home is another far more critical part. Many children with ADD have low self-esteem and low ambition, so a third valuable aid for children with ADD, especially in their teen years, may be psychotherapy to help them deal with their discouragement and fear of failure. Our psychologist is also teaching us, as a family, how to accommodate to the stress and disruption of ADD. At times, although we needed professional help, we couldn't afford it. To serve the same purpose, we organized a parent-support group. Parents met in our home and shared common experiences. We were relieved to learn that others shared our burdens. The collaboration of ideas from many homes helped all of us work better. The courage of other parents reinforced our persistence.

DISCIPLINE THAT WORKS

We strive to maintain good relationships between parent and child. "A good relationship with a child is a prerequisite to effective discipline. When the relationship is good, almost any form of discipline is effective. When the relationship is poor, however, almost no form of discipline works well. Never use discipline that damages your relationship with children."[4]

The key to effective discipline is to be in control of yourself. When I am calm, I can better judge the situation. If I get angry, I cannot discipline appropriately. So I calm myself first. At the moment of provocation, I pray for the Spirit to be with me so I can act the way I want my child to act. Children mimic our actions. After praying, I wait for the calming Spirit to come. If a child is physically out of order, I turn the child toward me, place my hands on the child's shoulders, look into the child's eyes, and then bow my head until I feel calm. I do not leave the situation. When I get myself under control and I speak softly, my children listen. (They react violently if I scream.)

Our children learn calming strategies from us. That is one of the most valuable gifts and skills we can give a child with ADD. Sometimes I lower the volume of my voice to a whisper to control my anger. I see results when I speak calmly, precisely, and to the point. Always I try not to lecture. Children disengage during a lecture—especially children with ADD. The first rule on lecturing is, The briefer the better. The second is, Take time to listen.

I never arise from bed in the morning without saying a prayer that the Spirit of the Lord will guide my actions. That helps me receive the words I should say during the day. When a provoking situation arises, I stop to think before I speak. (If necessary, I bite my tongue or my cheek.) And I listen to the child, but not until I've made sure he's calm. I listen only to calm and respectful messages from him.

I also recommend developing a detailed plan of discipline. Several years ago, Bill and I noticed that our discipline had become uneven. To the children, it probably seemed haphazard and perhaps arbitrary. So, my husband and I worked on a philosophy of discipline. We aimed to balance firmness with kindness—justice with mercy. Our children needed clear direction from parents who would not back down. They also needed an atmosphere of love and kindness. We agreed upon logical consequences for common misbehaviors to help us avoid excesses or indulgences. For example, when a child acted up at dinner, he lost the privilege of eating with the family for five minutes or until he became calm. When he damaged a toy either impulsively or in anger, we took toys away for several days. We used Thomas Phelan's "1–2–3 Magic" method with time-outs.[5]

Chore time is often resistance time. Our other children learned to complete their chores fairly easily. Our children with ADD were not task-oriented. They were not motivated to help, and they were easily distracted. Getting them to follow through was difficult. But we stuck to our guns. We assigned chores to each child every day after school. They had to earn the privilege of free time—after they completed their chores and homework.

As our children got older, discipline has included counsel about cars, dating, curfews, and reminders about morality. When our children wanted to disregard our counsel, we suggested they seek the Lord's counsel in prayer or in a priesthood blessing. We have found that our children with ADD listen to the Lord's counsel given in a blessing.

We adapted a response to disobedience that is similar to the Lord's when he chastened the Prophet Joseph Smith for procrastinating the start of the Kirtland Temple (see D&C 95). We tell the child what he did wrong. We say why it is wrong. We ask the child what would be right. If he doesn't know, we tell him. And we tell him we love him. We plant those good seeds in his mind.

CLASSROOM ADAPTATIONS

Current laws in this country require schools to provide extra resources to children with ADD. We took advantage of that extra help. Find out what is currently available and then develop a plan for your child. Generally, schools will not give your child help until you ask for it. Teachers may want to, but they are forbidden to diagnose disorders. So, parents need to take the initiative. You'll need to obtain a professional diagnosis in writing. Then call a conference with the teachers and school educators. Once a diagnosis is confirmed, the law requires that schools must prepare an individualized education plan (IEP).

If you like the plan, that's good. If you don't, speak up. Remember, as a parent, you are divinely called to be an advocate for your child. I've sometimes had to ask, and ask, and then ask again before I received the help that enabled my children to learn and prepare for life. Sometimes I've had to oppose the opinions of educators and experts. That was hard for me, but calm, informed persistence has always worked, even with people who seemed oppositional at first.

We found it best not to sound pushy or dictatorial. We always prayed before we entered a teacher conference. We tried to speak with calmness and peace, but we would not relent on being concerned. We asserted what we thought was best for our child. Once an IEP is in place, stay alert. Watch your child's progress in school.

Two notes about homework. It's often the *bane* of children with ADD and a *pain* for parents. Homework assignments can be lost, thrown away, or misplaced. Our children with ADD sometimes deceived us into thinking they had no homework. Other times, they honestly forgot or failed to write down assignments. Some years we had to call teachers every week to find out which assignments were missing. Those calls kept the child from falling behind. If your school has a homework hotline, use it.

Second, we learned early that some homework is terribly hard for our children with ADD to do. Because math and science are difficult for many minds with ADD, we spent much more one-on-one time with our children on that homework. It was draining. Their distractibility strained our patience. Worst of all, when we later learned that they didn't turn it in, we were sometimes provoked in the early years into fire-and-brimstone style ranting and raving. We regretted it immediately. Ranting and raving made *us* feel better, but it only hurt the child and our relationship. It did not change the behavior. Our attitude now is to try to serve the children as a coach. We encourage and motivate instead of lecturing. With persistent gentleness, we push the child to stay on task with homework. (A child with ADD can think of a dozen things to do with a pencil . . . except writing.)

We have also developed a reward system to motivate the child to do the homework *and* to turn it in. I had to devise a *new* reward system every few weeks to keep the child excited. That taxed my ingenuity, but it was always worth it.

Most teachers noticed that our children with ADD are intelligent, but many didn't understand why they were disruptive and did not complete their tasks. They logically concluded that these children could do better if only they'd try harder. With all the diplomacy we could muster, we explained that this conclusion was common but false. According to developmental child psychiatrist Daniel Amen, "telling people with ADD to try harder only disorganizes them, often to the point where they give up trying."[6] Ask teachers not to ask children to "try harder" or "hurry up." Call teachers and talk. Become a friend. Offer to help. Remember the teacher is overloaded, so offers to help make it easier for the teacher to help your child.

Usually, to learn a new skill or concept, the child with ADD needs more time, less distraction, more verbal testing, and less writing of tests. When given such help, they can succeed. Sometimes we forget that the point of schooling is for them to learn basic skills and come to love learning. Skills and attitudes are more important than grades—especially in the early years.

Once in a while, you'll get a reward, too. When our youngest son was in the third grade, we kept close tabs on him. We coached him. He worked hard. One afternoon, he came running through the front door. He whipped out his report card and shouted, "I *am* smart, Mom, I *am* smart." He had earned straight *A* grades on his report card. It was a great triumph for him. We hugged and cried together. I shall never forget that victory.

SOCIAL ADAPTATIONS

We had heard the comment, "Everyone notices when an ADD child walks into a room." It's not a *good* notice, so we wanted to teach our children social skills.

For years we worked on table manners, telephone calls, answering the front door, and sharing with others. We often used family home evening for role-playing. We let the children act out situations that were causing them problems. We carefully applied the rules to everyone in the family, not just the children with ADD. And we *expected* our children with ADD to succeed in social settings. That has helped them to improve.

When someone violated a rule at the table, we first warned him. On the second violation, we excused him from the table.

The child sat on the mat just inside the front door, "out of bounds." To prevent teasing, we ruled that anyone who teased him was also sent out of bounds. We fixed no limit to the time-out. As soon as the child got himself under control, he could return. Incentives and games to encourage polite manners were also part of our regular routine. For some meals, we had contests, judging who had the best manners. The winner won some treat or privilege. At others, we played manners games. The children delighted in spotting a parent in error. We persisted with this plan until now, as teenagers, they eat politely.

We also needed to reinforce manners in any social event that stressed or excited them. For instance, our sons had a hard time letting others take the first turn in a game. In the family, we made it a big deal when anyone agreed to take the last turn. When our children with ADD were younger, they would act wild when company came to the house. Such sudden changes in environment stressed them. I had to take them from the room and privately discuss their behavior. I found positive statements worked best: "You're polite boys. Polite boys don't act this way. You're capable of acting politely when company comes. You can play in your room for a while, or you can be with us in the living room and listen. Bring a quiet toy with you. [They needed something in their hands to play with.] You may not disrupt company." We had to repeat this ritual many times before they could act in more civilized ways around company. We persisted; eventually they got the concept.

I helped train our boys by setting up "dates" with them. Each boy and I would "go on a date" starting when they were about four. I helped them learn to treat a woman with respect. We had fun together, and they learned at the same time. By the time they were of dating age, they knew how to behave.

MOTHER ADAPTATIONS

I can't succeed as a mother if I don't nurture myself every day. Tough as we are, we mothers need daily breaks. Many frustrated mothers of children with ADD may say, "Taking time for myself is *impossible*." But I have discovered that it's not only possible—it's *essential*. We're not immune to burn-out. And if *we* burn out, who will volunteer to take our place? Even a short ten minutes can refresh my attitude toward mothering. If I've wanted to clean the bathroom that day, I may use my break to clean it. Looking at a clean sink pleases me. It's a visible accomplishment. Cleaning may not be your favorite break. You may prefer to do something creative. You may want to read, or exercise, or talk with someone who nurtures you.

The Lord wants us to see ourselves as worthy of care. He will sustain us, but he expects us to do our part in loving ourselves. He knows it isn't always easy. A degenerative joint disease in my feet (Charcot's) led to gangrene. Both of my legs below the knee had to be amputated four years ago. After the second amputation, I had to wear an intravenous tube for antibiotics. I felt nearly hopeless about returning to my former activities. On top of that, my diabetes damaged the nerves in my stomach. So I felt nauseated—day and night. For several months, I could keep little or nothing down, and I saw little hope for getting much better. I was at a low point emotionally. At that time, we had to switch our twelve-year-old to a new medicine. But first, we had to wean him from all his current medications. During that period without medicine, he was climbing the walls . . . literally! If he wasn't, I wanted to.

One day during this period, I fell down while in my bedroom. I lay there on the floor and just sobbed. Nothing seemed to be going right. I cried out in prayer, "Father, I cannot do this. It's just too hard!" In his great mercy, the Lord answered me. He gave me new understanding. I received this thought: "Pam, Josh has been brought to the earth to teach many people my characteristics—meekness, mildness, kindness, patience, love, and encouragement. You will learn much from him." When this thought entered my mind, I felt a swelling of great love and peace. The thought so deeply impressed me that I could hardly wait to hug Josh.

Afterwards, life stayed the same, but I had changed. I found I had more emotional muscle to handle the daily challenges of my health and my children. I had hope and courage. I could see differently now what the Lord expected of me as the mother of these children and what I am to learn from them. They came to help guide me home.

NOTES

1. See Edward M. Hallowell and John J. Raley, *Driven to Distraction* (New York: Simon and Schuster, 1987).

2. Even though the most current medical terminology is ADHD (Attention-deficit Hyperactivity Disorder), ADD is the more common term, and I will use it in this essay.

3. See Sam Goldstein, this volume, page 194.

4. Daniel G. Amen, unpublished manuscript in possession of the author.

5. Thomas W. Phelan, *1–2-3 Magic: Training Your Child to Do What You Want!* Videotape (Carol Stream, Ill.: Child Management, 1990).

6. Daniel G. Amen, interview with the author.

THE BALANCING ACT

MARGARET BLAIR YOUNG

Using talents wisely is a subject that has been much in my mind, especially over the last several years. Three years ago my good friend Buffy Cannon Wright visited me and my family. Mostly we talked about Buff's getting her master's degree in film and her goal of being a screenwriter. I was still writing. I had been teaching more than I wanted to at BYU–Hawaii during the previous year. We both had four children. She had a baby with Down's syndrome, and we both had three-year-olds and older children. We were going crazy doing too much, and Buff said, "I really don't know if I can handle all this. It is really, really hard. Annie screams all the time." Annie was her three-year-old. Mine was Michael. I said, "Well, Michael . . . Michael is Mr. Destructo. I follow him around with a broom and cloth." We went into my bedroom, and there was Michael with his box of cereal totally dumped out on the master bedroom floor like a visual aid.

That was on Thursday. The following Monday, my little brother called me early in the morning to tell me Buffy had been killed in a car accident. Her baby had been with her. The last thing Buffy did in this mortal life was to throw herself over her baby. She took all of the glass, and the baby had only burn marks from the car seat straps. Later her husband, who was

Margaret Blair Young teaches creative writing at Brigham Young University and is an author and playwright. She and her husband, Bruce Wilson Young, are the parents of four children. She teaches institute classes for Spanish-speakers in the Provo Utah Central Stake.

also an aspiring writer, had, as he described it to me, a vision in which he saw Buff. She led him to the bedside of each of their children. First, at Annie's bedside, she said, "This little girl matters more than anything else you are going to do. You'll publish, sure, but it doesn't really matter all that much. Look at this little girl. Have you ever seen anyone more beautiful? Do you know who she is?" Buff did the same at the bedside of each of their children. She let him know that they mattered more than anything else in this life.

That message came very powerfully to me. I feel strongly about not leaving my talents but much more strongly about not leaving my motherhood, about fulfilling my stewardship as it has been assigned. The balancing act is not easy. I am one who struggles. I can show you pictures of my laundry room as an illustration of how I struggle with this balance.

While we are developing talents, the choices, the accommodations that we have to make, often boil down to selective neglect. What am I willing *not* to do? I can't do everything. I used to do a lot of theater and have realized that I can't be away from my children three hours a night. So theater is not part of my life right now, though it may be when my children are a little older. But I give up laundry quite easily. And it is sort of a choice.

I'm grateful to live with a very good and supportive husband who understands. We lived in England for a BYU semester abroad, which is a fun thing BYU professors of English get to do periodically. I realized that during that time writing was not going to be a possibility for me. I had to home school my children, and there were just too many things going on. We noticed after a couple of months that I had started getting edgy, a little agitated, as if something was not quite right with me. Bruce said the sweetest thing finally: "I think if we had realized just how important your writing is to you, we would have found a way for you to do it." Then he started providing ways that I could go to the British Museum library to do some research on something I wanted to write about. That's an example of a supportive husband. That experience was also a real revelation to us both: My writing is really an essential part of who I am, and if we take that away from me, we get some consequences. I get agitated because I need that creative outlet.

My children understand that I do have a separate identity. I am not just the person who mops the floor and does the dishes. Mom is a writer, too. One of my novels is dedicated to my children, and they love to look at that and talk about it. My writing is a part of our lives. I have at least one child who wants to grow up and become a writer.

Occasionally I feel guilty or can't sleep, worrying that I am not balancing things well. My husband's support, though, helps me have the sense that I am heading in the right direction. We don't choose family over talent or talent over family. They have to balance. Sometimes the balance doesn't feel right, and I make adjustments so that it does. I really believe in trying to negotiate that balance, remembering that the most weight is with my family. But I really feel I am a better mother when taking care of my own creative needs as well. That frees me in a way to do my mothering duties and gives me some space in which I can be a better mother. I can't really feel guilty about that. Occasionally things take me away from my family. I do have a hard time when I've had to go do a reading far away and I've just been away from the family for a while. I do suffer with guilt, and it's probably guilt saying, "That's maybe a bit much. The kids need you at home."

So that's the struggle—the balancing act. And I'm right in the middle of it.

Let me return to Buffy now, briefly.

I spoke at her funeral, and after much prayer, said the things I felt she wanted me to. My entire talk was directed to her children. I said to them, "You matter more to your mom

213

than any of her screenplays, any of her classes, any of her workouts." And I knew I was speaking the truth.

Yet when I think of Buff, I think of her in all her aspects: wife, mother, writer, teacher, friend. Frustrated sometimes—even at her wits' end—but full of love and faith. Negotiating the balance, struggling with it just as I do. She was on her way to work on her master's thesis when she died. I believe she had it in the car with her. It matters to me that she was in the midst of that creative work when she died—I cannot imagine her otherwise. But it matters even more that Buff's final act was to shield, to save, her baby. In the name of love and grace and motherhood, that was how my friend finished her life. That was her last—and most important—statement in mortality. It's one that haunts and inspires me still as I continue in my own journey.

MY STRENGTH AND MY SONG

JANICE KAPP PERRY

I never sang solos until a few years ago when I was in Hawaii. A wonderful Hawaiian woman at church there said, "Will you sing a solo on our program today?" I replied, "Well, I've never really had any singing lessons. Singing solos is just not something I've done." "You know," she answered me, "that's a form of pride that President Benson talked about."

I didn't understand what she meant, but she went on. "He doesn't want us to have a fear of men or women. You're afraid there will be a better singer in the audience."

I thought, *For sure there will be.*

"President Benson said we should stand up, do our best, and look to the Lord for our approval and not to the world," she added.

I took that lesson to heart, and I have just been singing my best ever since, in the spirit of these words I heard at a Church music workshop years ago: "I'm not in rebellion against fine musicians. But as we admire orchids and roses, we also love sunflowers, asters, and wayside offerings."[1]

Did you know that both our Savior and our Prophet Joseph Smith wanted music in the last hours of their lives to bolster their strength? The Savior asked his disciples to sing a hymn with him before he went to the Mount of Olives (see Matthew

Janice Kapp Perry received her musical training at Brigham Young University. She and her husband, Douglas C. Perry, are the parents of five children. She has served as a ward Relief Society president and sings with the Mormon Tabernacle Choir.

215

26:30), and Joseph Smith asked his companions to sing with him and for him before his martyrdom. That puts those of us who love and find comfort in music in very good company. If the Savior wanting a hymn sung is important enough to be recorded in the Gospels, that convinces me that God gave us music to help us through this life.

An idea set to music stays with us in a different way than just the words. I was in a car accident a couple of years ago. Someone crashed right into my driver's side door and shattered every bit of the glass. At the very moment my life was in danger, here's what went through my mind: "When you hear the crash, think of Jones' Paint and Glass." It was useless information then, of course, but somebody had set it to music, and it came floating up at a very unusual time. If that type of music stays with us so long, it's really important to set the gospel to music so that gospel messages come to mind in times of need.

Music enhances every situation of our lives. During difficult times, music makes the burden easier. In happy times, music enhances our happiness. And as Elder Boyd K. Packer notes, "We are able to feel and learn very quickly through music, through art, through poetry some spiritual things that we would otherwise learn very slowly."[2] As we allow it, the Spirit of the Lord does soften and tune our hearts through worthy music.

Music can touch us and make things a little easier. My daughter, Lynne, tells the following story about music:

"I was probably about halfway through my mission when I was put with a new companion. After about a week together I began to realize that my companion had some serious problems. I found out later that chemical imbalances made her very unpredictable. She would fly off the handle and shriek in rage at me over simple things or even nothing that I could detect. Having been raised in a peaceful home, I was distressed by that kind of contention. I felt like I couldn't function as a missionary under those conditions. She always apologized for these outbursts afterwards. She'd say, 'I'm sorry. I couldn't help it,' and we'd work through it. But occasionally she would have an outburst when we were driving to teach a discussion. There was no way that we could have the Spirit with us after one of those outbursts.

"One morning I was in the shower, crying. It was the only place that I could be alone. I was just kind of sobbing and praying that somehow I could find a way to deal with this for the next few months. I knew my mission president wouldn't just transfer one of us, because that would just give the problem to someone else. I received the impression that music was going to be the key to my relationship with this companion. *Music?* I thought, because I had had no indication that she was musical. But the impression was very strong. That day as we left in the car to go quite a distance to a discussion, I thought, *Okay, that was a definite impression, so I ought to act on it.* I began to hum a song of Mom's called 'Song of Testimony.' My companion recognized it and joined in humming with me. Then I started singing, and she sang with me. Though she had no musical training, she loved to sing. We finished a few other songs by the time we arrived at our appointment. As we offered a prayer before going up to the house, we both felt a sweetness and calm that we sorely needed. Many times in the three months that we were together, we had to resort to humming—and sometimes the humming would start kind of loud and frustrated, but it never ceased to make a difference in our relationship. We ended up as very good friends. She died just a few months after we returned from our missions. Her father asked me to sing 'Song of Testimony' at her funeral. I felt honored to sing at her funeral and very grateful to the Lord for turning a very stressful, contentious situation into a good friendship."

Sometimes the songs I have written come back to haunt me. I may learn something from them as I write them, or learn it later when I return to a song and feel like a hypocrite because I'm not living what I wrote. This happened to me when I was a new Relief Society president trying as hard as I could. I went to a training session with President Barbara Winder, and for three hours she told us how to improve our Relief Societies. I felt overwhelmed. I thought, *How can we do more than we're doing?* At the end of her session, she said something that made it all right: "Just choose one or two things from what we've said. And above all, 'Do not run faster . . . than you have strength'" (D&C 10:4). I went straight home and looked up that scripture. It made me feel so good I decided to write a song about it. And I tried to live that principle.

One day, however, I was at Relief Society all day for a home-making meeting. My daughter's little girl had burned her hands badly, and I was wishing I was with her so I could see how she was. My mother was also ill, and I felt I should have been with her that day. But my nephew was here from Alaska to enter the Missionary Training Center, and I had promised to help him do his shopping all that afternoon and give an open house for him that evening for all the Utah relatives. I rushed from thing to thing, not doing anything well. Just before the open house, I remembered an item I had forgotten to buy. So I jumped into the car. The radio was tuned to an LDS music station, and when I turned the ignition key, there was my song "Do Not Run Faster Than You Have Strength." It was the strangest feeling. I looked at my radio and said, "Easy for you to say."

A few days ago I talked to Lynne about how her day was going. (Sometimes she calls up and says, "Mom, is this the complaint department?" "Yes, it is," I answer. "Go for it.") She'd had a day that rivaled one of mine. She was trying to phone people in a stake choir, write out a piece of music for their stake conference on Sunday, and prepare dinner for the missionaries. She needed to go grocery shopping, but she had also committed to do two hours of visiting teaching, and she was helping her husband get ready for a mule-packing trip. I said to Lynne, "Each generation improves on the last one," meaning busy to busier to busiest. We all do too much and get stressed. That's when music can help us gain perspective.

I thought that I could do it all, complete each task,
    accept each call.
I never felt my work was done, until I had pleased
    everyone.
I told myself I must be strong, be there for all to
    lean upon,
But in the end I came to see, that's more than God
    requires of me.
He has said:

Chorus:
Do not run faster than you have strength.
If you grow weary, what have you gained?
You will have wisdom and strength enough,
If first you remember to fill your own cup.

Music has helped me the most at the toughest times of my life—the deaths of my father, my mother, and one of our newborn babies. In each case, music helped me gain peace in specific ways. My husband and I had a serious Rh factor problem, and our last baby was two months premature and extremely ill with Rh complications. He was given a name and a blessing, and unsure that he would live, we watched through the night. He passed away by the next morning. At that point I remembered that I had four little children at home who needed reassurance, who needed to see that I was okay so that they would be okay. Even though I felt peace of mind, I didn't really grieve the way I needed to. I didn't fully acknowledge that loss or that I might never have another baby. Twenty years later, I was remembering that experience one night and decided that because it was still somewhat unresolved in my mind, I needed to write about it. Every day for a week or two, I relived the experience, writing lyrics and composing a song that I hoped would put it to rest for me. I cried then in a way I had not cried when it happened. Since then it has been a very happy memory. I look forward to rearing that baby, as Joseph Smith said we would.[3] My feelings are only happy ones. Here is the song I wrote then:

MY HEART SANG A LULLABY

Richie was born on a day in December,
I know it was Sunday—some things you remember,
Richie's first cries were like music to me,
But no one could promise how long he would stay.
And the night seemed so long as we watched him and
   prayed.

Richie was gone by the light of the morning,
Before his first sunrise, before the day's dawning.
So still in our arms, it was our turn to cry,
A memorized moment as we said good-bye.
And he looked like an angel in his blanket of white.

Richie, my son, only here for a moment,
He came and he went and the world didn't notice.
But nothing's the same, especially for me,
Eternity's promise is clearer to see.
He has just gone ahead to where we'll someday be.

Chorus:
And my heart sang a lullaby
To celebrate birth,
As he crossed the veil
Between heaven and earth.
My heart sang a lullaby
For this tiny one.
A song of forever,
Of things yet to come.
Just a lullaby to carry him home.
Yes, a lullaby to carry him home.

My father died when he was fifty-seven, one year younger than I am now. I thought that was awfully young to lose my father. I'd seen him go through a lot during his last few years, so by the time he died, I felt some relief. Even the day he died, I felt exhilarated, happy for him to be free of pain. I went through his funeral with that same feeling. I didn't cry but just felt peace. A couple of days after his funeral, I was driving alone from Provo to Logan, where we were moving. I turned on the radio, early on a Sunday morning, and the Tabernacle Choir was singing: "In my Father's house are many mansions. In my Father's house are many mansions. If it were not so I would have told you. I go to prepare a place for you." At that moment I felt the impact of losing my father. But I felt a sweet peace that he had gone to prepare for us to follow. I cried all the way to Logan. It was a great, therapeutic cry. Many years later, my mother died at age eighty-one. A song we had written together, "The Woman You'll Be Some Day," comforted me then and many times since when I've wished to be with her.

I started writing music when I was about forty. I also lost the use of my hand then and could no longer play the piano with it. I've been to forty different specialists, and they have no diagnosis, no cure. One of the last people I went to was Dr. Iliff C. Jeffery, a blind osteopath. He worked hard to help me regain the use of my hand. I sometimes complained to him as he worked about how inconvenient this was and how hard to write music when I couldn't play the piano. One day I realized the irony of my complaining to a blind man. It was a significant moment in my life. I said, "Well, Doctor, I don't think you can fix my hand, but thank you for trying."

"I may not be able to fix it," he said, "but I may be able to help you accept a handicap a little more gracefully." I met with him two more times, and he taught me what we can learn from disabilities. We have more purpose and more humility in our prayers. We learn to trust the Lord's timing. He said, "There is a healing for every problem we have on earth, whether it be now or in the next life."

"Well, I hope for you there will be a blessing in this life," I said, "so that you can see again." He chuckled and then explained that because of pain in his eyes, he had had them removed some years before. "But," he assured me, "there will come a time when you wouldn't trade having the use of your hand for what you have learned from not having it." I couldn't see that at the time, but through the years I have come to that point and have gained peace of mind about it. I wanted to write something to honor him, and it turned into a song called "The Test." One verse is for him, this blind man that I love so much, but the song is for me and for all of us who have prayed in faith for healing or relief and the answer hasn't come in quite the way we'd hoped.

Tell me, friend, why are you blind?
Why doesn't he who worked the miracles
Send light into your eyes?

Tell me, friend, if you understand,
Why doesn't he with power to raise the dead
Just make you whole again?

It would be so easy for him.
I watch you and in sorrow question why.
Then you, my friend, in perfect faith reply:

Didn't he say he sent us to be tested?
Didn't he say the way would not be sure?
But didn't he say we could live with him forevermore,
Well and whole, if we but patiently endure?
After the trial, we will be blessed,
But this life is the test.

Music can sometimes help in unusual situations. Years ago when our children were young, I had a family home evening lesson to prepare. I had a slight grudge against each person in my family that day, including my husband. I thought, *I've got to find a way to get my points across and maybe music will make them more palatable.* During the day, I wrote a verse for each of our four children and one for my husband. My irritations with them were little things, such as Steve spending an hour in the shower. So I sang his verse, and then at the end of each verse I had the family join in to sing the chorus,

> Steve, Steve,
> We all love Steve,
> More than we can say.
> We love the bad,
> We love the good,
> We love him any old way.

I sang a verse for each family member, and then everyone joined in the chorus with the appropriate name inserted. I figured that the chorus made up for the verse. I mentioned it to Steve years later, and he said, "Oh yeah, I remember that. Our favorite verse was the one you wrote for yourself." And I said, "Well, I wouldn't have had a grudge against myself." He said, "No, quite the contrary." And he reminded me of the words I had written for myself:

> There's a sweet and gentle woman
> And her age is thirty-eight.
> She's more wonderful
> And kind than any other.
> You might even say she's perfect
> And so very humble too.
> We are blessed to have
> Saint Janice as our mother.

And then they all sang,

> Mom, Mom,
> We all love Mom,
> More than we can say.
> We love the bad,
> We love the good,
> We love her any old way.

Have fun with your talents. Don't let everything be too serious.

One of the most complicated adversities many of us face is marriage. We work at this relationship our whole life. It never is perfect. My husband keeps asking me to write him a beautiful love song, and I never have gotten to it. I've tried, but I can't get it right. I thought that he deserved *a* song after thirty-six years, though. This is what I wrote:

After thirty-six years I have learned quite a lot
About what things will please him
And what things will not.
So our marriage is blissfully calm and serene
Except for a few insignificant things:

In raising our children we certainly clicked
Except I'm too easy and he's much too strict.
But a little of his way, a little of mine,
And it seems that the kids have all grown up just fine.

We both enjoy movies, but know in advance
That he'll choose adventure and I'll choose romance.
Yes, we do have a few problems like these—
Like he says half his time is spent finding my keys.

He loves his computers, he bought one for me.
He wants me to learn it, but I won't agree.
He'll talk about floppies and hardware and ROMS
When I don't even know how to turn the thing on!

When it comes to music, we're solid, it seems
Except he loves classics, and country suits me.
But in this decision we've compromised fairly—
No high-brow, no low-brow, just Janice Kapp Perry!

When it comes to TV, we're exactly the same.
We love basketball, football, all BYU games.
But I prefer watching one game at a time
While he flips the channels to watch eight or nine.
If I had the chance I would willingly choke
The guy who invented remote!
But we found a solution that works usually
His TV is upstairs, mine downstairs, you see.
And we are united each time our team scores—
I whistle and clap, and he stomps on the floor.

I'm sure he's observed I'm a little too round,
But he says he just loves me more by the pound.
Then I can't resist pointing out lovingly
That while I've gained thirty, he's gained forty-three.

Just lately he's noticed my hair's turning gray
Then quickly pretends that he likes it that way.
So I pat his bald spot and say with a flare:
"At least I am blessed with a full head of hair!"

Except for these few little things I have mentioned,
Our marriage is really quite nearly perfection.
We've had disagreements, but as I recall,
We just did things his way—no problem at all!
He may see things differently, I could be wrong,
But I get the last word 'cause I wrote the song!

Music helps us ease everyday tensions and can also strengthen us to face very serious challenges. Yesterday I received a letter from a man about the song "I Am of Infinite Worth." He wrote: "I've had a very hard life of abuse and ill health. The first time I heard this song, I broke down in tears and the Spirit of God shot through me like an arrow. I realized for the first time just who I really was—that I am a son of the most High God and am of infinite worth. . . . I was so abused through my life. I can overcome. I do not have the song, but it is impressed in my soul. And in times of tribulation and temptation, I sing that song as I put on the armor of God. Your song is my shield." Music can help us in thousands of ways. Our hymnbook is as scripture to us, and our beautiful hymns can shield us.

A few years ago, I was going through the most difficult challenge of my life. At times, alone in my room, I pleaded with Heavenly Father for some help, some comfort. I kept saying, "Just let my mom come and talk to me. Just let me see her a minute." I pleaded in many different ways. Through my prayers, I finally gained peace. But while I struggled, I kept

225

finding myself singing the first part of a little Primary song that I had written much earlier. I wrote it, but now I was living it. I needed it.

A CHILD'S PRAYER

Heavenly Father, are you really there?
And do you hear and answer every child's prayer?
Some say that heaven is far away,
But I feel it close around me as I pray.
Heavenly Father, I remember now
Something that Jesus told disciples long ago:
"Suffer the children to come to me."
Father, in prayer I'm coming now to thee.

I have never sung those words without having a witness that he is really there, that he was hearing my prayer, and that in his own way and in his own time my prayers would be answered. And they have been answered. The things I was going through then have been resolved. I know that as you look through your hymnbook, your Primary songbook, or other music that you love, you will find comfort there to meet your challenges.

NOTES

1. Attributed to Minnie Hodapp, notes in possession of author.

2. Boyd K. Packer, *That All May Be Edified* (Salt Lake City: Bookcraft, 1982), 275–76.

3. "You will have the joy, the pleasure, and satisfaction of nurturing this child, after its resurrection, until it reaches the full stature of its spirit." Joseph Smith, quoted by Joseph F. Smith, *Gospel Doctrine: Selections from the Sermons and Writings of Joseph F. Smith,* 5th ed. (Salt Lake City: Deseret Book, 1939), 455–56.

FINANCIAL PLANNING FROM A WOMAN'S PERSPECTIVE

KATHLEEN E. VOORHEES

Money is a difficult topic because it seems hard and cold and somehow worldly. But paying attention to money is necessary. As an old saying goes, "I don't like money actually, but it quiets my nerves." This essay isn't intended to make you a millionaire, but it will, I hope, educate and motivate you to prepare for the future. Taking control of your finances can quiet your nerves, I promise you. Money makes a terrible master but an excellent servant. We don't want money to be our master, but with proper planning and use of resources, money can help us be better servants. Financial resources free us to serve missions and help in numerous other ways.

The Lord would have us practice economic constancy. N. Eldon Tanner, when he was a member of the First Presidency, identified five principles of money management:[1]

1. Pay an honest tithe.
2. Live on less than you earn.
3. Learn to distinguish between needs and wants.
4. Develop and live within a budget.
5. Be honest in all your financial affairs.

Kathleen Egan Voorhees is an investment advisor at First Western Advisors in Salt Lake City. She and her husband, Hugh D. Voorhees, a general surgeon, are parents of nine children. She teaches the ten-year-old girls in Primary.

What special advice do women need beyond this general counsel? What makes our situation unique?

Generally, both genders have the same concerns: Will I outlive my money? Will I be able to afford a college education for my children? How can I set aside extra money for savings and investments? How can I get good investment returns without too much risk?

Women have a few concerns besides those.

First, women live an average of five to seven years longer than men. So we are going to need more money because we're going to live longer.

Second, women earn less. Though the earnings gap is narrowing, women still earn substantially less than men doing the same jobs. Women earn approximately 73 cents on the dollar compared to men doing the same work.[2]

Three, retirement income is substantially lower. Retirement benefits—Social Security, company pensions, 401(k) plans, and so forth—are based on time in the workplace. Women experience significant workforce disadvantages because we are the caregivers: we care for children, grandchildren, and elderly parents. No one debates the importance of the nurturing years, but the sad fact is the average Social Security benefit paid to women in 1993 was just $571 per month—25 percent lower than the average received by men.[3]

Many will experience what I call the "suddenly single" phenomenon. Either through widowhood or divorce, women are forced to make decisions alone. The suddenly single encounter many complex issues. Will you be ready? My heart goes out to those in this situation; it is very tough. My advice is to avoid major decisions for a while. It takes at least a year to adjust to major change. When in doubt, procrastinate. Divorce is financially crippling for women, who stand to lose 73 percent of their standard of living after the breakup.[4] But suddenly single women might take heart from this statement of Nancy Reagan's: "A woman is like a teabag [herbal, of course]—you can't tell how strong she is until you put her in hot water." Women may end up in hot water, but if we can give birth, we can do anything.

Nine of ten women will be solely responsible for their own financial well-being at some point in their lives.[5] Using money to make money may sound like man's work, but I believe it is our responsibility, too. It should not be left to someone else. Financial management is not something women can turn their backs on. And believe it or not, an Oppenheimer Management survey indicated that 93 percent of married men felt confident their wives could handle finances alone if they had to.[6] The chances are nine out of ten that you *will* have to, so you might as well be ready.

Besides, making money can be fun. If you don't participate and don't learn to understand financial principles, you may find yourself in old age settling for whatever is left, and it may not be enough. Besides that, women make good money managers. Women ask smart questions and insist on understanding before they buy something. They want to be educated about investment options. Women are excellent planners. I see women all the time making lists of things that they need to do for their family—their grocery lists, school shopping lists, and so on. Financial planning is the same orientation: making lists and taking care of them, checking them off. Whereas men tend to view money as an extension of their masculinity, a sign of their virility, and a symbol of power, women understand that money is what you buy things with, including security.[7]

Finances are a shared opportunity, not a male talent.

You may be starting to get math anxiety. Studies show that girls who did not do well in math in school, or who do not like math, have a difficult time handling their finances later in life. It's their attitude. I was one of those. I didn't like math, and I didn't do particularly well in it. Yet here I am in the money management business. Calculators and computers do all the work. My fear was unfounded. A twenty-dollar financial calculator with just a couple more buttons than the ones you are used to will take maybe twenty minutes to figure out. Then all you need to know is which buttons to push at the right time. Or call your financial advisor and get the answer you need in five minutes. Don't let math scare you.

Let's get to financial-plan basics. A sound financial foundation includes six elements: cash, health insurance, life insurance, a home, retirement savings, and college savings.

Cash. Cash for emergencies is considered a basic—three months' worth of your monthly expenses is the rule of thumb.

Health insurance. Health insurance is a basic because of the consequences if you don't have it. I have a married son who is going to China for six months. His health insurance through his current employment will lapse during that time. He is okay with the idea of dropping his coverage temporarily, but I won't let him. His family could be devastated financially if he doesn't have at least major medical coverage.

Life insurance. Life insurance is owned by 78 percent of Americans.[8] It's one of the largest industries in every developed nation in the world, because the product they sell fills a basic need. If you have dependents, you need to insure the life of your breadwinner for income protection.

Life insurance looks complicated, but actually it is based on one thing: a 1980 mortality table, which is essentially a table that indicates normal life expectancy for each age and gender. The insurance industry, to be competitive, has little gimmicks, like add-ons, riders, or options. They have different ways to pay the premium and different ways to take out the money, all of which just make it complicated. Look at it as if you were buying a car, say a Ford Explorer. You go to the dealership and see the car. At ten different dealerships the same car will have different financing terms and a different price. You can add different options, such as a sun roof or CD player, but the basic vehicle is the same at every dealership. Insurance is the same way. You might buy a term product, a universal life policy, a variable life product, or a single premium. But it's still a Ford Explorer; it's still the 1980 mortality table. You just have to decide how you want your cereal: toasted, sugar coated, fat free, hot, cold, or just plain.

Which insurance plan should you buy? Discuss it with your financial advisor. He or she can tell you what is available. How much insurance do you need? It's a simple mathematical equation. Your insurance agent can help you figure it out.

A home. Purchasing a home is usually considered one of the basics in a sound financial plan. You might think, *We have a nice nest egg in our house.* But your liquid net worth usually excludes your house. You've got to live somewhere, so your home is not counted as part of your investment capital. Owning a home might not be counted as a financial asset when totaling your projected retirement savings, but it is certainly an important physical and emotional asset.

Retirement savings. We all dream of what it will be like when we retire. Consider this definition of retirement: twice as much husband on half the cash. In generations past, retirement was not in anyone's vocabulary. Our forefathers worked until they dropped dead. But Social Security and company retirement plans have given the employed public a new and luxurious hope for future rest and relaxation. Sources of retirement income include Social Security, pension plans with your company or your private pension, and your personal savings. Yet, the solvency of Social Security has been a concern for years. Forty percent of American women depend on Social Security for more than 90 percent of their income after age sixty-five.

A lot of people consider the Social Security card the lottery ticket of the future. In other words, it's likely to be worthless. In 1945, there were 42 payers to 1 payee; that is, 42 people worked for each person receiving benefits.[9] In 1984, 3.3 people worked for each person receiving benefits.[10] I'm a baby boomer, and economists are predicting that baby boomers will bankrupt the system. If you are a generation Xer (between age eighteen and thirty-four), a widely publicized study suggests that more of you believe in UFOs than in Social Security benefits.[11] Social Security is not something you can count on, especially if you are young. You've got to start saving for yourself.

How much money, what kind of a nest egg, does it really take to retire? If you read the covers of *Money* magazine and the financial journals of the world, you know that for their readers it takes $1 million. A million would be nice—wonderful, in fact. But what does it really take to retire? Actually, how much you need depends on the kind of life you plan to lead once you retire. If you want to travel a lot or pay for grandchildren's education (my mother has seventy-seven grandchildren, so she's not going to do that!), you could well want an annual income that's equal to your highest earning preretirement year. If you expect to lead a simple life, you may need only 70 percent or less of preretirement income. That's assuming your home is paid for, your children are grown, you're not rearing any grandchildren, and so on.

Saving should be a habit. The Japanese as a group save 20 percent of their income, and Americans have a 3 percent savings rate.[12] That's because many of us have a bad attitude about saving: When we save our money, we feel deprived. We have to change that attitude. Saving money should bring a feeling of security and satisfaction, like the feeling you have when you know that down in your basement you've got food storage—you've got wheat, flour, and raspberry jam. Money in the bank and food in the basement are preparations for the future.

There are many options for savings: investment vehicles such as 401(k) plans, qualified plans, and IRAs; financial products such as stocks, bonds, mutual funds, CD's, treasuries. Financial savings are as individualized as the people who make them. Talk with a financial specialist to decide what is best for you. The important thing to remember is to start saving now. Don't wait. Believe it or not, when you retire most of your income is going to come from investment appreciation, not from contributions made by you. You need to give time a chance to work for you.

College savings. You may wonder why college savings is at the bottom of the basics list. After all, most children will go to college *before* their parents retire. If you can help your kids with their college education, great. Do it. But if you have to make a choice between saving for your retirement and putting your children through college, be self-serving and save for your retirement. You have to be a little bit selfish now if you want to be self-sufficient later on. Besides that, kids can learn a lot by putting themselves through college. They often study better if they know that they are paying the tuition with a part-time job. It won't hurt them. But if you decide to save for college instead of retirement, pick out which of your "well-educated" kids you plan to live with or borrow from when you are seventy-five.

We've got to talk about inflation, public enemy number 1 where your money is concerned. What is inflation? It might be best described as a dollar saved today is seventy-five cents tomorrow. An actual definition is that inflation is the rate of increase in the price of goods and services. Data about inflation in this country has been collected since 1720. During the Civil War, inflation was as high as 25 percent. In recent years, it was highest in 1979—about 13 percent. In the last six years, it has been very low, under 3 percent. We've been lucky. Inflation in the United States is quite moderate compared to that in foreign economies. In 1989, Argentina experienced 5,000 percent inflation, and in 1993, Brazil's rate was more than 1,000 percent.[13]

An example of inflation in more concrete terms is the cost of a stamp: in 1980 a stamp was 15 cents; today it costs 32 cents. That illustrates the loss of purchasing power of your money. A 4 percent annual rate of inflation will slice 55 percent off your purchasing power in twenty years. Inflation is important to consider when you think about what you are going to invest your money in, your retirement dollar, your

IRA, your savings. You have to invest your money in something that will fight inflation.

Do not confuse lack of financial familiarity with a lack of brain power. (Remember that old age is always fifteen years older than you are.) Believe in yourself. Rely on you to take care of you. Handling money can bring anxiety, but the result is that you can get a sense of power, control, and freedom— the best thing of all. Educate yourself. Trust yourself. Know good advice from bad, and stop believing that everyone else knows more than you do.

I can almost hear you saying, "Sure. Right after I make breakfast, shop for groceries, pick up the dry cleaning, attend PTA meeting, run the errands for my husband, deliver the kids to karate lessons, gas up the car, fix dinner, return the videos, let the dog out, and put the kids to bed, I *must* plan for my retirement."

Don't wait. Please plan for your financial futures. Make time to do what is important. You spend time with your family, you have a physical checkup, and you even make time for unpleasant things like going to the dentist. Charting your financial future is just as vital to your well-being. Take care of it. Take care of yourself.

NOTES

1. N. Eldon Tanner, *Constancy amid Change* [pamphlet], Salt Lake City: The Church of Jesus Christ of Latter-day Saints, 1979; address delivered at the welfare session of general conference, October 1979.

2. Former Labor Secretary Robert Reich, quoted in *Working Woman,* September 1996, 29–30.

3. Bureau of Labor Statistics: Institute for Women's Policy Research.

4. Oppenheimer Management Survey on Women and Investing, Two World Trade Center, New York, New York, 10048–0203.

5. *Credit Union Executive,* March 1994.

6. Social Security Bulletin, Spring 1994.

7. U.S. National Center for Health Statistics, Vital Statistics of the United States, annual 1990.

8. C. David Chase, *Chase Investment Performance Digest: 1960 through 1996* (Concord, Mass.: Chase Global Data and Research, 1997), 290.

9. Lili Wright, "On 60th Birthday, Social Security Sees Unhappy Returns," *Salt Lake Tribune,* 14 August 1995, A1.

10. Wright, "Social Security Sees Unhappy Returns," A1.

11. "Unidentified Flying Benefits," *Registered Representative* (July 1995): 34.

12. Wright, "Social Security Sees Unhappy Returns," A1.

13. Chase, *Investment Performance Digest,* 38–40.

STRESS AND COPING:
THE HASSLE HAYSTACK

ELAINE SORENSEN MARSHALL

Stress is one of the most overworked words in modern life. Yet, more than in any previous generation, our lives at home, work, and church are complicated—by contact with more people, increasing complexity of choices, and by a growing number of important but unrelated tasks and demands. Popular magazines promote "tests" to measure stress, with endless lists of "Ten Happy Habits" to reduce stress. Stress reduction is becoming a common prescription in clinical health-promotion and risk-reduction programs. Is all of this just a trendy sign of our time? No. Research in health and social sciences indicates that stress really can make you sick. Stress has been associated with stomach troubles, headaches, and many other health problems. It can make life miserable or even lead to early death from heart disease and stroke.

What is stress? I found twenty-nine different definitions lurking among library volumes in the social sciences. I am sure that there are more, but I stopped upon finding the following

Elaine S. Marshall serves as associate dean of the College of Nursing at Brigham Young University. She has been a missionary to Colombia and has served on a general Church writing committee. Her recent book on children's stress won an award from the National Council on Family Relations. She is married to Dr. John Marshall and is the mother of four children.

236

statement: "I would advocate that the word 'stress' be stricken from our vocabulary as soon as possible."[1]

Some have attempted to define stress according to an index of particular, difficult life events. Self-administered "stress tests" in checkstand magazines instruct the reader to check the number of stressful events in her or his life. The list includes everything from death, divorce, and jail terms to pregnancy, retirement, sexual difficulties, and Christmas—on the same list. Supposedly, enough of such events in one year threatens your health. One year, my score was so high I should have been in the coronary unit. Ironically, that was the year I seemed to cope best.

Actually, recent research indicates that daily hassles, more than major life events, most threaten quality of life and health. Some social scientists have noted that though major life changes, such as divorce and bereavement, are more dramatic, daily hassles may have greater influences on our actual health.[2] Somehow, we seem to marshal our resources and come through the "big" things in life. Certainly we suffer, but people bring casseroles; we seek help; we pray, and we grow stronger. It is the last-straw, flat-tire stuff that raises our blood pressure, increases muscle tension, and initiates all the physiological stress responses that scientists know make us sick and threaten our health and lives.

The hassle pile-up is what gets to us. A few years ago, I had endured separation and divorce, the loss of a son, reduction of income, selling my home, moving to a new town, getting a job, going back to graduate school, putting my children into a new school, staying up at night through four successive cases of chicken pox—all on the official "Life Stress Events" list (okay, maybe not the chicken pox). Then one day, when I arrived too late for my haircut appointment, after frantically running to children's lessons, my school, and my job, I became hysterical, thrashing and sobbing. The hairdresser stood stunned, but I couldn't stop. That last-straw hassle had toppled me over the edge. (Since that traumatic event, I cut my own hair.)

Psychologist Richard Lazarus defines stress as a "relationship between the person and the environment that is appraised by the person as taxing or exceeding his or her resources and endangering his or her well-being."[3] That subtle phrase "appraised by the person" means that whatever *I think* is stressful *is* stressful. Events that exhilarate one person may devastate another. We may each decide whether something challenges us to grow or threatens our very sense of survival. Women, men, and children all experience stress and hassles uniquely. Life is stress! The goal is not to eliminate stress but to cultivate effective ways of coping with it, growing from it, and perhaps even thriving on it. Researchers are thus turning away from studying the sources of stress to observing how people respond, cope, and grow. Many of their findings are well-known. Let me focus on three that may be less familiar to you.

VIEWING LIFE AS A JOURNEY

One basic strategy for effectively coping with stress is to see that life is the journey rather than a way to a final rewarding end or even to a continual series of better-than-now destinations. I am just discovering this, after living nearly half a century saying, "Life will be better after the final exam . . . after I graduate . . . when I go on a mission . . . when I get home from my mission . . . when I am married . . . after the baby is born . . . after the bills are paid . . . " I have a friend who says, "Life is what happens while you are making other plans." I know today that my stress *is* my life.

We hear the generic "life is a journey" metaphor everywhere from billboards to popular self-help books. If that metaphor has lost its power for you, try a different word: Your life may be an expedition, an adventure, an assembly line, a book in progress, a pilgrimage, an excursion, a parade—whatever image best conveys the process for you. But it *is* a process, moving through time, offering interesting insights, challenges, and pleasures along the way. It is not a quick, straight shot to heaven and perfection.

FAITH AND LOVE

Latter-day Saints know that health is enhanced, healing happens, and hassles are put in perspective when we vigorously exercise faith in God. Current scientific studies are also reporting that prayer correlates with higher numbers of positive outcomes to physical illnesses. Treatment programs for addicts encourage faith in a higher power. Popular authors and television talk-show hosts are promoting daily gratitude journals. They have proven effective: list five things for which you are grateful every day, and by the end of the year you will feel more energy and less stress. Life is better when we are responsive to our daily blessings, sensitive to spiritual moments, and honor the sacred things waiting to be noticed in our daily life.

Another intangible but documented stress reducer is love. In study after study, people with a variety of physical, psychological, and emotional illnesses fared better than expected if they had meaningful supportive relationships. Loving relationships improve health and reduce stress.

In the health sciences, we call this "social support"—that is, nurturant people who are important to you, who love and need you, and who help you when you need it. There are some people who nourish our souls, whose very presence makes life better. My friend Martha is like that to everyone who knows her. I see her only occasionally, and seldom talk for long, but I need only be near her, and life is easier. On the other hand, some people swallow the energy out of a room, drain us, or make us feel less competent, more tense. When our hassle level is high, we need to be far from these people for a time.

Soon after my grandmother died, my grandfather had a stroke that left him unable to speak. Already predisposed to perfectionism and solitude, human interaction became uncomfortable and tense as he struggled to be understood. His simplest request to move a chair became an irritation to him and the person trying to help. By a lovely miracle of sensitivity, a friend gave him a long-haired, white cat. Soon the cat responded to his strokes, seemed to love him as he gave love, and made him feel competent and needed once more. Tension lessened as we all learned to communicate again. This was a miracle of the power of giving and receiving love at the simplest level.

We need love from others, and we need to give love. Giving love and service promotes mental and emotional health. To give freely does not mean being a martyr, however, or giving from an empty reservoir. Some people give beyond their strength, beyond wisdom, and tax their health. Listen to Anne Morrow Lindbergh's words on the danger to women of giving in ways that do not replenish the spirit: "Is this then what happens to woman? She wants perpetually to spill herself away. All her instinct as a woman—the eternal nourisher of children, of men, of society—demands that she give. Her time, her energy, her creativeness drain out into these channels. . . . Woman spills herself away in driblets to the thirsty, seldom being allowed the time, the quiet, the peace, to let the pitcher fill up to the brim." Lindbergh does not argue for a stance of selfishness, however, but for "purposeful giving": "Purposeful giving is not as apt to deplete one's resources; it belongs to that natural order of giving that seems to renew itself even in the act of depletion. The more one gives the more one has to give—like milk in the breast."[4]

Another way we combat stress is by loving in a special way that developmental theorists call "generativity"—giving to and guiding the next generation. Those who feel a sense of "parenting," though they may not be parents, have a larger perspective and purpose beyond today's hassles. Teaching and mentoring the next generation in any part of our life lends

240

purpose and reduces competitive stress in our own lives. A recent popular magazine listed the four hundred "best" physicians for women, according to peer nomination. My husband, who has spent a career teaching physicians, was not on the list, but he delighted in counting a dozen names who were "his residents" with the same joy as if they were his own children. I realized at that moment that drawing energy from such generative giving promotes health and wisdom.

WORK

Among the most common effective antidotes for stress is work. That may be hard to believe because for many of us work is a primary source of stress. To be a stress reducer, work must be loved, and not everyone can find that in the work of their employment. To find a vocation that you love would surely add years of health to your life. But if you are not fortunate in your employment, you must find some activities, both physical and mental, over which you have a sense of control and achievement. You may find you need to balance the satisfying mental exertion of your workplace with a physical interest or vice versa.

Though I love my work, I spend hours in a building, at a desk, among students, in meetings, or near a computer. Eventually such work, though intellectually stimulating, adds to my stress. I need some physical work or play. Though I claim to be allergic to formal exercise, I know activity could reduce my sense of stress and help me be healthier. I love gardening and even housecleaning, and I usually take the stairs at work, but I fall far short of a healthy, stress-reducing lifestyle. My father, who drives cattle, lifts bales of hay, and literally sweats for fourteen hours a day, never complains of stress.

IMAGINATION

The strategies I've mentioned so far may be familiar to you, but the last remedy may be new: imagination. To use

241

imagination to cope does not mean to fantasize and escape into a more comfortable alternative reality. Facing truth, speaking truth, and respecting truth are the foundations of physical and emotional health. Among cancer patients, for example, guided imagery and positive affirmation have both been shown to enhance health, but not until the individual has first faced the truth of his or her medical diagnosis, treatment, and prognosis.

Once we are able to confront and integrate the truth of our lives, however, imagination can be the soul's medicine. Imagination, that uniquely human attribute, allows us to find meaning in the challenges of our lives, whether traumatic events or daily hassles.

While my mother was dying, her body was terribly swollen, and for a time she moaned as if, I perceived, in childbirth. As I washed her and combed her hair, I imagined myself midwife to the one who bore me. I was attending to her as she labored for another passage. I treasure that image. It helps me tolerate the grief of her loss. I have since become aware that this is a common metaphor in poetry, literature, and personal stories. A daughter's care of a dying mother is a return to the essential maternal story of passage.

Two other words, *imagery* and *magic,* are found in the word *imagination.* Imagery can expand our reality and positively reframe stressors almost too harsh for endurance. Coping images are everywhere, if we search among the ordinary, expecting magic and miracles.

In a startling, often-told psychology project, three groups of subjects were assigned a different activity. One group was asked to spend one-half hour a day practicing free throws on a basketball court; the second, to spend one-half hour a day off the court, without a ball, imagining successful free throws in the mind; and the third group was to do nothing. At the end of two weeks, the three groups were brought to a basketball court and asked to make ten free throws. The scores of those who did nothing remained the same. The scores of the group who practiced and the group who imagined the practice both improved and performed equally. Imagery became magic.

Faith, love, work, and imagination are powerful tools, important gear, for coping with life stress on life's journey. So are moderation in life habits of diet, exercise, sleep, and personal maintenance. No matter how well equipped we are, there will be times we simply cannot forge ahead, and we must slow down a while to rest and reflect. We may even choose to reroute our course. I have found life to be a journey forward, and sometimes backward, or even sideways, toward perfection. Striving, progress, stumbling, repentance, and growth have been important milestones on my eternal path. But if I accept life as a journey, then I can expect and accept the rocks and the slippery spots as well as the smooth pavement.

NOTES

1. Joseph T. Mullan, "The (Mis)meaning of Life Events in Family Stress Theory and Research," paper presented at the Preconference Theory Construction and Research Methodology Workshop, National Council on Family Relations Annual Meeting, October 1983, St. Paul, Minnesota, 11.

2. See Richard S. Lazarus and Susan Folkman, *Stress, Appraisal, and Coping* (New York: Springer, 1984); Anita DeLongis, James C. Coyne, Gayle Dakof, Susan Folkman, and Richard S. Lazarus, "Relationship of Daily Hassles, Uplifts, and Major Life Events to Health Status," *Health Psychology* 1 (1982): 119–36.

3. Lazarus and Folkman, *Stress, Appraisal, and Coping*, 21.

4. Anne Morrow Lindbergh, *Gift from the Sea* (New York: Random House, 1955), 45, 47.

ONLY THE WATER MOVES ITS FACE

NANCY BAIRD

I no longer look at people's faces
when I run—
smeared moons in the dark caves
of their cars.
The sight is too instructive
in the subtle ways of wickedness.
Ask Jeremiah, down in the stinking pit,
looking up at the blinded circle of sky,
the children of darkness peering
down its crumbling lip like
rotten teeth.
And the hands are important. . . .
It is possible, while driving, to use
both hands to show contempt
and violence—
those hands—elegant, fluid creatures
of heart and brain
reduced, degraded to this purpose.

It is so still in the canyons . . . deserted,
but for the slick of snake in rocks,
the occasional astonishment of deer.

Nancy Hanks Baird was named Utah Poet of the Year in 1996. She received her bachelor's degree in English from Brigham Young University and has worked as a freelance writer and editor. She and her husband, John K. Baird, are the parents of five children.

244

Only the water moves its face,
and the hands of a deeper mind
than this world can remember
push the wind around the rock,
shake the loosened leaves to the road,
are busy in the fragrant, steadfast
work of life.

DAILY WALKS

ELAINE S. DALTON

Mine is not a spectacular life. Most days the many things I have done that day do not show. Once, in a group of friends, a mother of eight remarked, "I wonder how many pairs of shoes I have bought, sought, and polished in my lifetime?" Another mother speculated about the number of meals she had prepared. I personally wonder about the number of socks that have gone through my laundry room—and where half of them are! I am the facilitator who enables a busy family to go and do and accomplish. I am not usually known by my own name. I am the bishop's wife or Zach's or Jess's mom. And those labels are just fine with me because those people are my life. At times I have resented the dailyness of my life; but as I look back, I see that dailyness has patterned and schooled me. Daily doings add up, and they can make an eternity of difference.

I am a long-distance runner. In preparing to run a marathon, dailyness is vital. The daily runs strengthen you and prepare your body to go the 26.2 miles. It also teaches you much about yourself. Watching the Boston Marathon reminded me of those hills at mile 20. Just when you think you are

Elaine S. Dalton received her bachelor's degree in English from Brigham Young University. She and her husband, Stephen E. Dalton, are the parents of five sons and one daughter. She has served as stake Young Women president and executive secretary to the national presidency of Lambda Delta Sigma and as a member of the Young Women General Board.

almost finished, with only six miles to go, here come the hills. There will always be those hills at mile 20.

One almost overwhelming hill came when my father died of viral pneumonia. It was my first experience with deep sorrow. Much of what I have to come to understand of obedience, sacrifice, and grace as a daily gift I learned from my mother at that time. She was left a widow at the age of forty-five with three children. I was the eldest and had just begun school at Brigham Young University. My brother Rob was nine, and my brother Jim was sixteen.

After the funeral, we gathered around the kitchen table to talk and to cry. What were we to do now? My mother said that we would need to be good—to obey the Lord. We would need to keep saying our family prayers because without our father to lead us, we needed the Lord as never before. She reassured us with the scripture, "I, the Lord, am bound when ye do what I say" (D&C 82:10). That became our family motto. She told us that she knew we would be fine and Heavenly Father would watch over us and help us if we were obedient to him. She testified of his grace in our life. It was what I needed to hear.

We discussed our future. My mother would teach school, and we would continue to help her by doing the work around the home. My younger brothers would do the yard work. I volunteered to come home from BYU for a time to assist also. My heart wasn't in my school work; I was behind, and I was lonely. Mother looked me in the eye and said, "You will continue, and you will make your father and all of us proud. I will see that you all graduate from college and serve missions if it means I have to get a morning paper route and take in laundry at night." That was when I understood the meaning of sacrifice. And something in the way she said it made me know that sacrifice involved not only going without but doing so with great love.

My pleadings with the Lord to help me understand why my father died went unanswered for about a year. Then, in a devotional address, a scripture from Proverbs pierced my heart, and I knew it was my answer: "Trust in the Lord with all thine heart; and lean not unto thine own understanding. In all thy ways acknowledge him, and he shall direct thy paths" (Proverbs 3:5–6). It became my life's motto. Guided by that motto, I continued on at BYU. There both my mind and my spirit were schooled. There I received answers to important prayers. There the direction of my life was determined.

Other hills in my life—sickness, death, unemployment, back surgery, broken bones, broken hearts—many of you are also acquainted with. At those times I have trusted and tried not to lean to my own understanding. Looking back, I would not trade these experiences. They have schooled me, refined me, and strengthened me. Some have proved to be shortcuts to my goal; they changed my path and brought me closer to the Lord.

In the New Testament Paul refers to life as a race. He tells us to "run all" that we might "obtain" (1 Corinthians 9:24). That means to keep running until we "obtain" the goal. Though Mosiah cautions us not to run faster than we have strength, he also tells us to run diligently (see Mosiah 4:27). Life is a marathon, a paced race toward an eternal and sure goal. Diligence—our daily obedience—allows us to progress and move steadily toward our goals.

On morning runs I recognize individuals from a long distance away by their walk or run—by their stride or the bounce of their hair or just the way they hold their arms and body. Mormon said that he, too, knew those to whom he spoke, the followers of Christ, by their "peaceable walk" (Moroni 7:4). Not unlike strength for a marathon, I believe a "peaceable walk" is developed daily. Those who have peaceable walks are learning of the Savior and also listening to him. They walk in the meekness of his Spirit. They do the right things for the right reasons. They are willing to pay the price for personal revelation by living the covenants of obedience and sacrifice.

In Doctrine and Covenants 19:23 is the formula for how I will accomplish the next phase of challenges, opportunities, events that the Lord has in store for me. What a comforting set of instructions with a promise: "learn of me . . . listen to my words . . . walk in the meekness of my Spirit . . . and you shall have peace." I do have peace! I know that whatever happens, he is there. He is aware of each of us. He has a plan that involves us. And he will prepare us for whatever lies in our future—gently, over time, with patience and great love. That is grace, true grace.

He will help us. And I have learned how to be grateful and what to be grateful for. I am grateful for the dailyness. In subtle, quiet ways, these patterns prepare us to grow, as Christ did, from grace to grace, in obedience. Nature shows the strength and joy of dailyness. I am grateful for daily sunrises and sunsets, for the stars' and moon's appearance daily. In times of great stress and trial, the routine things sustain us— daily prayer and daily scripture study.

In dailyness we learn obedience and practice sacrifice. What have my life's uncommonly common experiences taught me about obedience and sacrifice? That to be truly obedient, we must have great love, and that our sacrifices, however small, large, or individually tailored, will make us holy.

So I am grateful for mothers and talks and prophets and prayers and kitchen tables, which become altars whereon obedience and sacrifice can be learned. I am grateful for *daily* experience, reminders that the Father sent his Son on a mission and that he was obedient in all things. Most of all, I am grateful for his atoning sacrifice. My prayer is that we may someday have that walk that will identify us as one of his—that someday we might be worthy to receive the invitation "Walk with me" (Moses 6:34).

IT'S ABOUT TIME

MARY ELLEN EDMUNDS

In the Book of Mormon, Alma teaches his son Corianton that only men measure time, God doesn't (see Alma 40:8). I'm an earthling, and so for me—at least for now—I have to measure time. That is no small thing, trying to measure time. President Ezra Taft Benson has said: "Time is numbered only to man. God has your eternal perspective in mind."[1]

We use the word *time* in so much of our conversation: leisure time, part-time, full-time, overtime, prime time, high time, daytime, springtime, Father Time, once upon a time, time after time. Have you heard yourself say things like "I remember the time when . . . " "Where did the time go?" "Take your time," "Have you got a minute?" "I'll have it ready in no time," "Timing is everything," "What time is it?"

We all know what time is, and we speak of it constantly, but it is a little hard to define or describe. I found this definition in one dictionary: "A finite extent of continued existence."[2] So you can ask someone, "Do you have a finite extent of continued existence that you could share with me?"

Have you ever in your whole life run out of time?

Time is a gift. It's a gift from God. We can't demand more, and we can't insist on less. We can't buy more, and we can't

Mary Ellen Edmunds has served as a director of training at the Missionary Training Center in Provo, Utah, and as a member of the Relief Society General Board. A graduate of the College of Nursing at Brigham Young University, she has been a faculty member in that same school and has served full-time proselyting and welfare missions in Asia and Africa.

sell any (otherwise, it wouldn't really be a gift). Everyone in the world receives the same amount of time every day. "I have told you many times," Brigham Young said, "the property which we inherit from our Heavenly Father is our time, and the power to choose in the disposition of the same."[3]

Time is our life—it's our day to prepare to be with God forever and ever. Time is given to us for that preparation, for repenting and forgiving and trying to be good and do good. Alma taught his son Corianton, further, that "there was a time granted unto man . . . a probationary time, a time to repent and serve God" (Alma 42:4).

In the hymn "Improve the Shining Moments," there is this statement: "Time flies on wings of lightning."[4] Sometimes that is so true that it makes me sick. Remember when summer used to be three months long? Remember when Christmas vacation was days long instead of just a few hours? Last year we didn't have July. I don't know what happened, but we didn't have July.

In President Gordon B. Hinckley's biography is an insight into this reality of so much to do and how quickly time passes: "Apparently the tendency to shoehorn too much into any twenty-four-hour period was a Hinckley family trait. During one month when Virginia had her hands full with a heavy load of family and Church responsibilities, Marjorie outlined the list of things pressuring her second-oldest daughter and concluded matter-of-factly, 'Life gets that way every once in a while when you belong to the true church.'"[5]

Is life that way for you? Are you busy? Are you tired? Are you weary, empty, depleted, cross? Has hurrying and being too busy become a habit with you?

So much of my life is "management by crisis." I feel sometimes that I don't know how to slow down, or sit down, or get out of the fast lane—and I don't really know how I got in it. I missed an off-ramp!

We all have a long list of things to do, whether written

down or rattling around in our brain: pray; study; exercise; plant a garden, eat it; raise brilliant, cheerful, reverent children; clean a basement; write in a journal; avoid fat, calories, movie theater popcorn, and evil thoughts; pray for your enemies; do visiting teaching; store a year's supply of food (but not on your body! We're not supposed to look like Welfare Square); say yes to everything anyone asks you to do and hunt for more things to do; plant trees; remember the pioneers . . .

And we want to do everything so quickly. We hunt for fast-food, shortcuts, one-hour photo developing, express elevators, condensed books, instant soups, and ten-minute oil changes. Personally, I look for labels that say "Just add water." I can do that. And I have a 72-minute kit.

But there's much in life that isn't instant and isn't fast. Mothers don't sign up for an easy plan to have a baby in a few weeks. It's almost always around nine months—longer for elephants, shorter for guinea pigs. Skills and relationships and testimony and character traits—there are a lot of things that take time. For the most part, the things in our life that matter the most will have to be attended to. We will have to budget some time—make and take some time—for them. It's a process, sometimes a lifelong process. Enoch and his city were taken up "in process of time" (Moses 7:21).

One of our challenges is to figure out which are the most important things in our life—where we should be putting our time and our energy and our other resources—right now, in this season of our lives. President Harold B. Lee taught: "Most men do not set priorities to guide them in allocating their time [maybe he meant women do?] and most men [and women] forget that the first priority should be to maintain their own spiritual and physical strength [don't forget that]; then comes their family; then the Church; and then their professions."[6]

Elder Dallin H. Oaks warns us that "the treasure of our hearts—our priorities—should not be the destructible and temporary things of this world."[7] How do we set priorities? Elder

M. Russell Ballard taught: "Find some quiet time regularly to think deeply about where you are going and what you will need to do to get there. Jesus, our exemplar, often 'withdrew himself into the wilderness, and prayed' (Luke 5:16). We need to do the same thing occasionally to rejuvenate ourselves spiritually as the Savior did."[8]

As I was thinking of my life and priorities, it occurred to me that if I had spent as much time that particular day reading the scriptures as I had spent going through the newspaper, the *TV Guide,* junk mail, or catalogs, and so on, I could have built a ship and crossed an ocean or had some other adventure in the scriptures. But there are just those days when junk mail is all I can handle.

What are the things in your life to which you are intensely devoted and dedicated? What are the things you spend your time on—not just the amount of time, but your best time? Your children? The scriptures? Pondering? Exercising? Eating? A book club? Visiting? Attending the temple? Reading?

Let's say you had to drop four things from your life to free up some time. What would you drop? And how would you decide? For what would you drop everything? Your answers would reveal much about your priorities.

We don't put first things first to get them done and out of the way—we put them first because of the critical effect they have on everything that follows. It's like building a house on a rock rather than on sand. And if we're always putting third things first, perhaps our foundation is too sandy and not rocky enough.

First things first isn't only about importance. It's about order—what we do first, what we focus on and make time for and in which order. When I first read in the Doctrine and Covenants about creating "a house of order, a house of God" (D&C 88:119), I thought that meant that all the cupboards and closets and shelves in heaven were neat and orderly. Of course, it's more a matter of things happening at the right time and in the right order, first things first.

Some things are fundamental and foundational in our lives—soul builders. Doing the right things in the right order, as much as we are able, increases our capacity to use time well. That is the way we can stretch seconds and magnify minutes.

Here are some phrases from hymn 226 again:

> Improve the shining moments;
> Don't let them pass you by.
> Work while the sun is radiant;
> Work, for the night draws nigh.

We must improve the shining moments—improve our time. That means we increase the value of, take advantage of, or make good use of those moments. For the word *improve,* one dictionary even listed, "make use of for spiritual edification."

So how do we *improve* our time? Part of that has to do with how we choose to spend it—in what order and how much for which task or which project. President Ezra Taft Benson taught us that "when we put God first, all other things fall into their proper place or drop out of our lives. Our love of the Lord will govern the . . . demands on our time, the interests we pursue, and the order of our priorities."[9]

First things first, and everything else falls into place.

We have lots of chances to choose among a lot of things that are good, enjoyable, important, and exciting, not just between good and bad. If it were always a choice of doing good or bad, choosing would be easier, but mostly it is a choice between many things, all of which are good, important, valuable, and enjoyable. "The highest challenge we have in mortality," Elder Neal A. Maxwell said, "is to use our free agency well, making right choices in the interplay of time and talents."[10]

We perhaps become more like God in our choice of how

to use our time and other resources than we realize. We've heard a lot about how long it took the pioneers to walk to Zion and some of the suffering they went through. I think of who they became, who they were, as a result of their experiences, and I ask myself, "Who am I becoming? Who and what am I becoming by my experiences and my choice of time as I rush through life pulling not a handcart but one of those little suitcases with two wheels. Who am I becoming?" I thought about that one Sunday as I was racing over Iowa and Nebraska in a jet at hundreds of miles an hour. I couldn't even see the trail.

I wonder how my use of time fits in to Moroni's invitation to "come unto Christ, and be perfected in him, and deny yourselves of all ungodliness" (Moroni 10:32). Are there things that are ungodly about the way I use time?

What does it mean to deny myself? As I'm thinking about how to use my time, what does it say or show about me if I can delay some less-important things and work really hard to keep first things first? It's worth thinking about, and when I have some free time I will.

"Time cannot be recycled," President Spencer W. Kimball said. "When a moment has gone, it is really gone. . . . Wise time management is really the wise management of ourselves."[11] It's true. Much of managing our time has to do with self-discipline and self-control.

Here are just a few suggestions. Maybe you can pick out one or two that might be helpful for you.

Make appointments with yourself. You look on your envelope or your seventeen-holed paper and see if you have made any appointments with you (or in my case, MEE). Make appointments with yourself just to do what you need to do, and then if someone calls, you can say, "Oh, I have an appointment that day."

Simplify. I like the idea, or the concept, of simplifying. It can be a time-saver. I spend a lot of time in my basement, where there's matter unorganized, trying to find a 1983 *Ensign*

255

or a particular toy that I want to play with or a box of stuff. I get emotionally attached to things and it is very hard for me to give them away. I have much, much, much precious trash, but if we simplify, we could have more room in our closets—and imagine a home with an empty drawer! I get sick of hearing myself say, "I've got to get organized!" I think the last words I'll utter before I die are, "I've got to get organized!"

Have a bag to take with you. In that bag you can put some things you could work on for a few minutes if you find yourself waiting: you could read a lesson or write a note or sew on a button or paint an oil painting. (Big bag.) Think of it—if you could just capture and protect an "extra" few minutes every day . . .

Plan. It's wise to use some of our minutes to plan—to anticipate—to look ahead and think ahead and figure out what might be happening, or what we *want* to have happen, and then ask ourselves, "When can I do this?" and "How shall I accomplish that?" to bring about what we most need and want to do. Sometimes emergencies have a way of jumping right into first place. If we're not careful and aware, some of the time we had tried to guard for visiting someone, for pondering or contemplating, or for communicating with our Heavenly Father, might get eaten up with the crises that come along. If we give some thought to how and when (and if) we're going to do something, it may reduce the number of crises we have to deal with.

For me the right time to plan is in the morning. That's when I seem to be the most optimistic, the most awake. It may be exactly the opposite for you—your best planning time may be right before you go to sleep, or in the middle of the day—or twice a year. Whatever it is, figuring out your own best time will save you time. I find that when I'm tired, when my battery is running low, when I'm exhausted and weary, is not a good time to plan because I don't always make my best decisions then. Everything looks bigger and harder.

256

Write things down. For many of us writing things down is critical. Some people can do without pencil and paper. They know the date of everything that ever happened in the history of the world, and everything that is going to happen, and they can recall the names of all the general authorities with their middle names and their wives' maiden names, and all the temples. Some people can remember without writing things down, but for the rest of us, writing a few things down helps.

I recommend making lists as a result of prayerfully, carefully, thinking. Often we receive promptings and reminders of things that are important to us. If we don't write them down, we might forget them, and we might miss an opportunity or a good idea or some important spiritual guidance.

I don't know that having something really fancy to write in makes much difference. One day I was writing something in my planner, and my mother said, "I have a planner." "I didn't know that," I said. "Can I see it?" She said, "Sure." She handed me an envelope; on the back she'd written a few things she needed to do that day, or soon. It worked just as well for her as my seventeen-holed, neatly ruled planner worked for me!

Don't waste time. Don't get in the habit of wasting time, or "killing" time— as if you could kill time without injuring eternity![12] There are so many more ways to waste time today. "I deplore the terrible waste of the intellectual resources of so many people . . . who devote countless hours watching mindless drivel," President Gordon B. Hinckley said. "This old world needs straightening up."[13]

I'm often extremely busy, and yet I'm wasting time. How about you? Other times I can be relaxing, thinking and feeling, pondering—and I'm using time very, very well! I don't want to mistake busyness for being effective or using time well. More busyness is not evidence that I'm good at using my time. In fact, doing the right things at the right time more often than not means being quiet and listening and feeling. So whatever you do: Don't let lists run your life. Sometimes it feels so good to be list-less. Just listless. Take a break! Give it a rest! Slow down! Turn off the machines. Be quiet. Be still.

My friend Peggy has a clock with hands that have sort of collapsed and a lot of numbers that are haphazardly scattered toward the bottom. You never can say, "The big hand is on the . . . and the little hand is on the . . . " because the hands are just sort of twitching. They never go anyplace. Across the clock's middle is written, "Who cares?"

Elder J. Richard Clarke said that the "proper use of leisure requires discriminating judgment. Our leisure provides opportunity for renewal of spirit, mind, and body. It is a time for worship, for family, for service, for study, for wholesome recreation. It brings harmony into our life."[14] How long has it been since you walked anywhere slowly, just thinking and feeling? Or gone outside and looked at the stars? Or watched the sun rise or set? Or played in the sandpile with a child, or laughed at the jokes from *Boys' Life?* I repeat, just being busy is not a sign that time is being used well.

One important thing in my life that troubles me, because I'm not good at it yet, is that I don't want to seem too busy for people, to help or just be with people. That's hard for me. It's hard to be interrupted when I'm "on a roll." People are a high priority, and the most important things in our lives—our highest priorities—are not interruptions: they are our air, our water, our bread, our life, our eternity! Jesus was willing to stop and help people. He didn't act too busy or too rushed to stop and be kind. I want to be more like the Savior, and I find that I don't exactly know how to do that always. I'd love to sit with some of you and find out how you handle that.

Elder Hans B. Ringger has taught us: "Money alone does not lift the burdens of our fellowmen. . . . The world is in need of time, and if we have but one hour to spare, we are wealthy. It takes time to listen and to comfort, it takes time to teach and to encourage, and it takes time to feed and to clothe."[15]

Yet, there are times when I have to say, "I wish I could, and

I would if I could, but I can't." Anne Morrow Lindbergh said: "My life cannot implement in action the demands of all the people to whom my heart responds."[16] That's how I feel. I realize I can't do everything asked of me, even if I want to. So how do we kindly and sincerely say no to things we cannot do, and how do we say yes to things we need to do even if they are hard things?

And what about all the things that we don't get done? How stressed should we be about all the things we meant to do and weren't able to do? Let's suppose that you're doing your best on a day that is really busy. The phone keeps ringing, your cat eats your list, and your baby's teething (on your arm), you drop a gallon of milk, someone selling magazines comes to the door, and certain things you were supposed to do just aren't getting done. On those days it's comforting to remember what Elder Russell M. Nelson has said: "When priorities are in place, one can more patiently tolerate unfinished business."[17]

In Mosiah 4:27, King Benjamin teaches us about the use of time: "And see that all these things are done in wisdom and order; for it is not requisite that a man should run faster than he has strength. And again, it is expedient that he should be diligent, that thereby he might win the prize; therefore, all things must be done in order."

We are told to liken the scriptures to ourselves, so put your name or your circumstance in the verse. Let's see how it might read: "And see that all these things are done in wisdom and order; for it is not requisite that a [mother of young children] should run faster than [she] has strength [amen!]. All things must be done in order." You fill in that blank: wife of the bishop, caretaker of aging parents, Relief Society president, mother of a child with a disability, woman who has to search for water and fuel every single day, full-time student, single parent, and on and on. Or perhaps you are thinking, *Well, I wonder which five I should put in my blank!*

In the biography of President Gordon B. Hinckley is an insight into Sister Hinckley, which I love: "Her general outlook, however, was more practical than self-critical. 'I have a new project,' she wrote . . . , 'one chapter a day from each of the standard works. I have been on it for four days and am only 3 days behind. Better to have tried and failed than never to have tried.'"[18]

Good for her! Don't beat up on yourself. There is always, for almost everyone on the planet, so much to do and not enough time. That's why we have to choose and do our best to plan wisely. But maybe one of the things we need to do is relax a little bit more, to do the best we can every day and not get mad at ourselves if we can't do it all right now.

Let's be supportive and kind to each other because we may be in a different season than our neighbor, our sister, our mothers at our age, or whatever. We can't judge each other because we're in different seasons and situations. If we're not doing what others are doing right now, or if someone isn't doing what we're good at or doing, back off. Let's back off and not judge. Sometimes we harshly—even if we don't say it out loud—think, *Surely she could be more organized, have less dust, read every lesson ahead of time, never be late to anything, dress her children better, have them behave better, and be in better physical condition!* Oh, how we need to be understanding and kind.

I feel sure there will be enough time for all that we most need and want to do in this life, however long or short. But I'm also certain that there will never be a season where we'll just sit with nothing to do. We may enjoy a few do-nothing days, but there are no do-nothing seasons. I am convinced that our Heavenly Father is aware of the season each of us is in. He is not just *aware* of what that season is; he *understands* it. And our burdens will never be heavier than we can bear if we let him help and let others help.

Amulek, in testifying to the Zoramites, teaches us a great

principle: "Now is the time and the day of your salvation. . . . For behold, *this life is the time* for men to prepare to meet God. . . . I beseech of you that ye do not procrastinate the day of your repentance until the end; for after this day of life, which is given us to prepare for eternity, behold, *if we do not improve our time* while in this life, then cometh the night of darkness wherein there can be no labor performed" (Alma 34:31–33; emphasis added).

If there are critical things that we fail to do today, either they'll still be waiting tomorrow, or they won't be there anymore. They might go away, and the opportunity or the moment may have passed. Procrastination is deadly. It can destroy time, energy, and other resources. And it can become a very strong habit—hard to break.

In hymn 229, "Today, While the Sun Shines," we sing:

> Today, today, work with a will;
> Today, today, your duties fulfill.
> Today, today, work while you may;
> Prepare for tomorrow by working today.

Joseph Smith counseled: "Let us this very day begin anew, and now say, with all our hearts, we will forsake our sins and be righteous."[19] Eventually, the night will come and the day will be finished when we could have done our work. We will either have used our time well and done the things that mattered most, or we will not have done.

We must also remember that we who love the Lord have covenanted to give him time. Brigham Young said: "I want everything that the Lord places in my possession, my time, my talents, every ability I have, every penny that he has committed to me to be used to his glory, and for the building up of his kingdom on the earth."[20]

Perhaps we can consider advice, which has been given by many, to tithe our time. (Cherry, my friend, and I were wondering on one of our more exhausted days if that 10 percent could come, part of the time at least, when we're asleep; or does it have to be an "out-of-bed" experience?) Miraculously, nine minutes go further than ten, just as nine pennies go further than ten. You can't get out paper or use a computer to figure this out scientifically. It's one of those heavenly things that just is—nine minutes can go further than ten. Somehow, when we do what God asks us to do, the best we can, keeping first things first, our time seems to come back to us, added upon and multiplied. It's a miracle.

In Doctrine and Covenants 88 there's a wonderful verse about the end of time, the earth's last day. (My mother says it's evidence that I won't be there. See what you think.) "And there shall be silence in heaven for the space of half an hour"—they'll probably have to put me in my room—"and immediately after shall the curtain of heaven be unfolded, as a scroll is unfolded after it is rolled up, and the face of the Lord shall be unveiled" (v. 95). Oh, what a feeling! We'll know. We'll know in that space of half an hour what is about to happen, and then we'll have the chance to think back, *How did we use our day? How did we use the day that God gave us before the night came?*

I think, during that half hour, as I anticipate seeing the Savior, I will perhaps think more deeply about what he did for me in a very personal way in the Garden, such that he can understand everything—everything we feel, everything we experience, everything that makes us feel lonely and heavily burdened.

He knows. He understands. He's been there. He loved us that much then, and oh, how he loves us right now. There is nothing we can do to cause him to stop loving us. Nothing. And just because I don't understand unconditional love doesn't make it unreal. It is real. God loves us, the Savior loves us—they love us unconditionally. They love us right now.

Let him help you! Let them help you. Let the Savior encircle you in the arms of his love.

I pray that we will live as happily and positively and

enthusiastically as we possibly can the great plan of happiness, the gospel of Jesus Christ; that we will do as much as we possibly can, in any season in which we find ourselves; that we will use this precious time that our Heavenly Father has given us, this day of our lives, to do all we can to be more like him, closer to him, and to build up and defend the kingdom of God.

And now I'll turn the time over to you. Use it well. Enjoy it. Appreciate it.

NOTES

1. Ezra Taft Benson, "To the Single Adult Sisters of the Church," *Ensign,* Nov. 1988, 97.

2. *The New Shorter Oxford English Dictionary* (Oxford: Clarendon Press, 1993), s.v. "time."

3. Brigham Young, in *Journal of Discourses,* 26 vols. (London: Latter-day Saints' Book Depot, 1854–86), 18:354.

4. "Improve the Shining Moments," *Hymns* (Salt Lake City: The Church of Jesus Christ of Latter-day Saints, 1985), no. 226.

5. Sheri Dew, *Go Forward with Faith: The Biography of Gordon B. Hinckley* (Salt Lake City: Deseret Book, 1996), 347.

6. Harold B. Lee, quoted in James E. Faust, "Happiness Is Having a Father Who Cares," *Ensign,* January 1974, 23.

7. Dallin H. Oaks, *Pure in Heart* (Salt Lake City: Bookcraft, 1988), 74.

8. M. Russell Ballard, "Keeping Life's Demands in Balance," *Ensign,* May 1987, 14.

9. Ezra Taft Benson, "The Great Commandment—Love the Lord," *Ensign,* May 1988, 4.

10. Neal A. Maxwell, *Deposition of a Disciple* (Salt Lake City: Deseret Book, 1976), 68.

11. Spencer W. Kimball, "Jesus: The Perfect Leader," *Ensign,* August 1979, 6.

12. Henry David Thoreau, quoted in *Bartlett's Familiar Quotations,* 16th ed. (Boston: Little, Brown and Company, 1992), 477.

13. Dew, *Go Forward with Faith,* 457.

14. J. Richard Clarke, "The Value of Work," *Ensign,* May 1982, 78.

15. Hans B. Ringger, "Choose You This Day," *Ensign,* May 1990, 26.

16. Anne Morrow Lindbergh, quoted by Neal A. Maxwell, *The Smallest Part* (Salt Lake City: Deseret Book, 1973), 46.

17. Russell M. Nelson, "Lessons from Eve," *Ensign,* November 1987, 88.

18. Dew, *Go Forward with Faith,* 346.

19. *Teachings of the Prophet Joseph Smith,* sel. Joseph Fielding Smith (Salt Lake City: Deseret Book, 1938), 364.

20. Brigham Young, in *Journal of Discourses,* 18:248.

The original presentation of this essay is available on audiocassette from Deseret Book or on the Internet at http://coned.byu.edu/cw/womens.htm

THE FIRE OF THE COVENANT

GERALD N. LUND

The time was fall 1838. The place was Caldwell County, Missouri. Tensions were running high. In the previous two years, more than five thousand Latter-day Saints had moved into what had been a sparsely populated county. The old settlers were getting nervous. Too many Yankee Mormons were moving in. Missouri had entered the Union as a slave state, and it wanted to stay that way. The militia and mobs began to prowl. On the night of 24 October, a mob broke into an isolated settlement, burned the haystacks, torched the barns, and then kidnapped three Latter-day Saint men and threatened to take them back to Jackson County to execute them.

When word reached Joseph Smith in Far West, he called out the Mormon militia under the direction of David Patten, who was second senior member of the Quorum of the Twelve. He gathered a group of men to ride out and intercept that group.[1] On the way, they stopped at James Hendricks' home and asked him to join them. While he prepared, his wife, Drusilla, filled with great fear but also faith, got his gun down from the fireplace and handed it to him. As he left she said, "Don't get shot in the back."[2]

Gerald N. Lund, author of several books, is a zone administrator in the Church Educational System, with which he has been associated for more than thirty years. He has led tours to Europe, the Holy Land, Central America, and LDS Church history sites. He and his wife, Lynn Stanard Lund, have seven children. He serves as the teacher development leader in his ward in Bountiful, Utah.

They rode all that night. Just at morning they came upon a little place called Crooked River. They didn't realize at first that the mob was camped right across the river. The little band of Mormons was coming from the west, and the rising sun was in their eyes. The Saints couldn't see the mob as they began to cross the river. One of the Missouri picket guards first saw the brethren coming and opened fire. Patrick O'Bannion was hit immediately and died before noon. A fierce battle erupted. Another man, Gideon Carter, was shot in the face and killed instantly. As David Patten tried to fall back across the river, he was shot in the stomach. He died before nightfall, the first apostle martyred in this dispensation.[3] And James Hendricks? As the furious fire erupted, he turned, ran for shelter, and caught a ball in the back of the neck. He fell to the ground paralyzed from the neck down.[4]

On October 27, two days later, in Jefferson City, Missouri, Governor Lilburn W. Boggs received a wildly exaggerated account of what had happened at Crooked River. He was told that the whole Missouri militia had been massacred when actually they had lost only one man. The Mormons had lost three dead and seven wounded. In great anger, Governor Boggs issued an executive order that, among other things, read, "The Mormons must be treated as enemies and must be exterminated or driven from the state."[5]

About twelve miles west of Far West was a small settlement named Haun's Mill for its founder, Jacob Haun, who had built a grist mill there on Shoal Creek. October 30 was a beautiful Indian summer day.[6] About four o'clock in the afternoon, the women were sitting on their porches shucking corn or doing other things to prepare for the winter. The men were out doing the last of the work in the fields, and the children were playing close by. Suddenly they heard a low rumble and looked up. Across the meadow and the trees, they saw about 240 men riding toward them. The captain of the Haun's Mill militia ran out, waving his hat and crying, "Peace! Peace!" Instead, the riders opened fire. The scene of tranquillity erupted in terror. Children screamed. Women ran to rescue their children. The invaders fired at everyone in sight. Fathers grabbed their sons and ran for the blacksmith's shop, the strongest building in the settlement. The mob showed no discrimination whatsoever. One woman, Mary Stedwell, darted across the road, headed for the millpond. Bullets pinged all around her as she ran across the millrace. Finally one bullet found its target: Mary was shot through the palm of her hand, and, fainting, fell behind a log. Later, the Saints dug out between fifteen and twenty bullets from the log that sheltered her.[7]

Far more serious, the men and boys who had run into the blacksmith shop had made a terrible mistake. The heavy logs making up the walls had never been chinked, leaving great cracks all the way around the building. As the Saints barricaded the door, the mob dismounted, stepped up to the walls, put the muzzles through the cracks, and opened fire. In the deadly hail of bullets, most of the men were killed outright, and others were wounded. Finally the mob broke through the door and walked around, systematically shooting the survivors. Warren Smith had taken his two sons in with him for protection: Sardius was ten, and Alma was seven. In terror the boys dived beneath the blacksmith's bellows. They watched as a man put a gun to their father's head and pulled the trigger. A member of the mob heard them cry and looked underneath the bellows where he could see Sardius. He tried to pull the boy out, but when he couldn't, he simply put his rifle under the bellows, against Sardius' head, and pulled the trigger. Alma, whimpering in terror, burrowed deeper beneath the bellows. Another man reached in with his muzzle, couldn't quite reach Alma, but fired anyway, blowing away Alma's hip joint. Twenty minutes later, when the mob rode away with clothing and treasures they had looted from the cabins, they left seventeen dead and thirteen wounded. The Haun's Mill massacre became a tragic event in our history.

The day after the Crooked River killings in Far West, knowing the great tension and danger, Joseph Smith had sent word to all those in outlying settlements and villages to come into Far West for protection.[8] On October 26, Jacob Haun had driven into Far West and looked up Joseph Smith. John D. Lee, who happened to be standing there, wrote the following: "The morning after the battle of Crooked River, Haun came to Far West to consult with the Prophet concerning the policy of the removal of the settlers . . . to the fortified camp. Col. [Lyman] Wight and myself were standing by when the prophet said to [Mr. Haun], 'Move in, by all means, if you wish to save your lives.' Haun replied that if the settlers left their homes, all of their property would be lost . . . and burn[ed]. 'You had better lose your property than your lives; one can be replaced, the other cannot be restored; but there is no need of you losing either if you will only do as you are commanded.' Haun said that he considered the best plan was for all the settlers to move into and around the mill, and use the blacksmith's shop and other buildings as a fort in case of attack. . . . [Finally the Prophet said], 'You are at liberty to do so if you think best.' Haun then departed, well satisfied that he had carried his point. The Prophet turned to Col. Wight and said: 'That man did not come for counsel, but to induce me to tell him to do as he pleased; which I did. Had I commanded them to move in here and leave their property, they would have called me a tyrant. . . . ' [And then sadly the Prophet said], 'I am confident that we will soon learn that they have been butchered in a fearful manner.'"[9] The irony is that Jacob Haun went back to Haun's Mill and didn't tell the settlers the whole truth of what had taken place between him and Joseph Smith.[10] Jacob Haun was not one of the seventeen who were killed. He was one of the thirteen wounded and thus had to live out his life knowing the dreadful consequences of his refusing to follow counsel.

Let's go back a few years to the fall of 1830. Four missionaries were called by direct revelation to go to the western border of the United States in Independence, Missouri, on what is now known as the mission to the Lamanites. Parley P. Pratt, Oliver Cowdery, Peter Whitmer Jr., and Ziba Peterson all left New York and, at Parley P. Pratt's recommendation, stopped at a place where Parley had once lived called Kirtland, Ohio. There they received a warm and wonderful reception. Many accepted their message, including names well known in Church history: Frederick G. Williams, Sidney Rigdon, Isaac Morley, John Murdock, and so on.[11] In Kirtland, an eleven-year-old girl named Mary Elizabeth Rollins lived with her uncle. She heard that these missionaries had left what they called the Golden Bible with Brother Isaac Morley. She records: "I went to his house just before the meeting was to commence, and asked to see the Book. Brother Morley put it in my hand; as I looked at it, I felt such a desire to read it, that I could not refrain from asking him to let me take it home and read it, while he attended meeting. . . . He finally said, 'Child if you will bring this book home before breakfast tomorrow morning, you may take it.' . . . when I got into the house, I exclaimed, 'Oh, Uncle, I have gotten the "Golden Bible."' . . . We all took turns reading it until very late in the night—as soon as it was light enough to see, I was up and learned [by heart] the first verse in the book. When I reached Brother Morley's . . . , he remarked, 'I guess you did not read much in it.' I showed him how far we had read. He was surprised, and said, 'I don't believe you could tell me one word of it.'" She then quoted him the first verse she had memorized and told him the story in detail of everything they had read up to that point. "He gazed at me in surprise, and said, 'Child, take this book home and finish it. I think I can wait.'"[12]

This eleven-year-old is the same Mary Elizabeth Rollins who was living with her family in Independence three and a half years later. In July 1833 a mob of some five hundred men, angry at the influence of the growing community of Mormons, attacked the printing office of *The Evening and the Morning*

Star, run by W. W. Phelps. Living close by with her uncle, Mary Elizabeth and her sister Caroline saw the mob coming in and turned and ran for shelter. They ducked behind a split rail fence some distance away and watched as the mob demolished not only the press and the type but the very building. They tore the roof off and then tore the walls down. As the two girls, ages fifteen and twelve, huddled there in terror, Mary Elizabeth saw huge stacks of paper being thrown from one of the upper windows. Because she knew W. W. Phelps well, she knew the papers were the Book of Commandments, a collection of revelations sent from Kirtland to be printed. "Caroline," she said, "we must save those." Her twelve-year-old sister replied, "If we do, they will kill us." Mary Elizabeth said, "Nevertheless we must do it." They jumped up, ran to the building, and picked up as many of those sheaves of paper as they could carry. Two men took after them. The girls darted through the fence, ran deep into a cornfield, threw down the papers and themselves on top of them, and began to pray mightily when they heard the men tromping through the cornfield. Eventually the men gave up and left. Thanks to Mary Elizabeth and Caroline Rollins, we now have a few copies of the original Book of Commandments.[13]

Mary Elizabeth is one of my favorite people in Church history. One night, Mary Elizabeth awakened to see a figure standing in the air at the foot of her bed. She did what any wise girl would have done: she pulled the covers over her head. When she finally got the courage to look out, the person was gone. The next day, on the street, she passed Joseph Smith. The Prophet said, "Mary Elizabeth, I understand you had a visitation last night." She said, "How did you know that?" And he said, "Because the angel came to me. He said he had come to you and could not deliver the message because you had hid under the covers. He also said that he was greatly offended."[14] I guess angels aren't used to that kind of treatment.

Let me relate another story. Vilate and Heber C. Kimball

were driven out of Far West to a swampy bend on the Mississippi River. They lived in terrible conditions. For a time, they lived in a log lean-to built onto the back of someone else's house. After a year or so of that, Heber was finally able to build Vilate their own one-room log cabin. Then Heber spent years in missionary work, often in England. Finally after all the years of sacrifice, they reached a point in 1845 when Heber was prosperous enough to be able to build a beautiful two-story, brick home. Vilate and Heber moved into that home in November 1845. They locked the door and walked away without receiving a dime for it in February 1846.

They were not the only ones who left painfully. In the middle of April 1846, Bathsheba and George Albert Smith faced a similar situation. On her last day in Nauvoo, Bathsheba tidied up her home, swept the floor, put the broom in its accustomed place behind the door, and then stepped outside to a waiting wagon, leaving behind rooms full of beloved items and a house ready for occupancy by strangers.[15] I have wondered what kind of woman would walk away from her home, leaving it to her enemies and be sure it is swept clean before she does so.

Ten years later, in October 1856, the Willie Handcart Company had been caught in the first of some furious storms on the high plains of Wyoming. They suffered terribly. Finally in the last week of October, the first relief wagon from Salt Lake appeared. The handcart pioneers were given a limited amount of flour and food but were told the rescuers could do little more until they found the Martin company. Help was ahead, however: waiting at Rock Creek, only sixteen miles away, were other wagons filled with blankets, medicine, food, and beef. But that sixteen miles was through a howling blizzard. The Willie handcart company was camped at the base of Rocky Ridge, which is a three-mile pull, some of it very steep and the last part extremely rough. In the midst of a howling blizzard, they set out to cover that sixteen miles to the supply wagons. It took them almost twenty-four hours from the time they left camp till the last one of the company finally arrived at Rock Creek.

Two people in the Willie Handcart Company were Jens and Elsie Nielsen, well-to-do converts from Denmark who had sold their farm to travel to Zion. When they reached Iowa City, Jens had enough money to buy wagons and teams and outfit his family very comfortably, but the Church agents there asked if anyone had anything extra to help those who did not have enough. Jens Nielsen took enough money to buy one handcart, supplies for himself and his wife, his son, and Bodil Mortensen, a young girl they were responsible for, and gave the rest to the Church agents.[16]

The Nielsens started up Rocky Ridge. The children, Jens's own son and the girl accompanying them, were so weak and sick that they were riding in the handcart. Jens Nielsen pulled for fourteen or fifteen hours in snow until his feet were so badly frostbitten that he barely hobbled along. Somewhere between Rocky Ridge and Rock Creek, Jens collapsed. "Elsie, I can go no farther. You go on without me."

"I will not leave you, Jens," Elsie said, and she helped him into the cart with the two children. Jens Nielsen was six foot two and weighed two hundred and thirty pounds. Elsie Nielsen was four foot eleven and weighed one hundred pounds.[17] She pulled them all the rest of the way to Rock Creek. Jens lived, but both children died before morning.

As I read those stories and journals and diaries, I have many questions. Why was the cost in human lives so high? If these were the Lord's people, why weren't the storms tempered? Why were the innocent people in Haun's Mill, who didn't know what had taken place between Jacob Haun and the Prophet, allowed to become part of what happened in that tragedy? What happened to a Sardius Smith, who was killed at age twelve and, because of wicked men, never had the opportunity to grow to adulthood, marry, and have children in this life?

What about the calendar of the exile? When the Church moved from New York to Ohio, it was January. The Saints were forced to flee from Kirtland in December and January. They were driven out of Jackson County in November and December. They were driven out of Far West in January and February, and they left Nauvoo in February. Is that accidental? If the Lord really loves his people, why is no one driven out in May or June occasionally?

Some of the hardest questions for me are these: Why didn't they give up? What was it about this people that drove them on? And, I suppose most sobering, What would I have done in those circumstances? That question comes up over and over again. Would I have been strong enough? Would I have remained a believer?

These stories are the *whats* of the Restoration story; and they are astonishing, remarkable, incredible, and inspirational. But of far more value to us than knowing what happened is knowing the *why*. Why did this happen? Why were these people so remarkable? Why did they go on? To answer these questions we have to go back further even than Joseph Smith. These people had a tremendous love for and loyalty to Joseph Smith, but that's not what drove them. That's not what made them what they were. One thing I've learned in all my research is that they didn't think they were remarkable at all. I really believe that if we had a chance to ask them, "Why did you do such great things?" They'd say, "What things?" or "Who, me? You can't be talking about me." They didn't view themselves as unusual in any way.

Why was the way so hard? Why was the cost so high? Part of the answer is in Moses 1:39: "For behold, this is my work and my glory—to bring to pass the immortality and eternal life of man." That is what these stories are all about: God's work. They are God's story, and it is an incredible one. He says in his own words that his purposes are twofold: to bring to pass our immortality and our eternal life.

President Boyd K. Packer described our existence as a three-act play: the premortal life is act one; mortality, where we are now, is act two; and the postmortal life will be act three.[18] If a person comes into a play during act two, it is not surprising for him to be puzzled. Unless he knows what has happened in act one, and unless he has a sense of what will happen in act three, a lot of act two will not make sense. So let's talk briefly about God's plan for us. Some time in the distant past, we were born spiritually. Before that we were intelligences. As spirit children, male and female, we lived with our heavenly parents in the celestial kingdom. If we were with God and our heavenly mother in the celestial kingdom, what ever would have possessed us to leave? Isn't that what we are after—to be back in the celestial kingdom with God? So why did we have to leave? This is a very important point. Most of the Christian world's idea of heaven is to return to live with God, but we believe there is something far more significant. Not only do we want to live *with* God, we want to be *like* God. That is what eternal life, God's life, means. What was God like when we were there living with him in the celestial kingdom? Three things are significant. First, he had a glorified, immortal, physical body. We did not; we were only spirits. Second, he had a divine nature, every attribute in absolute perfection. We did not. Third, he had an eternal wife, and they were able to have eternal children. Thus we were living with God in heaven, but we certainly were not like him.

To move forward, to become like God, we had to have a body. Having a body is not just an incidental by-product of mortality. It is one of its central purposes. Until we can be connected with a physical, elemental body, we cannot have a fulness of joy (see D&C 93:33–34). In addition, to be like God, we have to acquire divine attributes. Those two objectives brought us to earth. As I understand it, to prove ourselves, we needed four things: first, an imperfect world; second, a mortal body that could endure sickness, irritation, tiredness, and other ills so that we could gain experience; third, agency, for without choice there is no morality; and fourth, opposition, as Lehi explained (see 2 Nephi 2:11), because we can't exercise agency with nothing to choose between and no conflicting enticements toward good or evil. The Fall was necessary to gain a battlefield, and thus began the plan of God. In scriptural terms life comes down to one word: *warfare*. Metaphors of war— from "put on the armor of righteousness" (2 Nephi 1:23) to "rejoice not against me, O mine enemy: when I fall, I shall arise" (Micah 7:8)—are found everywhere in scripture. The Spirit helps us in many ways—instructing, comforting, and strengthening us—but the ultimate battle is absolutely individual. It is not a team event. It is not a spectator sport.

That is what those early Saints knew. This vision in their hearts drove them to do what they did. Joseph Smith was the means. He was the one chosen to open the Restoration so that we could have the priesthood and the Church, the ordinances and the covenants. But what those people saw was the *why* behind it all.

So what drove these people? Why did an eleven-year-old girl want to read the Book of Mormon? Why did she and a twelve-year-old risk their lives to save a batch of papers? Why did fathers and husbands leave their desperately ill and poor families to serve missions? Why did a cultured and refined woman walk away from a beautiful two-story brick home and never look back? Because these people had a clear vision of God's plan for them, and it never wavered in their hearts.

Let me explain. By September 1846, most of the Saints had crossed Iowa at a terrible price and were preparing to winter at Winter Quarters. (Before that winter was over, about six hundred died at Winter Quarters.) On September 25, Brigham Young received word of the Battle of Nauvoo from a group who had just come from Nauvoo. The last ones still in the city were the poor, the widowed, and the orphans who had not been able to find a way to leave. Mobs finally came in and drove them out, picking up the men and throwing them in the river, driving the women and children with bayonets, threatening to kill them if they crossed back over the river. When Brigham Young received word of that, even though the rest of the Saints were in the most destitute and terrible of conditions themselves, he gathered the brethren and said: "The poor brethren and sisters, widows and orphans, sick and destitute, are now lying on the west bank of the Mississippi, waiting for teams and wagons and means to remove them. Now is the time for labor. Let *the fire of the covenant,* which you made in the house of the Lord burn in your hearts like flame unquenchable."[19]

Brigham Young didn't talk to them about the suffering of those poor people. He called to their minds the covenants they had made with God in the house of the Lord. He went on: "[I want every man who is able to] rise up with his teams and go straightway. . . . This is a day of action and not of argument." Before too many days had passed, almost a hundred wagons were moving east to go and rescue the poor.[20] I love that phrase, "the fire of the covenant," because that is what drove these people. That is why they did what they did.

Why was the way so hard then? Why is it still so hard today? We have to remember what God is about. Remember, his work and his glory is to bring to pass our immortality and our eternal life. To make us like him is not something that is done by waving a wand. At a time when the Saints were driven barefoot across sleet-filled prairies, when it was reported that women and children were marched thirty miles and left bloody footprints in the snow from their lacerated feet[21]—at that very time in our history, the Lord said in revelation: "Whoso layeth down his life in my cause, for my name's sake, shall find it again, even life eternal. Therefore, be not afraid of your enemies, for I have decreed in my heart, saith the Lord, that I will prove you in all things" (D&C 98:13–14). Why? Because a god doesn't buckle under pressure. When things get really rough a god doesn't say, "Hey, I'm outta here. I don't want to do this." Who "will abide in my covenant, even unto death,. . . . may be found worthy," he says (v. 14). Worthy of what? Worthy to be with God. Worthy of godhood.

The early Saints had the fire of the covenant in their hearts. That fire helped them demonstrate faith, and out of faith came great power. Mary Elizabeth Rollins, after she read the Book of Mormon, after she saved those papers, wrote of yet another experience in her journal. When she and her group of Saints were driven out of Jackson County, they camped in the low bottomlands of the Missouri River. Mobbers threatened the Mormons with death if they didn't leave the county. One or two families, when it was all finished, were left on the south side at the mercy of the mobs because there was not money enough to ferry everyone across the river. Greatly fearing, those who were left decided to fish during the night, hoping to sell their catch, if any, to get enough money to ferry over. The next day, they brought in three small fish and a catfish that weighed fourteen pounds. From her journal Mary Elizabeth says, "On opening it, what was their astonishment to find three bright silver half dollars [in its stomach], just the amount needed to carry the rest" of them across the ferry to join their brothers and sisters.[22] Coincidence? No, the power of faith.

Amanda Smith was the wife of Warren Smith and the mother of Sardius and Alma, who was so brutally wounded in Haun's Mill. When her little son was carried out of the blacksmith shop, she said, "I looked at the wound. It was the size of a small melon. There was no hip joint, there was just shattered bone and a huge gap." She laid him down and asked her son, "Alma, do you believe the Lord made your hip?"

"I do, Momma."

"Alma, do you believe he can make you another one?"

"I do, Momma."

She then bowed her head and prayed. She asked the Lord, "If it's your will that my son be taken, then take him now in his innocence, but if it is not your will, then help me." No sooner had she finished that prayer than words began to flow into her mind. She directed her son Willard to go to a firepit, get some ashes and pour water over them, and bring that water to her. She directed another child to go down to the millstream and find the roots of some slippery elm. She bathed the wound, the ash making a lye that bleached the flesh until, she said, it looked as white as chicken flesh. And then she packed the wound with a slippery elm poultice, following the directions of the Spirit.[23] Nine years later, in the spring of 1847, Alma Smith, his mother, and other family members left for Utah. Alma Smith walked every step of the way, without a cane, without a crutch. He was preserved for a long life of service. I can imagine him telling his story and walking back and forth without a limp to show his listeners what God can do for those who keep their covenants.[24]

So, if God can work miracles, what of those who died or whose limbs were not restored in the exodus to Zion? In a Sunday School class in southern Utah some thirty years after the Willie and Martin Handcart Companies reached Salt Lake, a Sunday School teacher was being critical. What a foolish decision it had been to leave so late in the season and to be caught in the winter storms, he noted. How easily the tragedy could have been avoided. An old man in the back of the class stood up and said, in substance, the following: "I ask you to stop this criticism. You are discussing a matter you know nothing about. Cold historic facts mean nothing here for they give no proper interpretation of the questions involved. Was it a mistake to send the handcart company out so late in the season? Yes! But I was in that company and my wife," and he named some others. "We suffered beyond anything you can imagine and many died of exposure and starvation, but did you ever hear a survivor of that company utter a word of criticism? No one of that company has ever apostatized or left the church. . . . I have pulled my handcart when I was so weak and weary from illness and lack of food that I could hardly put one foot ahead of the other. I have looked ahead and seen a patch of sand or a hill slope and I have said, 'I can only go that far and there I must give up, for I cannot pull the load through it.' I have gone on to that sand and when I reached it the cart began pushing me! I have looked back many times to see who was pushing my cart, but my eyes saw no one." And then he said, "I knew then that the Angels of God were there. Was I sorry that I chose to come by handcart? No! Neither then nor any minute of my life since. The price we paid to become acquainted with God was a privilege to pay, and I am thankful that I was privileged to come in the Martin Handcart Company."[25] This brother had not lost the vision, the fire of the covenant. Doctrine and Covenants 84:88 reads, "Whoso receiveth you, there I will be also, for I will go before your face. I will be on your right hand and on your left, and my Spirit shall be in your hearts, and mine angels round about you, to bear you up."

In 1842, a few weeks after organizing the Relief Society, Joseph Smith made a most remarkable statement. He said to the sisters: "If you live up to these principles, how great and glorious will be your reward in the celestial kingdom! If you live up to your privileges, the angels cannot be restrained from being your associates."[26] That is the promise to all. That is why we too—the inheritors of the fire of the covenant—will continue in carrying out God's work and his glory. That is the legacy left to us by these remarkable people who were driven by a vision of what they could become and did not falter from it.

NOTES

1. Ivan J. Barrett, *Joseph Smith and the Restoration: A History of the Church to 1846* (Provo: Brigham Young University Press, 1973), 391–92.

2. Leonard J. Arrington and Susan Arrington Madsen, "Drusilla Dorris

Hendricks: 'Mother's Little Christian'" in *Sunbonnet Sisters* (Salt Lake City: Bookcraft, 1984), 29–30.

3. Barrett, *Joseph Smith and the Restoration,* 392.

4. Arrington and Madsen, *Sunbonnet Sisters,* 30. See Carol Cornwall Madsen, *In Their Own Words: Women and the Story of Nauvoo* (Salt Lake City: Deseret Book, 1994), 161–68, for the rest of Drusilla Dorris Hendricks' story.

5. Joseph Smith, *History of The Church of Jesus Christ of Latter-day Saints,* ed. B. H. Roberts, 2d ed. rev., 7 vols. (Salt Lake City: The Church of Jesus Christ of Latter-day Saints, 1932–51), 3:175.

6. Much of the description that follows is drawn from Barrett, *Joseph Smith and the Restoration,* 399–401. See also B. H. Roberts, *The Missouri Persecutions* (Salt Lake City: Bookcraft, 1965), 232–37.

7. Smith, *History of the Church,* 3:186.

8. Leland H. Gentry, "History of the Latter-day Saints in Northern Missouri from 1836 to 1839," Ph.D. dissertation (Brigham Young University, 1965), 432.

9. Gentry, "Latter-day Saints in Northern Missouri," 432–33; spelling standardized.

10. Gentry, "Latter-day Saints in Northern Missouri," 432.

11. *Church History in the Fulness of Times* (Salt Lake City: The Church of Jesus Christ of Latter-day Saints, 1993), 79–82.

12. Adapted from "Mary Elizabeth Rollins Lightner," *Utah Genealogical and Historical Magazine* 17 (July 1926): 194. For more details, see "Mary Elizabeth Rollins Lightner: A Mormon Girl with Courage," in Arrington and Madsen, *Sunbonnet Sisters,* 13–20.

13. Adapted from "Mary Elizabeth Rollins Lightner," 196. See also Barrett, *Joseph Smith and the Restoration,* 250–51.

14. Adapted from Mary Lightner, "Testimony of Mary Elizabeth Lightner," address to Brigham Young University, 14 April 1905, Provo, Utah, BYU Archives and Manuscripts, typescript, 3.

15. Susan Easton Black and William G. Hartley, ed., *The Iowa Mormon Trail: Legacy of Faith and Courage* (Orem: Helix, 1997), 112.

16. Adapted from "Bishop Jens Neilsen: A Brief Biography Prepared by Albert R. Lyman," unpublished manuscript in possession of the author, 2–3.

17. As reported to the author in an interview with two grandchildren of Jens and Elsie Nielsen, 17 October 1996.

18. Boyd K. Packer, "The Play and the Plan," Church Educational System Fireside for College-age Young Adults, 7 May 1995.

19. Black and Hartley, *Iowa Mormon Trail,* 163; emphasis added.

20. Black and Hartley, *Iowa Mormon Trail,* 163.

21. Barrett, *Joseph Smith and the Restoration,* 264.

22. Adapted from "Mary Elizabeth Rollins Lightner," 197.

23. Adapted from Jean Brown Fonnesbeck, "From an Old Diary," *Young Woman's Journal* 29 (July 1918): 386–87.

24. Fonnesbeck, "From an Old Diary," 388–89.

25. Maurine Jensen Proctor and Scot Facer Proctor, *The Gathering: Mormon Pioneers on the Trail to Zion* (Salt Lake City: Deseret Book, 1996), 196.

26. Joseph Smith, *Teachings of the Prophet Joseph Smith,* sel. Joseph Fielding Smith (Salt Lake City: Deseret Book, 1938), 226–27.

THE TEMPLE: TAKING AN ETERNAL VIEW

S. MICHAEL WILCOX

Have you ever gotten excited at a sporting event? Have you ever gotten so excited at a sporting event that you actually shouted? Perhaps because your team scored a point or got a touchdown or made a big play? Have you ever been so excited that you not only shouted but actually rose from your seat to shout? Have you ever been so excited because you won or the victory was at hand that you rose and shouted and waved something? Your fists or a towel or a hat or a program? What is it about a sporting event that can elicit such exuberant exclamations of joy from us?

Whether or not you have had that experience, I hope that you have had the opportunity to rise, shout, and wave in an exclamation of joy and triumph that cannot be kept inside at an event of deep and eternal significance. I am referring, of course, to the dedication of the house of the Lord, the temple. The idea behind the hosanna shout is, in a reverent and very sacred way, the same idea behind our rising and shouting and waving at a basketball game. The joy is so great that we can't keep it inside, and we rise and shout and wave our excitement

S. Michael Wilcox, a popular speaker and author, is an instructor at the institute of religion at the University of Utah. He received his Ph.D. at the University of Colorado. He and his wife, Laura L. Chipman, are the parents of five children. He serves as an ordinance worker in the Jordan River Temple.

and joy. A temple dedication is the only time we do the hosanna shout in the Church, though we sing about it frequently:

> The Spirit of God like a fire is burning!
> . . . .
> We'll sing and we'll shout with the armies of heaven,
> Hosanna, hosanna, to God and the Lamb![1]

If you have ever participated in that great hosanna shout, you will truly have sung and shouted with the armies of heaven, for the joy on the other side of the veil must be even greater than on this side.

A temple dedication is an occasion worthy of that one most significant exclamation of joy and happiness for many reasons. The temple is many houses all in one, like an accordion of houses folded together. The Doctrine and Covenants mentions many of those houses: a house of glory, a house of order, a house of fasting, a house of prayer, a house of thanksgiving, a house of learning, and a house of refuge and protection (see D&C 88:119, 137; 109:24–26). I would like to talk about one of those houses: a house of learning and instruction, where we are perfected in our understanding of theory, doctrine, and principle and also perfected in our understanding of our callings (see D&C 13–14).

I went to the temple to receive my endowments when I was eighteen years old and ready to go on a mission. I was unprepared for the temple experience, however. I don't know that anyone can ever be totally and completely prepared for that first visit to the temple, though we do a much better job preparing people now than we did thirty years ago. I was frightened and bewildered by the experience. To be absolutely honest, when I left the temple that day, I had to admit to myself that this did not seem like my church. The experience did not feel like anything I was used to, and I was a bit frightened by it. I have learned since that my first experience in the

283

temple was not unique, that a number of people have some difficulty and bewilderment when they go. I felt that way because I did not know how to learn in the Lord's house. I did not know how to receive the instructions that he was giving me. If I had known how to learn, I would have still been as confused and bewildered, but I wouldn't have been frightened or doubtful or wondering how this could be my church.

The Lord chooses a unique and specific way of teaching in his house. If I could take a pair of glasses and put them on anybody who ever goes to the temple, whether for the first time or the hundredth, I would write in big red letters across those lenses the word *symbols*. Everything we see in the temple, we should see with that idea in mind. The Lord has chosen to teach his children in the temple primarily through symbols. But in our culture and in our world, we are not particularly symbol-oriented people. We like prose, well-measured sentences laid out so that we can't misunderstand them, sentences with only one very logical and easy-to-assimilate meaning. We are not particularly enthusiastic about poetry. Poetry uses fewer words, and so the words must mean more. The words don't have to be particularly logical. They may have multiple layers of meaning. They can be viewed with different eyes, can mean different things to different people. Many Church members prefer the Doctrine and Covenants because it lays out the doctrines so clearly, line upon line, that it is hard to misunderstand them. Many of us struggle with the Old Testament, which is a little more difficult. First of all, it is longer. But it also has strange rituals and historical events that we sometimes can't figure out, and at the end are all those prophets who don't speak like prophets speak today. We prefer Nephi, whose "soul delighteth in plainness" (2 Nephi 25:4). We don't like Isaiah, who is much more difficult and who paints word pictures. The temple, however, is more poetry than prose, more Old Testament than Doctrine and Covenants, and more Isaiah than Nephi. If we are to understand it, we have to train ourselves to learn through that unique way the Lord has chosen to teach us in his house.

Why does he choose to teach us this way? The primary reason may be that symbols can mean different things to different people at different stages of their life. In the temple we receive an *endow*ment, a particular kind of gift. If I gave an endowment of five million dollars to a university, the university couldn't spend the five million dollars. They could spend only the interest that that money generated. How long would my gift continue giving and blessing the university and the students who went there? Forever. The temple endowment is similar. The symbols—the ceremony, the ordinances, the narrative— are the original gift, and because they can suggest different things to the mind, they continue to generate interest.

The endowment is like the five barley loaves that Jesus used to feed the five thousand. This wonderful story can help us understand the power of the temple. When Jesus first asked for the five loaves, the apostles could not conceive of how he could feed so many with such a small amount of bread. But he had them sit down on the grass, and he blessed the bread, broke it into pieces, and began to distribute it. As the apostles distributed it, the scriptures say, everyone could eat as much as they wanted until they were filled. Afterward twelve baskets of fragments were left over (see Mark 6:37–44). The endowment is like five barley loaves. We might not understand all that it can feed us the first time we see it, but we can eat as much as we will and be filled, and there will always be twelve baskets left over to feast on again and again. There will always be more to learn when you have finished feasting than you thought was there the first time you looked.

The Lord helps us to learn in his house. He prepares and guides us in a number of ways. Let me suggest four of those ways.

First, before we ever go to the temple, we are familiar with ordinances that have multiple layers of meaning—that are symbolic. The sacrament is a symbolic ordinance; baptism also is a symbolic ordinance—outward actions suggest inner truths. There really isn't a whole lot about a little piece of bread and a little cup of water that suggests to us a man's body or blood, but because the Savior told us what they should suggest to our minds and symbolize to our souls, we see past the everyday image, the symbol, to the reality that it represents. If you didn't know much about Christianity and you walked into a Latter-day Saint chapel and saw people sitting quietly, taking little pieces of bread and little drinks of water, you might think that is a strange way to feed people. When my daughter Megan was about four, she thought the sacrament bread was food. She was hungry, so she took a whole handful. We said, "No, Megan, just one piece," and she said, "Why?" And we answered, "Because there has to be enough for everybody." She accepted that until the deacons lined up, and they had bread left in the trays. Then she stood up on the bench, put her hands on her hips, and with great indignation declared, "They have lots left." She was too young to see past the symbol to the beauty and power of what it represents.

Baptism demonstrates in a wonderful way how an outward ordinance can suggest many different things. If I ask what baptism suggests to the mind, some might say, "A bath. It's a cleansing bath; our sins are washed away in the waters of baptism." Would we agree with that symbolism? We have to because it's in the scriptures (see, for example, D&C 39:10). Others might say, "To me baptism is a birth. The font is the womb, and the person being baptized is like a baby in its mother's womb in water. Just before the baby is born, the water breaks, and the baby comes out of the water, born into the newness of life, innocent. So, too, we arise out of the waters of baptism into newness of life." Would we agree with that symbolism? We have to; it's in the scriptures (see, for example, Moses 6:59). Somebody else might say, "Baptism suggests just the opposite to me. Baptism is a burial, and the font is the grave. We take the old man of sin, the natural man, and we put him off. As Paul says, we've crucified him. We bury him in the waters of baptism and resurrect a whole new being. So baptism is a burial and the font is the grave." Would we agree with that symbolism? We have to because that also is in the scriptures (see, for example, Romans 6:4; Colossians 2:12). What is baptism? Is it a bath, a birth, or a burial? It is all of them. In a similar way, the symbols in the temple may have many layers of meaning to suggest different and powerful truths to different people.

The second way the Lord prepares us to learn in his house is through the scriptures. Just as all three of those meanings of baptism are explained in the scriptures, so, for almost every symbol you encounter in the temple, verses of scripture will unlock some of its meanings. Sometimes as you sit in the temple being part of a session, a ceremony, or an ordinance, a verse of scripture will rise in your mind. The Holy Ghost will bring it into your thoughts, and you will say, "Ahh, now I know a meaning for that particular symbol."

The scriptures are full of symbolic language. Discussing scriptural meanings, we can practice learning the language of symbols. So even though I can't talk about the symbols or the narrative of the temple outside the temple, I can talk about Moses and the Exodus. The story of Moses leading the children of Israel out of Egypt into the promised land was designed by the Lord to be studied and applied exactly the same way the temple narrative is designed to be studied and applied. Everything that happened to the children of Israel I am to apply to my life. I must be led across the wilderness of life to the promised land of the celestial kingdom and cross the River Jordan, or the veil, to get there. In the wilderness I must feast daily on manna, the word of the Lord. I will be led across that wilderness by Moses, a prophet, and by the pillar of fire, the Holy Ghost, who will be there day and night to lead me always. I will go to Mount Sinai, the mountain of the Lord, there to receive his law and to meet with him. What's our Mount Sinai? The temple. In this way the scriptures, especially the Old Testament, give us the opportunity to practice with symbolic language and find deeper and deeper levels of meaning and application.

The Lord suggests that to us in the temple. In an ordinance room, what do you look at all through a session? The altar. And what sits on the altar? The scriptures. That's a hint. And do the ordinance workers hold them up occasionally? That's a bigger hint—that the meanings and the power behind so much of what we do in the temple will be found in the holy scriptures. It is also a suggestion, because an altar is a place of gift giving and offerings, that one of the greatest gifts God gives to us is the scriptures. His gift to us lies on the altars of the temple, and we also go to those same altars to give our gifts back to him.

There is a third way that the Lord helps us learn in the temple. Some of the symbols in the temple are very easy to understand. With a little thought, anybody can get them. Everybody wears white. What does that suggest? Purity. Can it also suggest equality in the sight of God? Can it also suggest that as white is a reflection of all the colors of the rainbow, all the beautiful spectrum, so too must my life, now that I have been to the Lord's house, reflect all the colors, all the spectrum, of God's gospel light? Mirrors in the temple face one another. What do they suggest? Eternity. For many years I went to the temple, looked down those mirrors in one direction, and thought, *This is my eternal past; I have always existed.* And I looked down the other way and thought, *This is my eternal future; I will always exist. This is eternity, and everything God does is eternal.* But it is dangerous to stop thinking about a symbol, or ever to think you know all of what it means. Symbols in the temple *mean,* and even the most simple symbols may have different, profound lessons at different times.

Let me give you an example. I was doing baptisms for the dead in the Jordan River Temple several years ago, and I was standing in the font with one of my children. I was waiting my turn. In the Jordan River Temple, mirrors surround the font. From the font I could look down those eternal mirrors and think about my ancestors who were being vicariously baptized. A verse of scripture came into my mind: "It is sufficient to know . . . that the earth will be smitten with a curse unless there is a welding link of some kind or other between the fathers and the children, upon some subject or other—and behold what is that subject? It is the baptism for the dead" (D&C 128:18). The words *welding link* reminded me of a chain. As I looked down those mirrors, the Spirit whispered, "You are looking at the chain." I thought about that. I looked down the mirrors again. You know, it does look like a chain. Each little box, each little reflection, is hooked to another. If I were looking at the chain between the fathers and the children, then who would be in the next link, the next box, the next reflection? My parents. And the next one, my grandparents, and then my great-grandparents, and so on. And each box would fan out too, in a sense. Who, then, is in the next link behind me? My children and then my grandchildren, and then my great-grandchildren, and so on. Then this thought hit me. I looked up the mirror at my ancestors, and who did I see inside of them, inside every link? I saw myself in my ancestors. And if they looked from their position up the chain down to my link, whom would they see in me? They would see themselves. If I were to look in my children, whom would I see in them? And if they were to look back into mine, who would they see in me? Themselves. When that thought hit, another verse of scripture came into mind: "I and my father are one. I am in my father and my father is in me" (see D&C 50:43). Why can I do work for my twelfth great-grandfather? I am in him and he is in me. That is why I can do the work for him—because we are one. And that is why Jesus speaks for the Father as though he were the Father. That is why I can do work for my ancestors as though I were my ancestors: I am in them and they are in me and we are one. Even the most simple symbols of the temple may hold beautifully profound truths personally for us. This personal truth made baptism for the dead a very wonderful thing for me.

A fourth way the Lord helps us learn is through levels of difficulty in the symbols of the temple. Because some symbols take more thought, more maturity, the Lord gives us at least one meaning for them as they are presented in the temple. In those cases, provided both a meaning and the symbol, we can see how the meaning arises naturally out of the symbol.

Other symbols in the temple are very difficult to understand, and the Lord doesn't tell us what they mean. We just see and experience them. But he says to us, in effect, "Before you came to the temple, I gave you symbolic ordinances with multiple layers of meaning. I've given you the scriptures, which contain symbolic language, verses, and ideas that will open up the symbols of the temple. I've given you some symbols that are very easy to understand. With a little thought, anybody can derive something from them. And I've given you some symbols that are more difficult, that require more maturity for understanding, but I've told you what they mean so you can compare the meaning with the symbol. In some cases I've given you more than one meaning for a symbol. Do you understand now how I teach in my house? You can spend the rest of your life on an adventure of discovery and revelation unveiling all the beautiful truths that lie behind the many and varied symbols of the temple."

We can be assured that everything in the temple is beautiful. If a symbol or anything in the house of the Lord has ever troubled you in any way, or if you have attached a meaning to any symbol in the temple that bothers you or makes you feel demeaned in any way, you will know you do not correctly understand the symbol. You did not get that meaning in the temple because everything in the temple is affirming and beautiful. When we come to understand the beauty and the power behind the symbols of the temple, we will always say, "Ahh, that is beautiful. Now I understand. That is beautiful and edifying and powerful." There is nothing that is not beautiful in any aspect of the Lord's ceremonies, and he wants us to understand what they mean.

Everything in the temple can teach us. Everything. The colors. Have you noticed how some temples get lighter and lighter as you move through? What can that teach? Think of the architecture, the clothing, the words, the actions, what we see, what we do, what we hear. Even the exterior can have symbolic significance. Next time you drive by the Salt Lake Temple, for instance, take off the spires in your mind. If you imagine the pointed parts gone, what remains seems to be a castle, a medieval fortress. The temple is also a house of refuge, protection, and safety. The very shape of the building suggests that to our minds, as it no doubt did to our pioneer ancestors who had fled persecution.

We can't talk outside the temple about many of the symbols of the temple and how they can teach. But a few architectural symbols are appropriate to talk about outside the temple. About every other year the *Ensign* prints pictures of the sealing rooms in various temples. When we go into a sealing room, we want to learn. The main teacher in the temple is the Spirit, but it is completely appropriate to sit down with our spouse, our parents, or our friends in the celestial room and in a reverent and a quiet tone share insights with one another or ask questions. The scriptural phrase, "He that hath ears to hear, let him hear" (Mark 4:9) does not mean that if you can figure it out all by yourself, go ahead. The expression means that those who have ears to hear—who *want* to hear—*may* hear. Every time Jesus was asked by his disciples what one of his parables meant, for instance, he told them what it meant. It is proper and appropriate to share and to want to know what is behind those symbols, remembering that the Spirit is the primary teacher.

When I look around a sealing room, I first notice the altar. What can the altar teach me? The Spirit begins to work with my mind. "What do you do at altars?"

"Well, I got married there."

"Good, I'm glad that you remember that. What else? In the scriptures, what did they do at altars?"

"They sacrificed, they gave gifts, they made offerings."

And the Spirit whispers, "Well, what gifts, what offerings, what sacrifice, what did you lay on the altar when you knelt with your spouse?"

I ponder and I reflect and I realize: I gave myself. I put myself on that altar, and my wife gave herself. We exchanged gifts with each other, and we accepted each other's gifts. And then we joined hands; we laid our hands on the altar. In that action we gave ourselves, as a couple, the two of us, to God and to his great work. Then we learned what that great work was, and we also learned what blessings and promises would be ours if we were faithful. Temple workers didn't tell us that. The altar told us that.

What's the second most prominent thing in a sealing room? Mirrors and a chandelier. I look at that chandelier and think, *What can that teach me?* It's almost too big for the room, isn't it? It hangs down low over the altar, over the couple that kneels. I begin to ponder, and the Spirit says, "What is associated with light in the scriptures?" Truth, the Spirit, the Savior. I stand up. I take my wife's hand. We look down the mirrors, and what do we notice going with us right down eternity? That chandelier. And the Spirit seems to say, "You must take me with you. You must walk always with the truth, with the Spirit, with the Savior. We will light your way to eternity. Never, never move out from under the chandelier."

I was standing in front of the mirrors once, bobbing and weaving to get a better look. It seemed an exercise in futility, and I thought, *I wish I could take myself right out of the mirrors and still stand in front of them. I could see eternity a lot better, but I keep getting in the way.* The Spirit whispered, "Truer words were never spoken." I was a bishop at the time, counseling couples with marriage problems, as most bishops do. When that thought hit me, I wanted to bring every couple from my ward that was struggling with a marriage—and those who weren't—into that room and stand them in front of the mirror, side by side, and say, "Can you see what the problem is? Do you understand? One of you or both of you are so focused on yourselves that you can no longer see eternity. The bigger you are in the mirrors, the less of eternity you can see. But if you look at a chandelier, or if you look at your wife, if you look away from yourself, you see much, much farther." No one teaches us that. The mirrors teach us that. Everything in the temple can teach us.

In 3 Nephi 17:2–3, we find a formula for temple worship. It isn't specifically designated as a formula for temple worship, but it serves wonderfully as one. Jesus has spent the day with the Nephites, and they are tired. They've listened a long time and heard a great deal, ending with Isaiah and Micah. Now Isaiah and Micah in the morning are tough, but they are even more difficult when the mind is tired. So Christ is going to come back the next day, and he'll go over those same verses two more times to make sure the people understand. But as he looks around, he realizes that they're just not grasping everything, and so he says, "I perceive that ye are weak, that ye cannot understand all my words which I am commanded of the Father to speak unto you at this time."

Do you feel that way after attending the temple? I still feel that way. I say, "Father, I am weak. I don't understand it all."

And he says, "That's okay. You were never supposed to understand it all at once. This is supposed to feed you for a lifetime. There will always be twelve baskets left over. Don't feel guilty," he says. "Don't think, *I'm the dumbest person here. Everybody understands here but me.*" On the other hand, he

293

also says, "Don't be apathetic. Don't stop going, or don't just go and sleep."

Instead, he instructs us to do five things. All five of them are in the third verse. "Therefore, go ye unto your homes." We say, "Lord, we can do that." The problem is that we do number one and that's it. We just go home. But the power is in two, three, four, and five.

So, what's the second thing? "And ponder upon the things which I have said." Ponder. If I want to ponder the scriptures, I can pull them out and read them again and again and go back and reread, look at individual words, and see how maybe one word in verse 5 matches a word in verse 20. I can really go over it. But I can't do that in the temple. I can't even take a little pencil to just write down a few thoughts. To effectively ponder the temple, I must have these things in my mind. The only way to do that is by consistent attendance. Some of us can get there quickly; others have to travel farther. But I believe the Lord will bless us according to our ability to go. Those who cannot go as frequently will have increased capacity to understand, if they go as often as they can. I ponder in my mind the phrases and actions and the things that I see and do.

The third thing the Savior tells us to do is this: "Ask of the Father, in my name, that ye may understand." I pray: "Father in Heaven, I'm going to the temple today. Why do we do this? What is the meaning and the significance of this thing?" When I first went to the temple, I thought some of the symbols were strange. That's the word I would have used then. Today I would use the words *unique* and *different*. It took me a while to realize that in God's great wisdom, he made the temple symbols unique and different. By their very nature they demand of us that we ask the questions the Lord wants us to ask. The first time I went to the temple, I thought, *Why do we do that? What is the meaning of this? Why is this significant?* These are the very questions the Lord wants us to ask. The danger is not that we will ask the questions; the danger is that we will become so familiar with the symbols that we will stop asking questions. We need to continue to ask the Father to help us learn.

The fourth thing to do is "prepare your minds for the morrow." How do we prepare our minds to receive revelation, remembering that the Spirit is the primary teacher in the temple and revelation is the primary mode of instruction? What prepares our mind to receive it? Let me give you a thought. I am a teacher by profession, but even if you're not a professional teacher, this Church is a church of teachers. You don't get out of the Church without teaching. What is irresistible to a teacher? Hungry students who sit at the edge of their chairs, looking, scriptures open, and saying, "Teach me." For those students you would open your soul. You want to give them everything you've ever thought or known. When Jesus came to the earth, what did he come as? A teacher. What is irresistible to him? Hungry students.

On the other hand, how do you feel as a teacher when you enter a classroom and the people are staring off in all directions, looking around, reading something else, or dozing? You want to get the lesson over with soon. You don't give as much of yourself. So, one of the best ways to prepare our minds to receive revelation is to go to the temple hungry to learn. Then we are irresistible to the teacher of the temple. Little by little he will open things to our minds. The Lord uses "teacher" words in the temple right at the beginning. He says "be alert"—that's a teacher word—and "attentive"—that's a teacher word—and "reverent." Those are teacher words, and if we're alert and attentive and reverent, we begin to learn.

The fifth and final part of our formula is "and I come unto you again." Go back to the temple. He will be there again. He will not cease to teach and instruct. That's the formula: "Go home, ponder, pray, prepare, return." So, the second time I'll understand it all? No. I'm still weak. "That's okay," the Spirit whispers. "Go home, ponder, pray, prepare, return." And as we do that time and again, to quote Ezekiel, the waters of under-standing begin to rise.

My favorite scripture on the temple is in Ezekiel 47. Ezekiel sees in vision the temple that will one day be built in Jerusalem. When it's all finished, he is brought around to the east doors (because the temple faces the east). The first verse says, "He brought me again unto the door of the house; and, behold, waters issued out from under the threshold of the house eastward: for the forefront of the house stood toward the east, and the waters came down from under from the right side of the house, at the south side of the altar" (v. 1). A spring of water bubbles up right at the east doors of the temple. We have water in front of many of our temples—reflecting pools. Every time you see that water, please think of Ezekiel 47.

The water in Ezekiel's vision of the temple forms a river that flows down eastward into the Judean wilderness. Ezekiel returns to the bank of the river and finds "very many trees on the one side and on the other" (Ezekiel 47:7). The water goes into the Judean wilderness and then empties into the Dead Sea. Everywhere the water flows in the Judean wilderness, it cuts a swath of green through the desert. Everywhere water flows, life springs up. He says in verses 8 and 9: "These waters issue out toward the east country, and go down into the desert, and go into the sea: which being brought forth into the sea, the waters shall be healed. And it shall come to pass, that every thing that liveth, which moveth, whithersoever the rivers shall come, shall live: and there shall be a very great multitude of fish, because these waters shall come thither: for they shall be healed; and every thing shall live whither the river cometh."

When I read those words, the Spirit whispers this thought: "That which will one day be temporally true of my house in Jerusalem, is spiritually true now of all my temples." Out from the east doors of the Jordan River Temple, where I go most fre-quently, is a river of water. It is not a river you see with the eyes, but it is there nonetheless. It will do two things: give life and heal everything it touches—our families, our friendships, our bruised and broken hearts battered by the trials of life. Nephi tells us that the fountain of living water is the love of God (see 1 Nephi 11:25). The river that flows from the temple is a river of light, truth, and power, but primarily it is a river of love; it will heal and give life to everything.

How deep is the river? That depends on how often you wade into it. In Ezekiel 47:3, Ezekiel walks down the river a thousand cubits and wades into ankle-deep waters. That's not very deep. But on a hot summer day, even ankle-deep water is refreshing, healing, life-giving. Even ankle deep, the power of the temple is refreshing and life-giving. The message is, Don't leave the river. Walk down another thousand cubits and wade in again. In verse 4, Ezekiel wades in, and this time it is to the knees. He says, in effect, "Don't leave the river. Walk down the bank farther, and wade in again." This time it is to the loins, the waist. And I love verse 5. He measures another thousand cubits down the river bank, and "it was a river that I could not pass over." The river was over his head now, "for the waters were risen, waters to swim in, a river that could not be passed over." He could now immerse himself in that wonderful, life-giving, healing river of light and love that flows from our Father's house. One day, the combined rivers from all the temples dedicated in all the lands will bathe this world in light and love and healing.

In your Martha-and-Mary life, in your careful, troubled, cumbered, and compassionate life of service that is so pleasing to God, occasionally take time to sit quietly at the feet of the Savior at rest and be taught. Remember it is needful, it is healing and life-giving, to sit quietly at the feet of the Lord in the temple and be taught by the Spirit. And when you attend a temple dedication and are invited to rise and shout and wave, may you rise and shout with all your soul that great expression of joy and triumph. Then another river begins to flow, and healing and learning and protection and order and prayer and

297

fasting and all the other blessings of the temple are made available to more people. May you love the temple.

NOTE

1. "The Spirit of God," *Hymns* (Salt Lake City: The Church of Jesus Christ of Latter-day Saints, 1985), no. 2.

OF BECOMING

NANCY BAIRD

The south wind wicks the mountain road,
carrying the storm on its back.
Wild oak rattles and groans, drowning
out the river.
It is comforting, how the earth sleeps—
the ferocious energy of becoming
turning to air, rousing
great clouds of starlings,
moving storms through a slippery sky.

Long ago as he died, Rachmaninoff mourned
his giant hands: "Farewell,
my dear hands, farewell," he murmured,
committing them to memory.
All we can do is remember
the ground will not consume us,
instead will take the broken flesh,
catapult the residue
as a whirlwind out of the south.

In the bitter months
we are tempted to grieve for better days—
a landscape of brightness and extravagance,

Nancy Hanks Baird was named Utah Poet of the Year in 1996. She received her bachelor's
degree in English from Brigham Young University and has worked as a freelance writer
and editor. She and her husband, John K. Baird, are the parents of five children.

the earth unbearably green—
better than this dragging, tiresome
desolation.
But I say, he was never so alive
as when going into death, clinging
to his hands,
he let them go.
In one shuddering instant
he could really play; learned
that by the breath of God
frost is given.

Out of the south cometh the whirlwind: and cold out of the north. By the breath of God frost is given: and the breadth of the waters is straitened.

—Job 37:9, 10

JESUS, THE VERY THOUGHT OF THEE

ANN N. MADSEN

I am convinced that the very thought of Jesus can change us. Let me explain.

In the spring of 1988 I had a unique experience. I was invited to teach the life of Christ in a classroom on the shores of the Sea of Galilee. For a year at the BYU Jerusalem Center I had been teaching indirectly of Christ in the Old Testament, but now I was to teach of his life directly. I had little time, and I knew I must prepare.

I sensed that this would be one of the most important experiences of my life. And it was. From the time I awoke each morning until I slept each night I was focused on Jesus Christ. There were ways in which I felt that I knew him there for the first time, though I already knew how it felt to love him.

When my two weeks of round-the-clock preparing and teaching ended, I wrote in my journal: "As I sit here I recall the glorious hours of study I spent . . . in a small, pre-fab cabin [which became a holy place to me]. . . . I spent every waking hour earnestly preparing and alternately gazing out our picture window at the many moods of this lake. I was filled almost continually with a spirit which is difficult to describe. I was *immersed* in the study of Christ's life—so much of which was lived nearby.

Ann N. Madsen, an Isaiah scholar and poetess, has taught ancient scripture at Brigham Young University for more than twenty years. She and her husband, Truman, are the parents of three children and a Navajo foster son. They are the grandparents of sixteen.

"I knelt each dawn before that picture window—before His sea—to plead for His Spirit to direct and organize my study efforts that day. Three hours each morning I would teach. Each time I felt helped. . . . As I look back, I realize how profoundly my understanding was enhanced and my soul expanded. The in-depth study of Jesus was a monumental, marathon task and remains unfinished. I must do much more!" I realize now that it will only be finished when I meet Him face to face.

My ten- to twelve-hour study days on the shores of the Galilee changed me forever. I could identify with Nephi when he exclaimed: "We are made alive in Christ because of our faith. . . . And we talk of Christ, we rejoice in Christ, we preach of Christ" (2 Nephi 25:25–26). I had come to know Jesus in new ways.

I know you cannot travel to Israel to duplicate my Galilee experience. How I wish you could! But just as surely as he walked that shore and that I traced his footsteps there nearly two thousand years later, you must have your own sweet encounters with Jesus Christ. Your experience will differ from mine. You must find him in your own way and in your own place. The gateway to such an experience is the scriptures.

You remember when he walked on that water and beckoned to Peter. "It is I," he said, "be not afraid." And Peter answered him, "If it be thou, bid me come unto thee." And Jesus said, "Come" (Matthew 14:27–29).

So many times he has bidden us to come.

In latter-day scripture he invites us: "Learn of me, and listen to my words; walk in the meekness of my Spirit, and you shall have peace in me. I am Jesus Christ; I came by the will of the Father, and I do his will" (D&C 19:23–24).

He invites us to come to him, walk with him, to remember him in all the moments of our lives. "Look unto me in every thought; doubt not, fear not" (D&C 6:36). I know that that remembering, promised each time we take the sacrament, adds his power to our resolve. Thus we grow towards receiving his "image in [our] countenances" (Alma 5:14), and, over time, a mighty change can take place in our hearts.

We can only remember someone we have known. "For how knoweth a man the master whom he has not served, and who is a stranger unto him, and is far from the thoughts and intents of his heart?" (Mosiah 5:13). It was my new discoverings about Jesus through study and prayer near Galilee which gave me so much more to remember.

I remember his finding moments to be alone. I remember his weeping. I remember his healing—always healing. I remember how he met temptation and paid no heed to it. I remember how he urges us to be one. I remember how he gave himself over and over again and finally completely. I remember how he called the children to him and blessed them. In all these rememberings, I find indelibly in my heart the memory of his unfailing, everlasting love, his tenderness and caring. All were alike to him. No matter where you find yourself at this moment, he loves you. He loves each of us.

Six hundred years before Jesus was born on this earth, he told Jeremiah: "Ye shall seek me, and find me, when ye shall search for me with all your heart. And I will be found of you" (Jeremiah 29:13–14).I know we can trust that promise. Let us search together, remembering how he lived, and examine the ways we can trace his steps.

JESUS HAD MOMENTS ALONE TO THINK, TO PRAY

I remember how Jesus made time to be alone, to pray. So can we. I learned some of that on the shores of Galilee: "And he said unto them, Come ye yourselves apart into a desert place, and rest a while: for there were many coming and going, and they had no leisure so much as to eat. And they departed into a [solitary] place" (Mark 6:31–32; JST Mark 6:32–33).

We can identify with dashing around in our busy lives, having no leisure so much as to eat, can't we? But how can we ever learn to be like him if we only wave as we pass? Jesus often pulled away to rest and pray: forty days in the Judean desert after his baptism; all night before he called his apostles; later on a high mountain with Peter, James, and John; and finally in Gethsemane.

Such rest and prayer time require privacy. These moments can be sliced out of our busy days. This kind of communing is more than just reaching up; it is our bright awareness of his reaching down. Isaiah describes this over and over: "His hand is stretched out still"; and the Book of Mormon echoes: "Mine arm is lengthened out all the day long" (2 Nephi 28:32; Isaiah 5:25; 9:12). He constantly reaches for us. We need only look up and take his hand. Remember, Jesus said, "It is I; be not afraid. . . . Come!" (Matthew 14:27–29).

When can we pull away for time with our Father? Where is our "place apart"?

You are the only one who can answer that. But he has given all of us a precious time. It has been there all along. Remember? "Remember the sabbath day, to keep it holy" (Exodus 20:8). He himself rests and on the Sabbath invites us to join him.

I love the Sabbath day. I learned to love it even more living among the Orthodox Jews in Jerusalem. It has been said that not only have the Jews kept the Sabbath but the Sabbath has kept the Jews. I felt a kind of holy envy for the quiet, kept Sabbaths I experienced living in Jerusalem. Judaism teaches that "the Sabbath itself is a sanctuary which we build, a sanctuary in time."[1]

I find it exciting to think of walling off that one day each week. (You can tell I don't have any little children at home, but you will all get to be my age some time.) We can wall off that day each week, like a building, a temple, and, after entering it, practice holiness in a day which was constructed for that very purpose.

When I awake early Sunday morning, I am thankful that somehow the day seems totally different to me. On my knees,

I take my gratitude, my sins, my petitions, my temptations, and my deepest desires to our Father with ample time before anyone in my household stirs.

Later, when I hear the words of the sacrament prayers spoken, my heart is prepared and waiting. These lines I wrote a few years ago express how I feel. I call it "The Sacrament Prayers":

> The words are repeated
> once again
> this sacred, Sabbath time.
> Words I can trace
> through the week
> but this time
> unique,
> spoken quietly
> in youthful
> intonation
> and the nourishment
> is proffered
> to me
> by a boy's hand
> in exchange
> for
> my changing.

I reach heavenward with all my heart and feel understood and loved. Suddenly, the burdens of the past week are gone or lightened. I feel fortified to meet the new week's challenges—fresh and clean.

We can each learn to build our own "sanctuar[ies] in time," even beyond Sunday. You must find time. It may be late into the night while you wait anxiously for your teenagers to come home. It may be just after your children leave for school. Start small. Take fifteen minutes before you tear into those items to be checked off on your list. It may be while you nurse the baby, which could be any time, night or day. It's your choice, but choose a time.

JESUS FORGAVE AND FORGIVES

One Sabbath in March 1994, I sat in our chapel waiting to partake of the sacrament. I remembered how Jesus forgave and forgives. I was deep in prayer when these *words* came to me with such clarity that I wrote them down. I keep them in my scriptures: "Forgiveness is one of our tasks as we partake of the sacrament. If we would be forgiven, we must, ourselves, forgive. To truly forgive, I must identify the hurt, the pain—honestly, not denying it—and then offer that pain as a willing sacrifice to God. Then it can disappear. Once I've given it away, my attitude toward the person who inflicted it is also changed; no grievance or wound remains, and he or she can be seen in a new Light. The other person need do nothing for this to happen. It is in my heart that the 'mighty change' can take place."

Three years later, almost to the day when I wrote those lines, I had a remarkable temple recommend interview with my bishop, which I recorded in my journal: "I had decided to ask his counsel as I tried to forgive someone for long-ago pain and hurt. I had the sense as I brought up the subject that the bishop was reaching up in prayer to know how to teach me." That was a wonderful awareness. I explained that even though the person had been dead for several years, I knew I couldn't ignore the problem any longer. He spoke with me of mercy, pity. I said I had tried to feel that and I was still trying.

"At one point he looked me straight in the eye and said that I should just *do it,* just let go and forgive, that I needn't keep trying but that I should just do it. It was like he opened a door for me and beckoned me to come through, not waiting a moment.

"Just before I left he said, 'Ann, you have been badly hurt and have been carrying that around with you all these years.'

[I remember thinking, compared to others', my hurt is small, but because I nurtured it, it has grown. In my mind I pictured a bundle of pain about the size of a basketball.] Just then he said, 'Throw it away!'" His words fit my imagery so perfectly that I figured I was in tune. Then he added, "'You say to yourself, "Someone should have to pay for this. It isn't fair." But, Ann, someone has paid for it.' I knew immediately that he meant the Savior, and I wondered how I had been so dense for so long, and I began to cry. I remembered the paper I had kept in my scriptures, my personal revelation, that I had been inspired to write down during that sacrament service in March of 1994, and I went home and reread it:

"Forgiveness is one of our tasks as we partake of the sacrament. If we would be forgiven, we must, ourselves, forgive. To truly forgive, I must identify the hurt, the pain . . . and then offer [it] as a willing sacrifice to God. . . . It is in my heart that the 'mighty change' can take place."

The Lord had told me once, all by myself, sitting, waiting to partake of his sacred sacrament. Then the bishop received the same message to give to me again. This time I could hear and understand. How patiently God ministers to us in our need, quietly repeating over and over again, until we have ears to hear and hearts broken enough to understand.

How do we forgive those who we feel have sinned against us? A noted educator and friend, Dennis Rasmussen teaches us one way: "Evil multiplies by the response it seeks to provoke, and when I return evil for evil, I engender corruption myself. The chain of evil is broken for good when a pure and loving heart absorbs a hurt and forbears to hurt in return. . . . Deep within every child of God the Light of Christ resides, guiding, comforting, purifying the heart that turns to him."[2]

We can turn to him. We can join Christ in his merciful task of remembering sins no more.

JESUS CARED AND HEALED

I remember Jesus wept with the broken-hearted and healed the sick and the sorrowing. So can we. He wept, overlooking Jerusalem from the Mount of Olives. "O Jerusalem, Jerusalem, . . . how often would I have gathered thy children together, even as a hen gathereth her chickens under her wings, and ye would not!" (Matthew 23:37). What sadness he reflects in this lament! It is akin to his cry in Isaiah: "What could have been done more to my vineyard, that I have not done in it?" (Isaiah 5:4).

On the other side of the Mount of Olives, he wept with his dear friends Mary and Martha just before he raised their brother, Lazarus. Before the miracle he wept with them in their sorrow, in their pain. We can do that.

I remember Jesus healing, always healing. He went about healing, not hurting. He was sensitive to those who surrounded him, sometimes crowding so closely that he might have felt smothered. He took those who came to him by their hands and lifted them up. The crowds that swirled around him always included those coming to be healed—the sick, the lame— whom some perceived as ugly, stinking, and misshapen. He did not recoil from them.

What did he see? He saw the beauty of the human spirit in those who were unwhole, unfinished. We can pray to see as he sees. "Be thou whole," he said (see John 5:6). He comes, indeed, with the power to make us whole. He healed sickness and sin interchangeably. When the leper called out to him, "If thou wilt, thou canst make me clean," he touched the untouchable and answered, "I will; be thou clean!" (Matthew 8:2–3).

Such sweet patterns of compassion for us to follow. Healing defines Jesus' mission. He has delegated his gentle, healing priesthood power to the men among us so that they might join him in fashioning *his* miracles, implementing *his* will, anointing all of us to wholeness. He asks us, as women, to follow him and to do as he did. We were born with the capacity to heal and soothe and lift, to "succor the weak" (D&C 81:5). How often we sense the need to soothe those around us! We know almost instinctively how to minister and heal through our loving touch. Every woman has knelt at the side of a child, perhaps not her own, to "kiss a hurt better." It works. Why? Is it because feeling loved makes everything feel better?

Even a tiny girl knows the secret. Our youngest daughter, when she was about two years old, caught her hand in our old Ironrite as the motor was on and the roller was rolling. Her tiny hand was badly friction burned. As I heard her cry and ran to free her hand and gather her up in my arms, I wept as I saw the wound and blamed myself for her pain. I rushed her to a basin and ran cold water over the burn, all the time sobbing until I became aware that she wasn't crying but was wiping away my tears and whispering, "Don't cry, Mommy. Look, I'll kiss it better." And she did. So can we.

JESUS PAID NO HEED TO TEMPTATION

I remember how Jesus experienced temptation and paid no heed to it. He exemplified the counsel of James: "Submit yourselves therefore to God. Resist the devil, and he will flee from you" (James 4:7). We can learn to be drawn to righteousness, repelled by evil. Eventually we can lose all desire for sin. To do that we must educate our desires towards righteousness.

Jesus can help us in this, too. He taught us to pray with sincere intent: "Suffer [me] not to be led into temptation, but deliver [me] from evil" (JST Matthew 6:14). This is the decisive moment in our prayers when we ask to be led away from temptation and into righteousness. It is at this moment we make the decision to walk away from the darkness into his light.

"What we are speaking about," Elder Neal A. Maxwell has said, "is so much more than merely deflecting temptations for which we somehow do not feel responsible. Remember, . . . it is our own desires which determine the sizing and the attractiveness of various temptations. We set our [own] thermostats as to temptation."[3]

I know this is true. We may be enticed in opposite directions in a tug-of-war between light and darkness, but we are always the tie-breakers. Even when we can't see the light clearly, we can always move away from the darkness. As Elder Maxwell explains: "There remains an inner zone in which we are sovereign, unless we abdicate. In this zone lies the essence of our individuality and our personal accountability. Each assertion of a righteous desire, . . . however small . . . , adds to our spiritual momentum. . . . Our loving Lord will work with us, 'even if [we] can [do] no more than desire to believe,' providing we will 'let this desire work in [us]' (Alma 32:27)."[4] Thus, by educating the desires of our hearts, the battle can be won, sometimes even before we find ourselves muddied in the trenches.

"No one who understands the Savior's agony can think sin and error are overcome easily," observes Elder Jeffrey R. Holland. "But when we are making our best effort, that's when the angels come. Our success is as certain as it is difficult."[5] I know this is true; the angels do come. We receive tangible help.

JESUS PERSONIFIES LOVE

I remember that Jesus prayed for us to be one, to be bound to one another by love.

Satan seeks to isolate us, to separate us from God and each other, while Jesus taught us to be one, supporting one another in our feeblest attempts at godliness. "If ye are not one ye are not mine," he said (D&C 38:27).

We learn more about this unity in the temple and through kept covenants. Not long ago, on our way home from the cannery, Emily, our eldest daughter, shared a glorious idea with me about temple covenants. "When I am not in the temple," she said, "when I am just walking down the street, I pass by people who share my covenants. All over the world there are such people, millions of us. We may not speak of it. In fact, there is much of which I can never speak. But it is there, just the same, in my heart and in their hearts. I am never alone."

Our gracious God allows us to qualify through personal righteousness for these binding, eternal covenants. By kept covenants, we link our arms in a circle of righteousness, bound to each other and to God by love. This became so real to me a few weeks ago. Just after a baby had been blessed in our fast meeting, a sister in our ward stood to bear testimony that the circle of priesthood that had surrounded that infant symbolically formed a circle of protection against evil throughout that child's life. In my heart I echoed a resounding yes. I left that meeting to rush across town to be a witness as our grandson Robby was ordained a priest. Another circle formed around him. His two brothers, his father, who was also his bishop, and his grandfather (my husband) closed that circle, and his father began, "We, your family, lay our hands upon your head . . . " You can picture them, one hand on his head, one hand on a shoulder, forming a solid ring. For me it was symbolic of linking our arms in circles of righteousness, bound to each other with an unspoken covenant of love and support." Our families are linked forever by covenant.

Jesus taught us of the covenant of love. Jesus loves us, and he taught his apostles: "Love one another, as I have loved you" (John 15:12). How does his love differ from ours or from what we call love? It is pure and tender, totally sincere, gentle, without guile or artifice, no respecter of persons. Sometimes what we call love is demanding, dominating, or manipulative. But his is selfless; free of ego needs, facing outward, not inward; reaching always outward. Sometimes there are those around us whom we love less. We can learn to love them more.

JESUS GAVE HIS ALL

I remember how Jesus gave himself for us. He taught us about sacrifice and consecration based on a spirit of obedience.

Obedience is the one gift we can give God. The giving of it can eventually result in our will being swallowed up in his. Elder Neal A. Maxwell, speaking of consecration, taught us so memorably: "The submission of one's will is really the only uniquely personal thing we have to place on God's altar. . . . It is the only possession which is truly ours to give."[6]

Consecration is thus an expression of mature love. As I consecrate, I ask myself, What has the Lord blessed me with? How can I contribute these blessings to build his kingdom?

Once when I was studying Ephesians 5, I saw something I had not seen before. Paul was listing ways to come closer to God. "Submit to one another out of reverence for Christ" (New International Version, Ephesians 5:21). Then he writes of how husbands and wives are to give themselves: "Husbands, love your wives, just as Christ loved the church and gave himself up for [it]" (NIV Ephesians 5:25; "up" is in the original Greek). Giving ourselves up is the pattern we learn from Jesus.

This kind of giving or submitting is not "giving in," a situation in which one wins and one loses. It is giving oneself up. Can you see the difference?

How do we give ourselves up? One kindness at a time. Forgiving each offense as it occurs, or, better still, not taking offense. As Sister Elaine Jack taught us: "If people drop an offense, don't pick it up!"[7] We give ourselves up by looking outward more, inward less; losing our lives in the concerns of others, rather than our own; just letting go of our self-serving, proud impulses.

We live in a world which cries out to us constantly of our rights and entitlements, as if our only duty is to pamper ourselves. But we have the privilege of learning how much we can give, not how much we can take. "Freely ye have received, freely give," Christ counseled his apostles as he gave them power to heal and bless (Matthew 10:8). Is it not our goal to also heal and bless freely? And in the giving, never feel deprived, but rather blessed in offering each other our abundance. "There is enough and to spare" (D&C 104:17).

We give in many ways. "We can give anonymously, not letting our right hand know what our left hand is doing." But sometimes knowing who the giver is, is part of the gift. An attitude, a way of life, is hinted at here. A wonderful Hebrew word *hinunee* embodies this attitude. It is the common answer of prophets when the Lord calls them to be his messengers. Samuel said it. Isaiah said it. It means "Behold, here am I," with an understood component of "I am at your service. What will you have me do?" It includes the notion of "Thy will be done." Christ said it first, when he offered himself in the heavenly council to do for us what we could not do for ourselves. In answer to the Lord's question, "Whom shall I send, and who will go for us?" Isaiah said powerfully: "Here am I; send me" (Isaiah 6:8).

When I was fourteen years old, I learned a rhyme that I didn't know was quoting Isaiah and Jesus, although the compelling last line sounded very familiar:

> Let none hear you idly saying
> "There is nothing I can do,"
> While the souls of men are dying,
> And the Master calls for you.
> Gladly take the task he gives you.
> Let his work, your pleasure be.
> Answer quickly when he calls you,
> "Here am I; send me, send me!"[8]

JESUS SAID, "BEHOLD YOUR LITTLE ONES"

I remember how Jesus called the children to him and taught us to be like them.

Last Christmas our forty-year-old Navajo son came home for a wonderful reunion with our whole family. Since his last visit, we had added many nieces and nephews, some still toddlers, one already on a mission. As we sat together on Christmas Eve, he told us that he had been taught that all the children in his tribe were considered his sons and daughters and were never addressed as nieces or nephews. In his culture, the children were the teachers, and adults were to observe and learn from them. He had seen the family picture we'd sent each year, he said, and had come home to meet and learn from all his new "sons and daughters."

I wondered if his ancestors developed this belief by kneeling at the feet of Jesus, watching him bless the children. Trying to describe that transcendent scene, I wrote a poem called "Behold Your Little Ones":

> The children know.
> They gather in bright bouquets around Him.
> Baby fingers reach to touch Him,
> Tiny tendrils waving toward Him.
> They listen.
> Some not tall enough to see can hear.
> Hushed in unexpected silence they stand
> Stretching souls to listen.
> He stands, as if to go,
> But upturned flower faces hold Him fast,
> The power of their love a match for His;
> Innocent, untrammeled, full of faith,
> They hold Him fast.
> Flowers He cannot bruise,
> Flowers He must not lose
> When years trample their innocence.
> "Be like a child," the Savior said,
> Because
> The children know.

(3 Nephi 17:23)

Jesus directs us to observe our children so that we can be like them. What do they know that Jesus wants us to emulate? If you do not have children of your own, or if they are grown,

314

where do you find them to observe? We are all surrounded by children. Sometimes we don't notice them. Sometimes, even as their mothers, we don't notice them. They are in grocery stores, waiting in line, sitting in grocery carts near us. They stand next to us in elevators, sometimes dwarfed and scared as big bodies crowd around them. They are not far from us in sacrament meeting, tiny babes smiling at us over their father's shoulder even though they don't even know our names. They play on the street in front of our house or on our lawns or in our flowers.

Do we observe and learn from them every chance we get? Do we smile and offer to play a little in the grocery line or quietly take a tiny hand over the bench in sacrament meeting? When we find them muddied in our garden, do we help them pick a bouquet while watching for the qualities Jesus asked us to find? Did you ever notice how fasting produces childlike feelings, even beyond hunger?

All of us remain the children of a loving Father, born innocent and making our way through a wicked world, tried and tested and healed through faith and love, arriving at last, again, purified—childlike.

"Behold, what manner of love the Father hath bestowed upon us, that we should be called the [children] of God: therefore the world knoweth us not, because it knew him not. Beloved, now are we the [children] of God, and it doth not yet appear what we shall be: but we know that, when he shall appear, we shall be like him; for we shall see him as he is. And [everyone] that hath this hope in him purifieth himself, even as he is pure" (1 John 3:1–3).

We have promised to take upon us the name of Jesus Christ. What a seal on our lives. Sometimes we speak his name hurriedly, absent-mindedly, or simply by rote. Elder L. Edward Brown cautions us: "When we use these sacred words, 'in the name of Jesus Christ,' they are much more than a way to get out of a prayer, out of a testimony, or out of a talk. We are on holy ground. . . . We are using a name most sublime, most

315

holy, and most wonderful—the very name of the Son of God.
. . . This conclusion to the prayer may, in many ways, be the
most important part of the prayer."[9]

May I suggest that we use those moments when his name
is on our lips to pause, speak it slowly, and remember him as
you and I have just done, with great reverence and love.

> Jesus, the very thought of thee,
> With sweetness fills my breast,
> But sweeter far thy face to see
> And in thy presence rest.[10]

Gethsemane was Jesus' last "place apart" where he knelt
alone and cried out to his Father to be strengthened. One day
I was in the garden called Gethsemane all alone. I had a great
desire to kneel near where Jesus had knelt to speak my personal thanks for what he had suffered there. Amidst a flood of
thoughts of him, I remembered his inviting Peter to come to
him across the water and how at another time he promised that
when he had been lifted up, he would draw all of us unto him.

I knelt and prayed. It was a sacred moment; one I'll never
forget. Before leaving the garden, I wrote down the last words
of my prayer and realized it was a poem. I offer it to you as
my testimony.

BENEATH THE VIOLET WINDOWS—GETHSEMANE

> Dear Lord Jesus,
> Thou who lovest
> The people of the Mosque,
> Who would have gathered
> The people of the synagogue,
> Whose arms continue open
> To each saffron-robed monk
> And searching nun,
> Lord of the children
> And the childlike,

Pulled by thy love,
Seized by thy suffering,
Drawn to thee
By everlasting cords,
I come!

NOTES

1. Abraham Joshua Heschel, *The Sabbath: Its Meaning for Modern Man* (1951, 1986), 29.

2. Dennis Rasmussen, *The Lord's Question* (Provo: Keter Foundation, 1985), 63–64.

3. Neal A. Maxwell, in Conference Report, October 1996, 27; or "'According to the Desire of [Our] Hearts,'" *Ensign,* November 1996, 23.

4. Maxwell, in Conference Report, October 1996, 26.

5. Jeffrey R. Holland, address to prospective missionaries (Provo: Brigham Young University, 6 November 1996); used by permission.

6. Neal A. Maxwell, in Conference Report, October 1995, 30; or "Swallowed up in the Will of the Father," *Ensign,* November 1995, 24.

7. Elaine L. Jack, "Spiritual Maturity," *Clothed with Charity: Talks from the 1996 Women's Conference,* ed. Dawn Hall Anderson, Susette Fletcher Green, and Dlora Hall Anderson (Salt Lake City: Deseret Book, 1997), 50.

8. Anonymous.

9. L. Edward Brown, in Conference Report, April 1997; or "Pray unto the Father in My Name," *Ensign,* May 1997, 79.

10. "Jesus, the Very Thought of Thee," *Hymns* (Salt Lake City: The Church of Jesus Christ of Latter-day Saints, 1985), no. 141.

The original presentation of this essay is available on audiocassette from Deseret Book or on the Internet at http://coned.byu.edu/cw/womens.htm

ON YOUR RIGHT HAND AND ON YOUR LEFT

HEIDI SWINTON

I grew up wanting to write for *Newsweek* magazine. When I headed east to graduate school in journalism, I recognized that graduate school was the door to writing the big stories, the important ones, the cover stories with the bylines in bold type. I loved the business of reporting: the pace, the research, and the writing of the articles. I had been enrolled only three days in one of the country's most prestigious journalism programs when I knew I had done the wrong thing.

It took months for me to muster the courage to abandon that direction. I now look back and see the Lord's hand clearly shaping another way.

Today, I write about people in the Church, about our history, our leaders, our prophets' teachings, our beliefs, and our experiences. Despite my earlier aspirations, much of what I do has no byline at all. But when you are writing the Church story, that doesn't matter. You aren't writing alone or for you. This is the Church of Jesus Christ, and he has promised, "I will be on your right hand and on your left, and my Spirit shall be in your

Heidi S. Swinton, a graduate of the University of Utah, has written, compiled, and contributed to many books on Church subjects. She and her husband, Jeffrey, are the parents of four sons. She serves as a member of the Melchizedek Priesthood/Relief Society writing committee.

hearts, and mine angels round about you, to bear you up" (D&C 84:88).

What a promise to a writer! That the Lord will be with you—on your right hand, on your left. And in your heart! No newsroom, no byline or cover story could ever compare with that assurance and association.

The Church story is told in both true accounts and in fictional narratives. The challenge to writing the Church story in fiction is to be believable. The challenge for writing the Church story factually is to be read. Many readers think that if the story is true, it's going to be boring. Not so. I have a greeting card that makes this point well. Greeting cards are sound-byte sermons. This one has a pioneer woman on the front, sitting in a wagon. She looks rumpled, worn-out. She's writing in what appears to be her journal: "I think it was one of my pioneering great-grand-mothers, on a trek across the Great Plains, who summed up my philosophy of life in a quote from her diary . . . "

The inside of the card reads: "June 14, 1847: Ate out again. It was good."

I believe that writing the Church story is not just writing history; it is writing truth expressed in the goodness of people's lives. It is teaching principles by example. It is weaving a thread, a teaching that is based on an experience or a commentary, expanding the concept with true teachings and scriptures, and then crafting a lesson on life. It is writing of hardship and great blessings, patience and obedience, righteous choices and personal testimony. Every era is a compilation of such mettle. For me the process begins often with a journal account, a description in a news article, or a letter.

Laleta Dickson, a member of the tragic Willie Handcart Company, is a great example. She wrote in her journal in 1856: "When morning came, Father's body, along with the others who had died during the night, was buried in a deep hole. . . . I can see my mother's face as she sat looking at the partly conscious group. Her eyes looked so dead that I was afraid.

319

She didn't sit long, however. . . . When it was time to move out, Mother had her family ready to go. She put her invalid son in the cart with her baby and we joined the train. Our mother was a strong woman, and she would see us through anything."[1]

We look around us today and see the Church story now cast in a different context. No handcarts or freezing feet forge their way to Zion, but the messages of faith and fortitude are the same.

A congregation of Saints on the plains of Paraguay lost their homes and all their belongings in a disastrous flooding of the Piclomayo River, which was followed by another. When the relief party from the area presidency's office arrived, one of the older sisters was offering this prayer: "Father, we have lost our beautiful chapel, we have lost our clothing, we no longer have homes, we have no food to eat, we don't have any materials to build anything, we have to walk ten kilometers to get a drink of dirty river water and we don't have a bucket. But we desire to express to thee our gratitude for our good health, for our happiness, and for our Church membership. Father, we want thee to know that under any conditions, we will be true, strong, and faithful . . . "[2]

One more story. A young man preparing to serve a mission was finishing up his year at college on a campus where he was the only Latter-day Saint. In a letter to his parents he expressed his feelings: "I've become so comfortable here with my friends and the goings-on that it will be hard to be uprooted, not knowing how things will be when I'm planted once again. . . . My friends will still be here at school—and they will change and grow over these next few years. So will I. But I'm going into a different greenhouse, being exposed to different light."[3]

I love the image he created. He wasn't writing for publication. He was writing home. The sister from Paraguay wasn't praying to be heard by mortal ears; she was praying to her Father. Their words are stirring. I can feel them, and as they are developed into a story, you can feel them, too.

When this young missionary, my son Cameron, returned home from his mission, he found that his friends at school had indeed moved on. But during the two years he was serving, he made a new Friend, described in Mosiah as "the light and the life of the world; yea, a light that is endless" (Mosiah 16:9).

That is the Church story.

These three accounts illustrate the power of true stories. You can't rewrite the opening or final scene of someone's life to make your point. In true stories, you can select material that supports the direction you are going, but you have to maintain the integrity of the experience. That's why true stories are so real—they're like our own lives. We can't make the story be the way we want; we have to accept the way it is. We have to find meaning and strength in reality. That's a powerful lesson, and all true stories teach it.

Look at the power of the true stories in the scriptures. Abinadi, Elizabeth, Hannah, Mary, Joshua, and Sariah teach us so much. I love the words of Caleb and Joshua, "Be strong and of a good courage" (Joshua 1:18) and of Mary, "Behold the handmaid of the Lord; be it unto me according to thy word" (Luke 1:38). They, too, are the Church story.

Let me share some things I have learned in the process of doing this singular form of writing. First, when we are writing the Church story, we must recognize that we are making an offering to the Lord. We are writing for the Lord's library. We are consecrating our gifts, our time, our heart, and our hands. I had to learn that lesson.

About twelve years ago, an experience helped me put my part in perspective. It was a Sunday, a great day. Deseret Book had just published a book of essays on the presidents of the Church edited by Leonard J. Arrington, former Church historian. I had written the chapter on Lorenzo Snow, and my name was right there on the cover to claim it; I was famous. I took my pen to Church, knowing that someone would want my autograph.

I had barely crossed the foyer when a ward member rushed up to me, holding out that familiar sack from Deseret Book. I could see a book inside. It was "my" book, and I beamed as I got ready to whip that pen out of my purse.

"Heidi," she said with a hint of expectation in her voice, "could you get Brother Arrington to sign this for me?"

That experience in the church lobby gave new meaning to this verse in the Doctrine and Covenants: "O ye that embark in the service of God, see that ye serve him with all your heart, might, mind and strength" (D&C 4:2).

It says nothing about signing your name.

Second, writing is a process. Writers are always in some phase of the writing process—drafting, researching, rewriting, editing, reworking, going to bed because it isn't working. Writing is a process, just as the life it describes is a process.

Writing in a journal is good practice, good training. It helps us to see the Lord's hand in our own lives, and that helps us to see how he touches others. My great-great-great-grandmother Bathsheba Smith kept a journal. Last year, when I was writing the PBS documentary *Trail of Hope,* I turned to Bathsheba's account of leaving Nauvoo to illustrate the tremendous faith of these Saints. She wrote: "We left a comfortable home, the accumulations of four years of labor and thrift and took away with us only a few much needed articles such as clothing, bedding, and provisions. We left everything else behind us for our enemies. My last act in that precious spot was to tidy the rooms, sweep up the floor, and set the broom in its accustomed place behind the door. Then with emotions in my heart which I could not now pen and which I then strove with success to conceal, I gently closed the door and faced an unknown future, faced a new life, a great destiny as I well knew, but I faced it with faith in God."[4]

Third, it's going to be hard. The heavens do not open and pour out manuscripts. If anything, writing about the Church and its members is the most difficult writing we will ever do.

It will also provide some of the sweetest, purest moments. Most of mine are recorded only in my journal. Still, the adversary will work overtime to distract us and discourage us. And we can expect many long days and long nights questioning our own ability—and our own inspiration.

In President Spencer W. Kimball's first general conference address in 1943, he described how he had struggled with his new assignment. When I was putting together the compilation *I Know That My Redeemer Lives: Testimonies of the Latter-day Prophets,* I found his account. It opened my understanding to this process. He had been called three months earlier to serve as an apostle, and in the long days and weeks before his first address at a conference, he "did a great deal of thinking and praying, and fasting and praying." He said, "There were conflicting thoughts that surged through my mind—seeming voices saying: 'You can't do the work. You are not worthy. You have not the ability'—and always finally came the triumphant thought: 'You must do the work assigned—you must make yourself able, worthy, and qualified.' And the battle raged on."[5]

Those words sit next to my computer screen on a now-battered Post-it note. His counsel—make yourself able, worthy, and qualified—has great significance. To write the Church story, we have to *merit* the Lord's being with us, on our right hand and on our left. We can't expect his guidance and inspiration if we aren't worthy. We can't take his help for granted. Nor can we expect to be successful without it.

I love President Kimball's concluding comment: "The battle raged on." When we are struggling to put the words on the page, it will help to remember that President Kimball prophesied of that pressure. Satan does not want this work to go forward. If he can stop us, he claims a victory.

Our Father calls for us to "search diligently in the light of Christ." To write about that light in others' lives, we must first seek it in our own and then sustain it. President Joseph F. Smith spoke of the need to make ourselves able, worthy, and qualified when he said, "It is a self-evident truth, that no one can give what he does not possess, and [one] who is lacking a testimony of the gospel can never inspire such testimony in [others]."[6]

Everything written about the Church, from within the Church, reflects on the Church. When I write, I think about that. Writing the Church story is finding meaning not just in what happens but in how we deal with it, how we live the commandments, how we stand as a witness of God in a world that misuses his name and misunderstands his power. As writers we have to be humble and teachable and yet certain about the direction we are going and why.

I love the commentary in Moroni 10 because of the beautiful promises, the gifts that give value to work in the Lord's kingdom. We may think we find ourselves in verses 9 and 10: "To one is given by the Spirit of God . . . that he may teach the word of knowledge." But I especially like verse 12: "And . . . to another, that he may work mighty miracles." The Church story is one of mighty miracles. We share them, one consecrated effort at a time. Being involved in the writing, the telling, of these stories may be the most mighty miracle of all.

NOTES

1. Laleta Dickson's History of William James of the Willie Handcart Company, 1856, Archives of The Church of Jesus Christ of Latter-day Saints, n. p.; spelling and grammar standardized. See also *Trail of Hope: The Story of the Mormon Trail* (Salt Lake City: Deseret Book, 1997).

2. Heidi S. Swinton, *Pioneer Spirit: Modern-day Stories of Courage and Conviction* (Salt Lake City: Deseret Book, 1997), 10.

3. Letter in the possession of the author.

4. Bathsheba W. Smith, "Autobiography," ed. Alice Merrill Horne, typescript, 14–15, in author's possession.

5. Spencer W. Kimball, in Conference Report, October 1943, 15–16, 18.

6. Joseph F. Smith, *Gospel Doctrine* (Salt Lake City: Deseret Book, 1939), 388.

THE BEATITUDES: CONSTITUTION FOR A PERFECT LIFE

CHRISTINE DURHAM

I'm not asked very often in my regular job to give sermons. Having once considered going to divinity school but being unable at the time to figure out what the world was going to do with a female Mormon preacher, I opted for the secular priesthood and became a lawyer. Poor second best, many of my friends would say.

Thus, it is a great pleasure to share with you a feast from the Savior's teachings in the New Testament and in 3 Nephi, a sermon we know as the Beatitudes. The theme for my sermon is that the Beatitudes are a constitution. In a seminar on constitutional law that I teach at the University of Utah law school, I begin by asking my students (mostly second- and third-year law students who have had the basics of legal training), "What is a constitution?" Some of them are surprised by that question, because even though they've been exposed to federal constitutional law, even though they have spent all their lives reading and hearing about so-called constitutional rights and defending and protecting the Constitution, it is frequently true that some of them have not thought very deeply about the meaning and purpose of a constitution. They tend to say things like "A

Christine M. Durham has served as a justice on the Utah Supreme Court since 1982. She and her husband, George H. Durham II, have reared five children and serve as Gospel Doctrine teachers for the young adults in their ward.

constitution is a charter" and "It's a framework for the life of a community." Those are actually very good responses. They do describe what constitutions do for us. They organize us. They allocate the powers and duties that are to be exercised and performed in any given community. They regulate the relationship between the governed and the government, and between one citizen and another. So those are two important functions of a constitution—to organize power and allocate duty and to regulate relationships. A third very important function of a constitution is to embody, and to seek to enshrine and protect, the community's fundamental values and deepest commitments. With that definition as a basis, let us consider the Beatitudes as a constitution for living.

The Beatitudes have been described as "declarations of blessedness." Like a political constitution, they describe principles or laws that regulate relations between men and women, between men and women and God, and between us and God and back to each other. Similarly, they contain the fundamental elements of spiritual refinement and ultimately of perfection. Structural examination is an important part of any constitutional analysis. As far as we know from the scriptures, Jesus gave this sermon at least twice. It's recorded in the New Testament in both Matthew and Luke in slightly different versions. But the version we have in 3 Nephi has some interesting and probably significant differences, especially when we focus on the language.

The portion of the sermon that we identify as the Beatitudes is very short, and because I am focusing on its language and structure, I would like to read through it. First of all, the context involves Christ teaching the Nephites. He has just called twelve disciples and is in the process of instructing them about their work in preaching the gospel. He says to them, "Yea, blessed are they who shall believe in your words, and come down into the depths of humility and be baptized, for they shall be visited with fire and with the Holy Ghost, and shall receive a remission of their sins" (3 Nephi 12:2). And then begin the eight Beatitudes:

"Yea, blessed are the poor in spirit who come unto me, for theirs is the kingdom of heaven.

"And again, blessed are all they that mourn, for they shall be comforted.

"And blessed are the meek, for they shall inherit the earth.

"And blessed are all they who do hunger and thirst after righteousness, for they shall be filled with the Holy Ghost.

"And blessed are the merciful, for they shall obtain mercy.

"And blessed are all the pure in heart, for they shall see God.

"And blessed are all the peacemakers, for they shall be called the children of God.

"And blessed are all they who are persecuted for my name's sake, for theirs is the kingdom of heaven" (3 Nephi 12:3–10).

Let us look briefly at differences between the Matthew 5 version and 3 Nephi. Matthew records, "Blessed are the poor in spirit: for theirs is the kingdom of heaven" (Matthew 5:3). In Nephi we read, "Blessed are the poor in spirit *who come unto me,* for theirs is the kingdom of heaven" (3 Nephi 12:3; emphasis added). The Book of Mormon tells us what "poor in spirit" means—those who are in need spiritually, who come to Christ and receive an answer. They will come to the kingdom of heaven. There's another difference in Matthew 5:6: "Blessed are they which do hunger and thirst after righteousness: for they shall be filled." In 3 Nephi 12:6, the sermon is clearer. It reads, "And blessed are all they who do hunger and thirst after righteousness, for they shall be filled *with the Holy Ghost*" (emphasis added).

The eight Beatitudes contain the fundamental elements of spiritual refinement and perfection. There's a beautiful harmony, a balance, and a symmetry in this very short, eight-verse sermon. The first four verses—which refer to the poor in spirit

327

who come unto Christ, to those who mourn, to the meek, and to those who hunger and thirst after righteousness—all reflect neediness, an emptiness or a need that requires filling. Each declaration acknowledges the blessedness of spiritual need as the state that each of us must occupy as a human being seeking spiritual growth and response. The reference in these first four Beatitudes is to the internal, to the way we see ourselves in relation to God, to the way we understand and define ourselves as spiritual beings. Are we poor in spirit who come unto Christ? Do we mourn? Are we meek? And do we hunger and thirst after righteousness?

The second four declarations have a slightly different emphasis, referring to those who are merciful, pure in heart, peacemakers, and persecuted for the Lord's sake. Whereas the first four Beatitudes emphasize neediness, the second four emphasize generosity, acknowledging not our neediness as spiritual beings but our obligations and responsibilities in our spiritual life: to be merciful to others; to be pure in heart, to have pure intentions as we interact with others; to be peacemakers, to do what we can to reduce dissent and contention and to bring peace into the hearts of others; and finally to take upon ourselves the name of Christ, even suffering persecution in his name if necessary. The second part of the Beatitudes reaches outward to focus on the way we see others in reference to God.

Someone once asked C. S. Lewis to explain what he meant by the light of Christ. He explained that the light of Christ was not something that he himself could see but something by which he saw everything else. Parts of the Beatitudes provide us with the same kind of light, either for seeing inside ourselves or for seeing outside of ourselves and seeing others as God may see them.

As "declarations of blessedness," the Beatitudes describe an inherent, inevitable, definitional connection between the state of blessedness and the dynamic quality of being blessed.

Blessings are descriptive, but blessings are also promises: the promises of connections between cause and effect.

Let us focus briefly on the blessings individually. First, "Blessed are the poor in spirit who come unto me, for theirs is the kingdom of heaven" (3 Nephi 12:3). Wherein lies the blessing? Does the blessing consist of being among "the poor in spirit who come unto Christ," or does it rest in owning, in belonging to, in being part of, and having ownership in the kingdom of heaven? Where's the blessing in verse 6: "Blessed are all they who do hunger and thirst after righteousness, for they shall be filled with the Holy Ghost"? Does the blessing lie in the state of being hungry and thirsty, of longing and yearning for enlightenment and fulfillment? Or does the state of being blessed lie in being filled with the Holy Ghost?

I've puzzled over the language, trying to understand exactly the nature of the intended blessing. We can read the Beatitudes as describing cause and effect or as a requirement and a promise—if you're merciful, you'll receive mercy. But I'm not sure that the relationship between the parallel structure of the blessings is that straightforward. In some respects, the "ifs" and "thens" operate very much like the two sides of an equation—whatever happens on one side of the equals sign is, although different in character, the same as what's happening on the other side of the equals sign. For example, to be merciful transforms us spiritually in a fashion that makes us available to be recipients of God's mercy. Which is more blessed—to be merciful or to be the recipient of mercy? Which contributes more to our personal growth?

Let's consider mercy as the capacity to put aside personal hurt, personal offense, distress, anger, hatred. If we scratch the surface of any woman or man, we would uncover hardship, suffering, even victimization, that might, logically, give rise to legitimate resentment, anger, and questions about why the world is the way it is and why God permits certain things in the world to happen. Can we enjoy that resentment or anger, or sustain that level of hostility toward the world, and simultaneously exercise any of the blessings that Christ identified in the Beatitudes? I suggest that we cannot and, conversely, that we cannot hunger and thirst for righteousness, or be merciful, without at the same time being eligible for receiving blessings from God.

One of the things I like about the first of the Beatitudes—those that are poor in spirit who come to Christ—is the metaphor of a spiritual journey upon which each of us is engaged. We all have some distance to travel and at the end of that distance is our coming to Christ. But second is the act of "owning the kingdom" in some sense. The scriptures say, "Theirs is the kingdom of heaven." I don't know if that means the kingdom belongs to us, the poor in spirit who come to Christ, in the typical sense of ownership, or if it simply means that that will be a place where we will be at home, where we will be comfortable, where we will be comforted, and where we will be able to dwell in a sense of complete harmony with the Spirit.

Similarly, consider the second Beatitude: "Blessed are all they that mourn, for they shall be comforted" (3 Nephi 12:4). Most of us do not think of the act of mourning, or the process of mourning, as a state of blessedness. Most of us who have been hurt, who have experienced sorrow, who have experienced loss, who have been bereft of something very dear to us and who yearned in vain for its return, would not understand that condition as being a state of blessedness. But those of us who have experienced that condition and who have used it to seek God's comfort in our lives begin to understand the way in which mourning may be a blessing. Mourning opens us up. Pain softens our hearts. Hurt renders us available to messages and teachings that we would otherwise not heed. We know from the scriptures that God, on occasion—usually occasions when he looks around and sees what we have made of his creation—weeps. If God has the capacity for sorrow and the capacity to weep, then the capacity to mourn is in some sense godlike. And it's very clear that grief opens us up to this notion of comfort in a far broader sense.

Think about the last time you were hurt in some fashion, whether physically or emotionally. What did you seek for comfort? We hear a lot these days about things like comfort foods; we all probably have some of those. But I read a beautiful poem not long ago that talked about the process of marriage and what a marriage of long standing could be like. It referred to the "cashmere comfort" of being with someone who knows you well and loves you well. That reminded me of experiences when I've received comfort from my husband, from my children, and in my childhood from my parents. For just for a few seconds, re-create the last time you had a sense of being comforted. Remember that sense of warmth, of being soothed? We sometimes talk about the process of comforting as providing balm for the soul. If you can re-create that experience even for a moment, you can get in touch with the state of blessedness that must be available to those who mourn in a righteous sense according to the Beatitudes.

What about the meek? There's a place in the Psalms where this language—"blessed are the meek for they shall inherit the earth"—is repeated (see Psalm 37:11). The same phrase is used a couple of verses earlier, but that verse says that *those that wait upon the Lord,* they shall inherit the earth" (Psalm 37:9; emphasis added). That reference to the capacity to wait upon God teaches us a lot about meekness. I've never been known as a meek person, and yet I don't think that the scriptural quality of meekness as described in the third Beatitude is unavailable to me. Meekness does not mean being without a voice or an identity. Meekness does not mean being unable to understand your own needs and desires, and, then, when they are appropriate and righteous, to pursue them. Meekness as a spiritual quality is in no way incompatible with striving for excellence, working hard, or seeking after the desires of a righteous heart.

But meekness does require that after we have done all that we can do—after we have prepared ourselves, striven, focused our efforts, focused our work, harnessed our ambitions, done everything possible in our lives to find the excellence that we believe our lives should have—then we must be willing, emotionally, spiritually, and psychologically, to wait upon God. That's what I think meekness means in the Beatitudes. It has to do with patience, long suffering, gentleness, kindness, in all of the traditional senses; at its core, however, meekness refers to the ability to turn our hopes, desires, and ambitions over to God, to accept God's time, to accept God's hand as it operates in our lives, and to let his words, his doctrine, his teachings, and his love affect our hearts and transform our spirits. Those who are not known for our meekness in the secular sense may have a little more trouble getting access to that kind of patience; nonetheless, it is available to us all.

And what state of blessedness is going to accompany meekness? The scripture says the meek shall inherit the earth (see 3 Nephi 12:5). Some people have a lot of trouble with this particular phrase in the scriptures because of the incongruity of it. If you think of meekness as being the same as wimpiness, why would the meek *want* to inherit the earth? What on earth would they do with it when they got it? But again, meekness does not mean weakness or powerlessness. Meekness means being patient and waiting on the Lord, and the promise implies that the capacity to wait will render us capable to receive. I don't know what it means to inherit the earth. I suspect it doesn't refer to instruments of worldly power; that would seem incongruous in the context of the Savior's teachings about differences between mortal life and eternal life. I think the phrase "inherit the earth" means that those who are capable of waiting upon God will come into full possession of all of their heart's desires.

Now consider the next verse: "Blessed are all they who do hunger and thirst after righteousness, for they shall be filled with the Holy Ghost" (3 Nephi 12:6). The phrase "hunger and thirst after righteousness" suggests images of neediness: yearning, striving, seeking, looking for something that we don't have but that we need. But what are we are looking for? Not answers to specific questions. The scripture does not say that we will find all the answers or solve all the problems of the world but that we will be "filled with the Holy Ghost."

I love the introductory verses in which Christ is talking to the disciples. He describes so vividly and so beautifully being filled with the Holy Ghost: "They shall be visited with fire and with the Holy Ghost, and shall receive a remission of their sins" (3 Nephi 12:2). My experiences of being filled with the Holy Ghost have been like being visited with fire. It's an experience of beauty, of transcendence, of moving up and outside of one's self, and of seeing one's life from a completely different perspective. It's an experience of going from emptiness to fullness.

Next is "Blessed are the merciful, for they shall obtain mercy" (3 Nephi 12:7). We know from the scriptures that God is rich in mercy. In 1 Nephi we read that the "tender mercies of the Lord are over all" (1 Nephi 1:20). In Alma we learn that "mercy can satisfy the demands of justice" (Alma 34:16), although elsewhere in the scriptures we read that mercy cannot rob justice. They must operate in a complementary way. I would suggest that the adjective *merciful* is yet another synonym for *godlike*. If God is rich in mercy, if his tender mercies are over all, and if he is responsible for the mercy that permitted—through the Atonement—the demands of justice to be satisfied, then to be merciful is in some sense to be godlike, to take on an attribute that is part of God's identity.

The next Beatitude speaks of the pure in heart. Why not just "the pure"? Why not those whose lives are stainless? Whose actions are blameless? Who are entirely free from any corruption or taint in the way they live their lives? We would call them

333

pure. But that is not what the sermon refers to. It refers to those who are pure *in heart*. It looks inward, to examine intentions. The word *pure* to my mind connotes something that is clear, clean, spotless, and bright—something that is very intense. What happens when you focus your eyes? You see. When you focus your intentions with that pureness, that distilled clarity and intensity, you will see God.

This teaching reflects an orientation to the world, to other people, and to all of our actions. We should act intentionally—with intentionality. I learned about the concept of intentionality from a friend, not of our faith, who is a very deeply spiritual man. "Life is like dancing," he says. "The point of dancing is not to finish." The point of living, at least for most of us most of the time is not to finish. The point of getting up every morning is not to rush through to the end of the day—or at least it shouldn't be. There are days like that, of course; we all have days when we get that first foot on the floor, and we feel like we've started a foot race that is not going to end until midnight. I suggest that when we are living our lives that way, we've lost track of what it is to be pure in heart, because we have lost track of doing what we do, thinking what we think, saying what we say, experiencing what we experience with *intentionality,* with focus, with the ability to remember who we are and what God wants of us. That's what I think the scripture means in saying, "They shall see God" (3 Nephi 12:8). When our hearts are pure and focused, we can see God.

The next Beatitude concerns the peacemakers. I had a little brother who, when we older siblings were squabbling, would say, "Now, don't fight. It's not nice." His advice didn't endear him to us at the time—a risk all peacemakers run. What does being a peacemaker mean? Is it someone who papers over every dispute, who refuses to acknowledge legitimate differences in people's perspectives? Is it someone who wants to squelch dissent in any form solely for the purpose of civility? In that case, some of the totalitarian governments around the world qualify as successful peacemakers. They do not tolerate contention or dissent, and, on the surface, the societies they manage are peaceful. Some of them are a lot more peaceful than democratic societies: they have less public contention, less violence, fewer opportunities for people to display tension toward each other. But that has nothing to do with the process of peacemaking that Jesus Christ taught.

We learn throughout the scriptures that the spirit of contention is not from the Lord but from the devil. How, then, can we disagree with each other? How can we see the world through our own prisms of experience, education, and individual learning? I suggest that this Beatitude has something to teach us in that regard. It says, "Blessed are all the peacemakers, for they shall be called the children of God" (3 Nephi 12:9). That language is interesting. It doesn't say for they *are* the children of God or that they *shall be* the children of God. It says they shall *be called* the children of God. They will be identified and labeled and understood in the larger community as having a function that has to do with God's doctrine, God's teaching, and God's peace.

My own opinion is that the peace described in the scriptures, and the peace referred to in this part of the Beatitudes, is not merely a passive peace, an absence of bad feeling or disagreement. Instead, I think, it is a very active, affirmative experience akin to being filled with the Holy Ghost. I hope that you have had the experience sometime in your life of disagreeing strenuously with someone you love and care about deeply, disagreeing about politics, about the solution to a problem, about an ethical choice that has to be made, about things as mundane and essential as the way to run a household, or manage family finances, or teach children. I hope that if you have had the experience of disagreeing with someone you value and love, you have also had the experience of coming to a state of toleration for that disagreement, of understanding that you can still love and value someone even when that someone does

335

not see the world exactly as you see it. When that happens, ideally, the Spirit can enter into our lives and teach us ways of accommodating the enormous and beautiful diversity of human beings and human opinion. Peacemakers are the people who diminish the suffering that is caused by hate, fear, insecurity, greed, carelessness, recklessness. Peacemakers discern beyond the language that we sometimes hear, beyond the actions we sometimes observe; they discern the needs of other human hearts.

I'm married to a peacemaker. He's a peacemaker on many levels, not the least of which is that he hates confrontation. How he ever ended up married to a lawyer, I don't know. We had to work out all kinds of techniques for disagreeing and valuing each other when we disagreed and were trying to solve problems. We had to agree on how to disagree. But it's not that part of his character which leads me to call him a peacemaker. It is his capacity for hearing the voices that speak from people's hearts. When we were newly married, we took a marriage class, and one of the sections was on communication. We discovered in that session that I am what is known as a "technical listener." Language means a great deal to me; I care deeply about it, and it is evocative to me. Language is one of the ways I get in touch with my spiritual life. My husband is not a technical listener, and he's not a technical talker. He is a discerning listener, an emotional listener. He picks up on body language, on tone of voice, on the "affect" of speech and language. I have to say, we've made a pretty good team. I don't know how either one of us would have survived without the other in rearing our five children because there were so many moments over the course of that process when one or the other of our sets of skills was needed. His skills for hearing what people's hearts are trying to express, first of all, makes him a very good pediatrician, gifted in his field. But it also allows him to protect himself in a healthy way from communications that might otherwise be hurtful, confrontational, or

336

hostile and to respond to the need underneath. That has been particularly valuable in our neighborhood, community, and family. I watch him and understand that his idea of a successful interaction with another human being is to understand what that human being needs and to give it to him or to her—to bring peace to people's hearts.

To be a peacemaker you don't have to get a degree in foreign relations and work for the United Nations. You don't have to intervene and terminate every dispute. But if you can facilitate communication between yourself and other people and between other people, you have the beginnings of being a peacemaker. You also have the beginnings, if you are capable and willing, of extending the gospel to the lives of the people around you, to teach them about what God's peace means and to help them incorporate it into their lives. And what does that get you, according to the scripture? It gets you a pretty impressive title: "children of God." That title is appropriate, I think, because children do their father's work, particularly in the spiritual sense. Christ did his Father's work, and we in turn try to do our Father's work.

We come finally to the last of the Beatitudes. On the surface, this is the most paradoxical of the eight and perhaps the most difficult to understand: "Blessed are all they who are persecuted for my name's sake, for theirs is the kingdom of heaven" (3 Nephi 12:10). Being persecuted is not my idea of a blessing. It stresses me a lot, and I would just as soon avoid it under all circumstances. I've lived long enough, however, to figure out that we can't avoid it and that by virtue of living in the world and putting ourselves out there we run the risk of encountering people who not only disagree with us but in many instances just flat out don't like us, what we stand for, or what we believe in.

Here is a personal example. I am a transplant to the state of Utah. I came here to live more than twenty-five years ago. I've now lived here longer than I've lived anywhere else in my life and it's home, but I was startled when I first moved here. Having grown up in the Church in cities all over the United States and abroad but never here in "Zion," I was startled when I moved here by the extent to which my identity as a Latter-day Saint seemed important to people around me. Not only was it important to the community of Saints that I joined in my neighborhood and ward but it also seemed important to the professional, social, and civic communities that I joined. Now, I had been used to being identified as a Mormon. In fact, in my undergraduate college, there were only three Latter-day Saints, and I was known as one of them. But in that setting I experienced curiosity, as much respect as the lack of it, and a certain degree of being special, or at least different, because of my faith. When I came to Utah, I discovered that the label had other connotations, some of which were not nearly so favorable.

When we live in communities where large numbers of us belong to the same faith, our neighbors sometimes feel wariness. I often found that when people in Utah identified my religion—and that was one of the first things that people wanted to know—they tended to make a whole series of assumptions about what kind of person I was. And they weren't always favorable assumptions, especially in some of the professional circles I moved in.

I realized how important it was for me in that setting to embrace my identity as a Latter-day Saint without foregoing any of the other personal attributes that were part of my identity. When people didn't respect the fact that I was a Latter-day Saint or, on the other side of the spectrum, expected me to be a certain kind of Latter-day Saint, I realized that I was being "persecuted" in a symbolic way for His name's sake. I say "symbolic" because it was reflected in attitudes, not in penalties or punishment. It was nothing like the experiences of the early Mormon pioneers, who literally risked their lives, or the historical experiences of the early Christians or the Jews. But it gives me an insight into what it's like to be reduced to a label. Carrying the name of Jesus Christ means that, among other things, you are willing to accept the judgments others may wish to place upon you as a result of that choice, however misguided those judgments may seem to you.

There is a very interesting symmetry in the Beatitudes. In 3 Nephi 12:3, we began with the "poor in spirit who come unto me, for theirs is the kingdom of heaven." And in verse 10 we end with those "who are persecuted for my name's sake, for theirs is the kingdom of heaven." The sermon and its teaching have come full circle from a willingness to come unto Christ to a willingness to accept everything that that means, even persecution.

Three verses at the very end of this sermon in 3 Nephi record Christ speaking to some of his people: "Therefore those things which were of old time, which were under the law, in me are all fulfilled. Old things are done away, and all things have become new. Therefore I would that ye should be perfect even as I, or your Father who is in heaven is perfect" (12:46–48). Latter-day Saints should take this sermon, and the Beatitudes that precede it and are part of it, more literally than traditional Christians. For instance, have you ever been told you aren't a Christian because you are a Latter-day Saint? That seems quite odd to us because the name of our Church is The Church of Jesus Christ of Latter-day Saints. We can understand this apparent paradox better when we place Christianity in its historical, doctrinal context. Latter-day Saints are doctrinally, in some respects, outside the definitional boundaries of Christianity. Why? Because we see existence on a continuum, and we believe in what we call eternal progression—that human beings can move along a developmental continuum, can progress from grace to grace and from capacity to capacity, from a state of alienation from God and mortality toward a state of godhood. That is the notion of perfectability. It's right here in the version of the sermon found in the New Testament, but it is not commonly understood by our fellow Christians as we understand it. They have a very different notion of the relationship between God and man and the nature of divinity and the nature of mortality.

This idea of perfectability is quite a radical tenet of the Restoration. As one of my teenagers would say, "It's an awesome doctrine!"—awesome in the sense that it should instill in us a sense of enormous awe about our responsibilities and obligations. People observe our lives without understanding the connection between our doctrine and our lives. Christ's teachings, wherever we find them, sustain us on that continuum of perfectability. It's not an accident that the Beatitudes, which can function as a constitution for living, are found in a sermon that concludes with the Savior's injunction, "Therefore I would that ye should be perfect even as I, or your Father who is in heaven is perfect" (3 Nephi 12:48).

People think we have a lot of chutzpah (a wonderful Yiddish word meaning incredible brass) to believe in the notion of eternal progression, to take literally the injunction at the end of this sermon, to think about, let alone try to work on, becoming perfect. I don't think we have even begun to approach the standard that the Savior set. In the Beatitudes, this "declaration of blessedness" recorded for us in the scriptures, Christ teaches us that there are things we can do, ways we can look at ourselves, and ways we can look at the world that will enable us to begin our own journeys on the continuum of perfectability. I pray that we can manage to maintain our humility and our capacity for meekness on that particular journey. I suspect that if we truly understand the magnitude of what I have called a radical tenet of the Restoration, we won't have any trouble with the meekness part and will be satisfied in the end to wait upon God for the result.

STUDYING THE SCRIPTURES: A SCHOLARLY APPROACH

GAYE STRATHEARN

In 1919 President Joseph F. Smith said, "The word and the law of God are as important for women who would reach wise conclusions as they are for men; and women should study and consider the problems of this great latter-day work from the standpoint of God's revelations, and as they may be actuated by his Spirit, which it is their right to receive through the medium of sincere and heartfelt prayer."[1] Closer to our own time, at the very first general women's meeting in 1978, President Spencer W. Kimball declared: "We want our sisters to be scholars of the scriptures as well as our men. You need an acquaintanceship with his eternal truths for your own well being, and for the purposes of teaching your own children and all others who come within your influence."[2] At the very next general women's meeting, he elaborated even further: "We want our homes to be blessed with sister scriptorians—whether you are single or married, young or old, widowed or living in a family. . . . Become scholars of the scriptures."[3]

The question, of course, is "What does it mean to be a scholar of the scriptures?" I sometimes compare studying the scriptures to a rich, multilayered piece of cake, heeding the

Gaye Strathearn, an instructor in the Department of Ancient Scripture at Brigham Young University, is a doctoral candidate in New Testament at Claremont Graduate University. She served a mission in Melbourne, Australia.

Lord's counsel to Isaiah to "make the heart of this people fat" (Isaiah 6:10). The layers of a multilayered cake can represent different experiences in our lifetime scripture study. For instance, some layers may represent personal study added on at various times in our life; other layers may represent family scripture study or institute or seminary classes; another layer may represent Gospel Doctrine, priesthood, or Relief Society classes and discussions. Each layer adds to the flavorful richness of our study experience. A scholarly approach to the scriptures adds to that richness, but I would like to offer two cautions before diving into our topic.

First, unfortunately, some people want to eat only this one layer. For a few, the scholarly debate can become more important than the spirit of the scriptures. Let me give you an example. In Helaman we read of the missionary experiences of the two sons of Helaman: Nephi and Lehi. At one point in the narrative, Nephi returned to Zarahemla from his mission in the north and found "the people in a state of . . . wickedness" (Helaman 7:4). A series of events followed that led Nephi to prophesy about the murder of the chief judge and the capture of his assailant. Nephi's ability to identify the murderer caused quite a stir. Let's pick up the story there. "And now there were some among the people, who said that Nephi was a prophet. And there were others who said: Behold, he is a god, for except he was a god he could not know of all things. . . . And it came to pass that there arose a division among the people, insomuch that they divided hither and thither and went their ways, leaving Nephi alone, as he was standing in the midst of them" (Helaman 9:40–10:1).

Do you see what happened? The people were so caught up in the argument about whether Nephi was a prophet or a god that they ignored him, and whatever great things he could teach them, so they could continue the argument! Surely a spiritually sensitive people would be flocking to him, whether he was a prophet or a god, so they could learn. Their response is in stark contrast to that of their descendants fifty years later who longed for Christ "to tarry a little longer with them" (3 Nephi 17:5). To "search diligently in the light of Christ" is the goal of all scripture study (Moroni 7:19). A scholarly approach to the scriptures is a tremendous tool, but it is only a means to an end, not an end in and of itself.

The second caution concerns assumptions people bring to a study of the scriptures. I like to distinguish between what I call academic as opposed to scholarly approaches to scriptures. I use *academic* to refer to "the philosophies of men, mingled with scripture,"[4] and *scholarly* to refer to the "philosophies of men, mingled with scripture" but viewed through the lens of the gospel of Jesus Christ. Both approaches use very similar tools, such as history, language, archaeology, literary and text criticism, but the academic approach often makes assumptions that prevent our viewing the scriptures through the gospel lens. Foremost among those assumptions is that we cannot objectively assess spiritual experiences such as visitations, healings, or prophecy; therefore, we must either not discuss them or treat them as unverifiable psychological phenomena—events that individuals believed they experienced but that we can't regard as factual. I believe that Paul was referring to this attitude when he warned of those who were "ever learning, and never able to come to a knowledge of the truth (2 Timothy 3:7), or Peter, when he warned of the spiritually "unlearned and unstable" who "wrest" scriptures "unto their own destruction" (2 Peter 3:16).[5] Yet, those very same tools of scholarship can be of tremendous value if they are used within the gospel framework.

With those cautions in mind, let's have fun with two scholarly tools—language and redaction.

LANGUAGE

When I think of studying language as an important part of a scholarly approach to the scriptures, my mind invariably

343

turns to the Prophet Joseph Smith. Here was a man who knew the scriptures. Divine and angelic beings were his tutors. Besides the Father and the Son, many others—Peter, James, and John, Moses, Elias, John the Baptist, and Moroni—visited the Prophet, conferred keys upon him and his associates, and instructed him in spiritual matters.[6] These visitations must have been wonderful, spiritual, learning experiences for the young Joseph. In addition, when he received the Book of Mormon plates, he had the Urim and Thummim to help him translate. Yet, when it came to studying the scriptures, the Prophet didn't rely solely upon divine messengers or the Urim and Thummim.

Joseph's journal reflects his commitment to study Hebrew (in particular), as well as Greek and Egyptian. In Kirtland, the School of the Prophets engaged the services of a Jewish scholar, J. Seixas, to formally teach them Hebrew. During this period, Joseph's journal frequently records blocks of intensive study time: "Spent the day [or the afternoon] studying Hebrew [or Greek]."[7] The things he learned from that study he incorporated into his sermons.[8] On 17 February 1836, the Prophet recorded the following in his journal: "My soul delights in reading the word of the Lord in the original, and I am determined to pursue the study of languages until I shall become master of them, if I am permitted to live long enough, at any rate so long as I do live I am determined to make this my object, and with the blessing of God I shall succeed to my satisfaction."[9]

Why was it so important for Joseph to read the scriptures in Hebrew and Greek? Why was he driven, despite many other pressing concerns, to master those languages? Could it be that the very pondering associated with the translation process prompted the Spirit? I think so, and for me the beauty is that those same promptings can be available to us.

What does the phrase "as far as it is translated correctly" in the eighth Article of Faith mean? Any translator faces a number of different possibilities, each of which could be justified. The one chosen may be decided as much by poetry or theology as by syntax. Sometimes, therefore, as we look at a text through the lens of the gospel, we find possibilities other than the one chosen by the translators of the King James Version of the Bible. Let me give you a couple of examples.

After Eve eats the forbidden fruit, God says to her: "I will greatly multiply thy sorrow and thy conception; in sorrow thou shalt bring forth children; and thy desire shall be to thy husband, and he shall rule over thee" (Genesis 3:16). The preposition translated here as "over" is the Hebrew letter *beth*. Its primary meaning is "in" or "with" rather than "over." That changes the last phrase to "he shall rule with thee." This alternate translation supports President Kimball's preference to read "preside" rather than "rule" in this scripture, and it would also better capture God's intent for the family.[10] The Proclamation on the Family declares that although divine responsibilities may differ, "fathers and mothers are obligated to help one another as equal partners."[11]

Unfortunately, the footnotes in the LDS edition of the Bible don't provide, in this case, this alternate translation of Genesis 3:16. Sometimes the footnotes do provide such information, and that can be extremely helpful. For example, the Psalmist declares: "What is man, that thou art mindful of him? and the son of man, that thou visitest him? For thou hast made him a little lower than the angels, and hast crowned him with glory and honour" (Psalm 8:4–5). A footnote to these verses indicates that the Hebrew text reads, "less than the gods," rather than "lower than the angels," which comes from the Greek Septuagint text. Perhaps those who translated from the Hebrew to Greek felt "gods" smacked of the plural gods of Greek and Roman theology. And perhaps the King James translators followed suit because the Septuagint was the preferred text for Christianity and they weren't comfortable with the theological implications of humans being only a little lower than the gods—but that implication fits very nicely with the Latter-day Saint understanding of human potential.[12]

Those are two examples. There are many more. Translating from the original text can also help identify words with greater depth and complexity than is readily apparent in the English translation. For example, whereas English has just one word for love, Greek has at least four, each with its own nuance: *agapē*—charity (1 Corinthians 13), which Mormon defines as "the pure love of Christ" (Moroni 7:47); *eros*—sexual love (which we don't find mentioned in the Bible); *philos*—brotherly love (Revelation 3:19); and *storgē*—family love, parents for children and children for parents (Romans 1:31; 2 Timothy 3:3; used in the negative sense, "without family love"). Knowing which word was originally used by the writer can add clarity or new perceptions when we are pondering and studying.

I hope these few examples give a feeling for why the Prophet Joseph felt that paying attention to language was important.

REDACTION

According to the LDS Bible Dictionary, "The four Gospels are not so much biographies as they are testimonies. They do not reveal a day-by-day story of the life of Jesus; rather they tell who Jesus was, what he said, what he did, and why it was important" (p. 683). As a result, it is extremely difficult, if not impossible, to merge the four accounts of Christ's life and teachings. The authors were not primarily interested in the time line of Christ's life. Each took some events and teachings out of chronological order to better emphasize a point. For example, when Matthew wanted to emphasize Christ's teachings on the kingdom of God, he brought together into a single chapter all the parables that Jesus had taught on that subject (see Matthew 13). In other words, Matthew, Mark, Luke, and John sometimes acted as editors of Christ's life and teachings as they wrote their Gospel.

That editorial process is called redaction[13]—something we are familiar with in the Book of Mormon because both Mormon and Moroni insert editorial comments into their works. Mormon tells us that "a hundredth part of the proceedings of this people . . . cannot be contained in this work" (Helaman 3:14). Obviously he and Moroni, under the direction of the Spirit, had to make some important choices about what to include or exclude and what order to put it in. That's what an editor does. Recognizing the editor's hand can be instructive. For example, in an article he wrote on Alma 30, Gerald Lund[14] asks two questions about Mormon's editorial decisions: Why did Mormon include the incident of Korihor in the Book of Mormon, especially when a detailed story of an anti-Christ seems to go against Nephi's "mission statement" to engrave "that which is pleasing to God"? (2 Nephi 5:32). Why did Mormon specifically place the account of Korihor between the account of the sons of Mosiah and their missionary efforts to the Lamanites and the account of Alma's great mission to the Zoramites? Brother Lund's ensuing discussion of the role of foils (persons or incidents that set off or enhance another by contrast) in the scriptures and the power of the word have added a wonderful new layer to my understanding of this great chapter.

As another exercise in studying redaction, compare Matthew's placement and use of the incident of the stilling of the storm (Matthew 8:23–27) with that of Mark and Luke.[15] What was Matthew trying to teach that led him, as an editor, to present the story differently from the way Mark and Luke presented it? Why did he include two short incidents (Matthew 8:18–22) that aren't found in Mark and don't come until a chapter later in Luke? Notice also Matthew's choice of words, for instance, in calling Christ "Lord" in contrast to Mark's and Luke's using the title "Master." Is there significance in that? In my study of these questions, I have come to feel that Matthew wants to emphasize the importance of turning to Christ during the trials that will invariably come as we, as Christ's disciples, leave behind the cares of the world and enter into the boat, symbolic for Matthew of Christ's church. Mark and Luke both have Jesus stilling the storm first and then questioning his disciples; Matthew reverses the order. First, he questions their faith, and then he attends to the storm. The faith of the disciples is the central topic in Matthew. Matthew wants his readers to understand the stilling of the storm as even more than the story of a miracle. He wants us to see it as symbolic of the trials of discipleship.

Asking questions about redaction—the editorial process of ordering events, selecting which details to include or exclude, and so on—can be very enlightening.

We have examined only two of many elements in a scholarly approach to the scriptures; we have barely scratched the surface. Not everyone can pack up and pursue graduate degrees in religious topics, of course, but other resources are available. We might be able to take language classes, as Joseph Smith did. Other resources—some on computer software—could help us add a scholarship dimension to our scripture study. Many books written for the nonacademic reader and readily available in bookstores and libraries teach about social context, redaction, and all the other wonders of a scholarly approach. The Lord commanded the Prophet Joseph to "seek ye out of the best books words of wisdom; seek learning, even by study and also by faith" (D&C 88:118). In learning by study and also by faith, we can use the scholarly approach to the scriptures as a wonderful aid to invite the Spirit to enlighten our understanding of these great texts.

NOTES

1. Joseph F. Smith, *Gospel Doctrine* (Salt Lake City: Deseret Book, 1919), 290.

2. Spencer W. Kimball, "Privileges and Responsibilities of Sisters," *Ensign,* November 1978, 102.

3. Spencer W. Kimball, "The Role of Righteous Women," *Ensign,* November 1979, 102.

4. Bruce R. McConkie, *The Millennial Messiah* (Salt Lake City: Deseret Book, 1982), 59.

5. I understand Peter to mean "unlearned and unstable" in spiritual matters.

6. See Joseph Smith–History 1:16–17, 33–42, 54, 72; D&C 27:12; 76:22–23; 110:2–4, 11, 13.

7. Joseph Smith, *The Papers of Joseph Smith,* vol. 2, ed. Dean C. Jessee (Salt Lake City: Deseret Book, 1992). See Friday 20th (November 1835) on page 87, Saturday 21st (November 1835) on page 87, Monday 23d (November 1835) on page 88, Friday 27th (November 1835) on page 90, Friday 4th (December 1835) on page 95, Saturday 5th (December 1835) on page 95, Monday 7th (December 1835) on page 97, Tuesday morning the 8th (December 1835) on page 97, Monday 14th (December 1835) on page 105, Wednesday 23d (December 1835) on page 120, Wednesday 30th (December 1835) on page 124, etc.

8. For instance, his sermon on Genesis 1 is a classic. See Joseph Smith, *Words of Joseph Smith,* comp. and ed. Andrew F. Ehat and Lyndon W. Cook (Orem: Grandin Book, 1994), 350–51.

9. Joseph Smith, *The Personal Writings of Joseph Smith,* comp. and ed. Dean C. Jessee (Salt Lake City: Deseret Book, 1984), 161.

10. Spencer W. Kimball, "The Blessings and Responsibilities of Womanhood," *Ensign,* March 1976, 72.

11. *The Family: A Proclamation to the World,* read by President Gordon B. Hinckley in General Relief Society Meeting, 23 September 1995, in *Ensign,* November 1995, 102.

12. See Joseph Smith, *The Teachings of Joseph Smith,* sel. Joseph Fielding Smith (Salt Lake City: Deseret Book, 1938), 35–36; see also Orson F. Whitney, "Lives of Our Leaders—the Apostles: Lorenzo Snow," *Juvenile Instructor* 35 (1 January 1900): 3–4.

13. I distinguish between "redaction" and "redaction criticism." The scholarly world uses the latter to indicate that later authors created stories and teachings of Jesus and incorporated them into the Gospel texts. I understand redaction as the Gospel writers using historical events and teachings to teach various principles of the gospel.

14. Gerald N. Lund, "An Anti-Christ in the Book of Mormon—The Face May Be Strange, but the Voice Is Familiar," in *The Book of Mormon: Alma, The Testimony of the Word,* ed. Monte S. Nyman and Charles D. Tate Jr. (Provo: Religious Studies Center, 1992), 107–28.

15. For a full analysis of Matthew's redaction of this parable, see Günther Bornkamm's article "The Stilling of the Storm," in Günther Bornkamm, Gerhard Barth, and Heinz Joachim Held, *Tradition and Interpretation in Matthew* (Philadelphia: Westminister, 1963), 52–57. This article is foundational for the development of redaction criticism.

THE LAST TO REMAIN
AND THE FIRST TO RETURN

JENI BROBERG HOLZAPFEL AND
RICHARD NEITZEL HOLZAPFEL

When our young son Bailey was four years old, he was assigned to set the table for dinner. As he moved around the big kitchen table, carefully arranging the settings, he stopped briefly to ask me about the "dishes" Nephi was commanded to go and get in Jerusalem. I could see his mind working on the first line of the Primary song "Nephi's Courage":

> The Lord commanded Nephi to go and get the plates
> From the wicked Laban inside the city gates.[1]

Plates, dishes—they were the same thing in Bailey's mind. What a curious story he must have made up in his head, imagining Nephi and his brothers returning to Jerusalem to get a stack of dishes!

We have found ourselves reading stories in the New Testament, thinking and visualizing one thing, only to find out later that we had the wrong image in mind. As with our son, the story made a lot more sense once we understood what was

Jeni Broberg Holzapfel and Richard Neitzel Holzapfel are the authors of several books and articles, and they are the parents of five children. Jeni serves as the Young Women president in the Jerusalem Branch in Israel. Richard is a teacher at the BYU Jerusalem Center and teaches seminary in the Jerusalem Branch.

really going on. That is especially true when we study the women mentioned in the New Testament. To fully appreciate the lives and discipleship of these women, we must see them in their historical and social contexts and understand the attitudes and norms of the larger Greco-Roman world and of the Jewish subculture.[2]

GRECO-ROMAN ATTITUDES

First-century Greco-Roman attitudes about women originated in ancient Greece. They were a deep-rooted tradition that mandated that only male citizens of Athens had rights. One of the earliest known Greek poets, Hesiod, tells in *Theogony* the story of the creation of the first woman. Because Prometheus had stolen fire from the gods to give to humans, Zeus punished humans by sending them Pandora, the first woman. She had every gift—beauty, charm, grace, skill in women's work—but she was a "tempting snare" and a "nagging burden." Before she came to earth, men lived happily, untouched by troubles and disease. Pandora, whom Zeus made "to be an evil for mortal man," was she "from [whom] comes the fair sex; yes, wicked womenfolk are her descendants."[3] *Theogony* became the standard Greek version of divine creation.

Greek parents often exposed (meaning abandoned without food or shelter) their unwanted newborn infants, mostly girls. Exposed children usually died of hunger or cold or both and became the lifeless prey of birds and dogs, unless they were found by someone—a mixed blessing because the children automatically became slaves subject to terrible humiliation, including sexual abuse, most often of the females.

A few hundred years later during the Hellenistic age (323–330 B.C.), profound changes in social and political life, influenced by philosophy and scientific ideas, transformed the Greek world. The legal status of women also changed, even

351

though long-held beliefs and customs tended to thwart these advances.

When Rome dominated the ancient world, the women of the elite greatly increased their freedom and independence, but the relatively small number of women who benefited from the changes must be weighed against the harsh and difficult lives of most women during this period. Slavery continued on a wide scale and gave occasion to cruelty and sexual license, again especially with female household slaves.

Roman law required a father to rear all his male children but only his firstborn female. The words of the comic poet Posidippus are surely an exaggeration, but they contain a germ of truth: "A poor man brings up a son, but even a rich man exposes a daughter."[4]

Obviously, we are emphasizing the worst treatment of women in these ancient cultures, which were both complex and diverse. Many women felt needed, loved, and appreciated. Yet, the number of harsh, negative statements about women in Greco-Roman sources vastly outweigh positive. Negative attitudes toward women were the norm.

THE JEWISH WORLD

Jesus, of course, lived in the Jewish subculture of the Greco-Roman world. From what we glean from first-century Jewish sources, family and public life revolved around the free adult Israelite male. These men owned wives, children, land, slaves, livestock, and other possessions. Jewish women were generally excluded from public life and were often required to cover their heads or faces or both when in the presence of men. Men were cautioned about talking too much to women. In a court of law, a woman's testimony, except relating directly to a woman's issue, was not admissible evidence. Some rabbis saw the woman's role as God's punishment of Eve visited perpetually on all generations of women.

Women were discounted or excluded from many religious

observances. Men, not women, were required to attend regular synagogue worship and the feasts at the temple in Jerusalem. Women were banned from the temple altogether during menstruation and to certain areas of the temple at other times. Women did not count toward the minimum number of people necessary for public prayer. Jewish men were expected to pray daily, wearing prayer shawls and phylacteries, and to wear fringes on their garments. Women were not simply exempt from this daily ritual and from wearing these religious articles; they were prohibited from taking part. Females could not be called upon to read the scriptures in the synagogue on the Sabbath. Many rabbis believed women should not be taught the Torah.

A Jewish woman, however, did have a respected role as "a mother of Israel." Despite social regulations that often excluded her, she had a sense of worth because Judaism assigned her rights and powers denied to non-Israelite ("Gentile") men. For instance, she could move beyond the "Court of the Gentiles" in the temple and enter the "Court of Women" and thus come closer to God's presence and witness the sacrifice offerings. Unlike the Gentile, the Jewish woman was an insider who, despite her limitations, possessed a defined status within Jewish society.

To be sure, Jews honored the memory of the "mothers of Israel": Sarah, Rachel, and Rebekah. They honored the prophetesses of old, especially Miriam, the prophetess, and Deborah, judge of the people. They revered the women who had freed the people of Israel, such as Esther, and such martyrs as the mother of the Maccabees. Yet not even the brilliance of these figures can blind us to this sweeping dismissal by Flavius Josephus: "Saith the Scripture, A woman is inferior to her husband in all things."[5]

While Jewish women certainly experienced love and respect from their fathers, mothers, brothers, sisters, husbands, sons, and daughters, Jewish traditions restricted their participation in

353

public activity and tended to demean their worth at home as well as in society. By Jesus' time, Jewish men might already have been praying three times each day this set prayer: "Blessed art thou . . . who hast not made me a heathen [Gentile], . . . who hast not made me a woman, and . . . who hast not made me a slave."[6] Similarly, Greek men were thankful they were "born a human being and not a beast; next, a man and not a woman; thirdly, a Greek and not a barbarian."[7] Thus, Jews were thankful for not being Greek Gentiles, and Greeks were thankful for not being Jewish barbarians—women, however, made both gratitude lists.

Those unfamiliar with Jewish Palestinian society at the beginning of the first century after Christ will miss certain important cultural details in the four Gospels. The unwritten part of the Gospels includes what the authors presume the audience already knows, what they can read between the lines of their story. Yet this unwritten part is often crucial to our understanding. Presumably the Gospel writers expected their readers would be first-century, eastern Mediterranean peoples who shared their social values and cultural understanding.

When Latter-day Saints read stories about women in the four Gospels, such as the young Mary betrothed to Joseph, we often see her as someone who lives in our own time with our own dreams and expectations. We filter the New Testament story through our distinctively modern American eyes. We could not be further from the reality of first-century Jewish Palestine.

MARY, THE MOTHER OF JESUS

The first disciple of the mortal Messiah was his mother. Mary's discipleship began when she was betrothed to Joseph. She lived in a small village with a population of not more than two hundred people. Typically, a young girl was between twelve and twelve and a half years old when she was betrothed. Mary, therefore, was a young girl just entering womanhood and living in a small isolated village when the angel Gabriel first appeared to her. Luke records: "And the angel came in unto her, and said, Hail, thou that art highly favoured, the Lord is with thee: blessed art thou among women." Mary was "troubled at his saying," but the divine messenger reassured her, "Fear not, Mary: for thou hast found favour with God," and then explained what God required of her. Mary responded, "Behold the handmaid of the Lord; be it unto me according to thy word" (Luke 1:26–38).

Accepting her call to discipleship, Mary went to visit her cousin Elisabeth in Judea.

Elisabeth knew as soon as Mary arrived and "the babe leaped in [her] womb for joy" that Mary's child was to be the promised Messiah. The record tells us that "Elisabeth was filled with the Holy Ghost: And she spake out with a loud voice, and said, Blessed art thou among women, and blessed is the fruit of thy womb" (vv. 39–45). Elisabeth, a woman, stands beside Simeon, a man and aged Saint, as an early witness to Christ's divine mission.

The young but spiritually mature Mary praises the Lord for his goodness: "My soul doth magnify the Lord . . . for, behold, from henceforth all generations shall call me blessed. . . . He hath put down the mighty from their seats, and exalted them of low degree" (vv. 46–52). For women to witness by the Holy Ghost as Elisabeth did and proclaim the purpose of God as Mary does in these verses was unusual. God had indeed "exalted them of low degree."

Some time after Jesus' birth, as was the custom, Mary and Joseph traveled to the holy city Jerusalem with the newborn infant. Before nightfall, Mary and Joseph probably visited one of the public pools, perhaps one of the forty-eight ritual immersion pools recently found alongside the temple esplanade in Jerusalem. The next morning, Joseph and Mary with the baby Jesus would have gone to the temple, entering through the eastern gate in the southern wall and emerging into the Court of the Gentiles, where the moneychangers located their tables for business each day.

The scriptures do not provide enough detail to give us precise information to know exactly where Joseph, Mary, and the infant were in the temple when Simeon found them. The scriptures simply inform us that the Holy Spirit led him into the temple and to the young couple and the baby. Simeon was a "just and devout" man who had waited all his life for this moment. He took the baby from his mother's arms and praised God: "Lord, now lettest thou thy servant depart in peace, according to thy word: For mine eyes have seen thy salvation . . . ; a light to lighten the Gentiles, and the glory of thy people Israel." Mary and Joseph "marvelled" at this prophecy from a man unknown to them. He next blessed the young couple who would be rearing this child of promise and then warned Mary of future heartache: "Behold, this child is set for the fall and rising again of many in Israel; and for a sign which shall be spoken against; (Yea, a sword shall pierce through thy own soul also,) that the thoughts of many hearts may be revealed" (Luke 2:25, 29–35).

Elder Jeffrey R. Holland has written about this event: "There is a profound . . . message in the one this dear old man gave to sweet and pure Mary in that first Christmas season. He was joyously happy. He had lived to see the Son of God be born. He had held the child in his very arms. . . . But his joy was not of the superficial kind. . . . His joy had something to do with 'the fall and rising again' of many in Israel, and with this child's life—or at least his death—which would be like a sword piercing through his beloved mother's soul. . . . Surely such [an ominous warning] was untimely, even unseemly, at *that* moment—when the Son of God was so young and tender and safe, and his mother so thrilled with his birth. . . . [But] it was appropriate *and* important. . . . It is the life at the *other* end of the manger scene that gives this moment of nativity in Bethlehem its ultimate meaning. . . . wise old Simeon understood all of this—

that the birth was ultimately for the death. . . . Lying among those gifts of gold, frankincense, and myrrh were also a crown of thorns, a makeshift royal robe, and a Roman spear."[8]

So the beginning (Jesus' birth) is inextricably connected to the end (Jesus' death). And women were prominent among the witnesses at both times. During the last week of Jesus' ministry (Jesus' last fateful hours among his disciples), women are depicted as aware of what was to come and loyal to his impending call to suffer and die as the servant spoken of in Isaiah 53—the suffering Messiah. The many women at the cross and the burial contrast markedly with some of the disciples who deserted Jesus. Certainly they were in as much danger as the men (the Romans customarily killed the family and servants of political criminals). The small group of weeping but brave women stood "afar off," not out of trepidation but because the place of execution was cordoned off by the military. With faithful women watching, Jesus died an agonizing and painful death. These female disciples of Jesus were the last to remain at the cross and the first to return to the tomb early on the morning of the glorious resurrection. They were the first to remember Jesus words' about his death and resurrection.

THE UNNAMED WOMAN OF BETHANY

In Mark's narrative, three disciples play a major role in the story of Jesus' final week. The first two were members of the Twelve: Peter, who denied Jesus, and Judas, who betrayed him. The third disciple, a woman unnamed by Mark, anointed Jesus with precious ointment in preparation for his coming burial (see Mark 14:3–9).

While the parts played by Peter and Judas during Jesus' final days are well known, the woman who anointed Jesus is seldom recognized as the only disciple who understood both who Jesus was and that he was to die for us. Although Peter had declared Jesus to be both Messiah and Son of God, he took Jesus aside and rebuked him for teaching that he must "suffer many things . . . and be killed" (Mark 8:31–32).

Peter, and probably all the Twelve, fundamentally misunderstood Jesus' mission. Not one could bring himself to imagine that Jesus' mission might end with suffering and death.[9] Fear seized Peter and the rest as they journeyed toward Jerusalem.[10]

The woman of Bethany reacted differently. She anointed Jesus' head as a king, and she also understood the anointing to be in preparation for his coming suffering and death. It should be noted, however, that even this woman (and this seems to apply to all who followed Jesus from Galilee) did not understand that Jesus would be resurrected three days after his death.

John not only provided a name—Mary—for the unnamed woman of Matthew and Mark but also added to the story of what happened (see John 12:1–8). Between the raising of Lazarus and this story, John tells about the conspiracy to kill Jesus. His enemies were determined to capture him at the upcoming feast, knowing full well that Jesus would come to Jerusalem to worship and teach.[11]

After his triumphal entry into Jerusalem and "six days before the passover [Jesus] came to Bethany, where Lazarus was which had been dead, whom he raised from the dead. There they made him a supper; and Martha served: but Lazarus was one of them that sat at the table with him" (John 12:1–2). The King James Version of the Bible states that Jesus and Lazarus "sat at the table," but the Greek text indicates that they followed Greco-Roman custom and "reclined," or lay, on a mat while leaning on the left arm, thereby keeping the right hand free for eating the food placed on a low table.[12] Martha served the meal, Lazarus ate with Jesus, and Mary, who was mentioned last, was again at Jesus' feet (a position she took in each of the three stories in which she appears in the Gospels).[13]

Mary took the flask of very expensive perfume, "ointment

of spikenard," and poured it over the feet of Jesus, who was reclining beside her brother on the cushions round the table (John 12:3). All of the elements of devotion and worship are present in her service—respect, affection, and tenderness. And even that was not enough; she wiped away the dust and oil from Jesus' tired and dusty feet with her hair. That was the task of the lowliest slave: the custom was for the master at the table to wipe his dirty hands on a slave's hair.

Such service would be incomprehensible to many women today—she did what no man would do—and it may even have shocked Martha and Lazarus. John emphasizes that Mary's act was an extravagant one: "a pound of ointment of spikenard, very costly" (John 12:3). John underscored the cost by the comment that the entire "house was filled with the odour" of the perfume (John 12:3). This fragrant oil, made of pure nard, is derived from the root and spike (hair stem) of the nard plant, which grows in the mountains of northern India. The extravagance of her gift—the sweet smell of which filled the house—signified the depth of Mary's love for Jesus.

The disciples, with Judas as voice, protested the apparent extravagance and waste: "Why was not this ointment sold for three hundred pence, and given to the poor?"[14] Mark's account emphasizes the anger of the disciples: "And there were some that had indignation within themselves, and said, Why was this waste of the ointment made? For it might have been sold for more than three hundred pence, and have been given to the poor. And they *murmured* against her" (Mark 14:4–5; emphasis added). The word translated *murmured* relates to the snort of horses, so in English the sense is of persons "snorting with inward rage or indignation."[15]

"Then said Jesus, Let her alone: against the day of my burying hath she kept this. For the poor always ye have with you; but me ye have not always" (John 12:7–8). The Joseph Smith Translation adds to the story: "Then said Jesus, Let her alone; *for she hath preserved this ointment until now, that she might*

359

anoint me in token of my burial" (JST John 12:7; emphasis added).[16]

Jesus clearly rebuked those present for assuming that their spiritual understanding was greater than Mary's, and he showed them that in this case the opposite was true. As Jesus' words to Judas suggest, the anointing anticipated Jesus' death and burial because one did not normally anoint the feet of a living person but rather the feet of the deceased as part of preparing the whole body for burial.

One aspect of the anointing story, so important in both Mark and Matthew, is missing from John's—Jesus' bold and far-reaching declaration: "Verily I say unto you, Wheresoever this gospel shall be preached throughout the whole world, this also that she hath done shall be spoken of for a memorial of her" (Mark 14:9; see also Matthew 26:13). This actually happened in the early Church: Mary is introduced earlier in John 11: "It was that Mary which anointed the Lord with ointment, and wiped his feet with her hair, whose brother Lazarus was sick" (v. 2).

Despite differences among the accounts of Mark, Luke, and John, all three Gospels reflect the same basic story: a woman anoints Jesus. The incident causes objections, which Jesus rejects by approving of the woman's action. While John speaks of the anointing of the feet, Mark and Matthew speak of the anointing of the head.[17] Did she anoint both his head and feet? Because, in the Old Testament, prophets anointed the head of the Jewish king, the anointing of Jesus' head may be seen as the prophetic recognition of Jesus as the Anointed (*Messiah* in English is equivalent to the Hebrew, and *Christ* in English is equivalent to the Greek for "anointed").[18]

When Jesus asked, "Who am I?" Peter answered, "You are the anointed one" (see Matthew 16:15–16) without understanding the implications of Jesus' calling. This woman's anointing of Jesus, however, clearly recognized that Jesus' messiahship involved death, not the overthrow of Roman rule and kingly glory that many Jews anticipated.

WOMEN: WITNESSES OF THE RESURRECTION

Luke's story of Jesus' burial and resurrection follows a particular line.[19] When the Lord's body was taken from the cross, Joseph of Arimathaea "wrapped it in linen," a common burial cloth of the period made of flax from either Egypt or Jericho (Luke 23:53). The body was then taken to a new tomb, "hewn in stone, wherein never man before was laid" (v. 53). Luke continues, "And the women also, which came with him from Galilee, followed after, and beheld the sepulchre, and how his body was laid."

The women who followed and noted how Jesus' body was laid in the tomb did so because they planned to prepare "spices and ointments" to offer their final act of devotion to Jesus by anointing his body (Luke 23:56). According to the Gospel of John, who focuses exclusively on Mary Magdalene, she, with a total disregard for Mosaic regulations, wanted to find Jesus' body herself and planned to "take him away" if necessary.

Yet, when they returned after the Sabbath, they found the tomb empty. Surely these women were perplexed as they entered the tomb and found it empty. The women's perplexity seems to have lifted when "two men . . . in shining garments" appeared and spoke to them: "Why seek ye the living among the dead? He is not here, but is risen: remember how he spake unto you when he was yet in Galilee, saying, The Son of man must be delivered into the hands of sinful men, and be crucified, and the third day rise again. And they remembered his words" (Luke 24:5–8). Nothing in the text indicates that their confusion continued. The observation, "and they remembered his words," implies that they suddenly understood Jesus' prophecy and what had transpired at the tomb.

The two phrases, "remember how he spake unto you when he was yet in Galilee" and "they remembered his words," are a key theme of the story. The women, especially Mary Magdalene, had heroines' roles as the first to recall Jesus' words

361

when he spoke about his pending suffering and death in the divine plan and as the first to grasp their fulfillment (see Luke 9:22–23). The women now had enough light to understand, seemingly for the first time, that Jesus not only had to suffer and die but that he also rose from the dead in fulfillment of his own words. Previously, Jesus' disciples, the women included, had not understood his instructions on these points.[20]

Luke emphasized, in contrast to Mark's account, that the women reported "all these things unto the eleven, and to all the rest" (Luke 24:9). Their testimony was clearly important to Luke and the early Church.

When the women first reported their discovery to the apostles, however, they thought "their words seemed to them as idle tales, and they believed them not" (see Luke 24:10–11). Remember that in Jewish culture women could not be witnesses.[21] Generally a woman's testimony, along with that of a slave, was not admissible evidence in court, unless it dealt with a "woman's issue." This was "on account of the levity and boldness of their sex."[22] Finally, two others—Peter and the beloved disciple (John)—returned with Mary Magdalene to the site. Once they examined the tomb, Peter walked away "wondering" (Luke 24:12). Both Peter and John returned to "their own home" (John 20:10), but Mary remained at the tomb, puzzled and grief-stricken at not finding Jesus' body. The world before the resurrection could not make sense of an empty tomb. The "eleven" and "all the rest" remained incredulous (Luke 24:9).

John's Gospel, differing from that of Matthew, Mark, and Luke, then relates in detail the well-known story of Mary Magdalene and the risen Christ. Take special note that after Mary's recognition of the risen Lord, Jesus exhorted her: "Go to my brethren, and say unto them, I ascend unto my Father, and your Father; and to my God, and your God" (John 20:17). Mary fulfilled messianic prophecy when she heeded Jesus' words and announced to the disciples, "I have seen the Lord."[23]

Remember that the Greek word for Lord (*kyrios*) is the same word rendered in the Greek Old Testament (Septuagint) for *YHWH* (Jehovah), which is the proper name of God.[24]

Mary Magdalene became an "apostle to the apostles." The term does not mean a member of the Twelve, of course, but rather that she is "one sent forth" to witness the good news of Christ's resurrection.[25] Mary Magdalene was the first witness of the resurrection in two important and significant ways. She was the first person to see the resurrected Messiah, and she was the first person to witness to others what she had seen. She was in a sense the first disciple of the risen Jesus.

According to Luke, the next event is the appearance of Jesus to two disciples (Luke 24:13–35). As the two walked "to a village called Emmaus, which was from Jerusalem about threescore furlongs [about seven miles]," Jesus "drew near, and went with them."[26] Nowhere does the text state explicitly that the two travelers are men. Again, the Jewish customs about witnesses (and possibly our own way of looking at the New Testament) obscure the fact that for Jesus, women can and do act as legitimate witnesses of these events. Therefore, we should not assume that both travelers were men. One is named and clearly male; one, unnamed and probably female.[27] The couple, who at first failed to recognize Jesus, may have been returning home to Emmaus that day, for when they arrived they invited Jesus to have dinner with them in their home (see Luke 24:29–30).

The two travelers had the women's report and yet were leaving Jerusalem and the assembled disciples, dejected and despondent (see Luke 24:17–24). Clearly they did not understand Jesus' identity and mission. They had lost hope because of his crucifixion, despite the women's report of "a vision of angels, which said that he was alive" (v. 23). These two disciples did not believe the report because of their poor understanding of the scriptures. The Hebrew scriptures should have prepared them for Christ's suffering, death, and resurrection. In conversation as they walked, Jesus patiently talked with them: "And beginning at Moses and all the prophets, he expounded unto them in all the scriptures the things concerning himself." They still did not recognize him until he accepted their invitation "to tarry with them" at their home in Emmaus before continuing on his journey. "And it came to pass, as he sat at meat with them, he took bread, and blessed it, and brake, and gave to them. And their eyes were opened, and they knew him; and he vanished out of their sight" (vv. 27–31).

On the road, their initial sadness had given way to joy as they eagerly listened to Jesus' explanation of the scriptures. Their "eyes were opened" fully at the breaking of bread, when once again he served the meal to them as of old (vv. 31, 35). "And they said one to another, Did not our heart burn within us, while he talked with us by the way, and while he opened to us the scriptures?" (v. 32). They heard, understood, and accepted this disclosure, and at the meal they recognized Jesus. The two, formerly dejected, now became harbingers of a joyful message. "And they rose up the same hour, and returned to Jerusalem, and found the eleven gathered together" (v. 33).

The testimony of these two travelers, the latest development reported to the eleven, corroborated what the entire congregation now knew and believed. Several independent witnesses, both men and women, now emerged among the followers of Jesus.

WOMEN AND CHRIST

The prominence of women in the early Christian church has long been acknowledged[28] both by early Christian writers and their opponents.[29] When the pagan critic Celsus denigrated Christianity in the second century as a religion of women, children, and slaves, he articulated a connection between women and early Christianity that has only recently received serious attention.[30]

According to the four Gospels, Jesus' relations with women

seem to have been remarkably open, given the reserve that Jewish culture and customs in his day required. It is certain that some of these women did not conform to the socially acceptable categories of virgin daughter, respectable wife, and mother of legitimate children. Many were unmarried or widowed.

Jesus broke down barriers in the most surprising ways. He rejected social customs, especially those of first-century rabbinic Judaism. Jesus dealt with the women he met during his ministry as individuals, treating women and men alike. Each could communicate with Jesus, follow him, be companions with him, minister to him, be ministered to by him, and love him. Although Jesus (and therefore the writers of the Gospels) in no way sought to deny or diminish the distinction between men and women, he emphasized their partnership; it is therefore difficult to find differences in Jesus' approach to women and to men.

In the end, a woman's qualification for discipleship was and is the same as a man's: all must accept him as their Lord and Master. Any person who truly accepts him consequently becomes a witness of him as the source of Living Water. As we now view these women of the four Gospels, sisters at the well—thirsty and weary, burdened with care and tradition, dropping their leather buckets into the well and drawing up unto themselves refreshment and strength—the parched ground bears fruit, and they turn to us with their clay jars filled with water. They witness to us of its goodness, through their model of discipleship, joining hands with the good men with whom they served.

Remember the prayer that was recited daily by devout Jewish men: "Blessed art thou . . . who hast not made me a heathen [Gentile], . . . who hast not made me a woman, and . . . who hast not made me a slave."[31] Paul, who had said this prayer himself from the age of twelve until he met Jesus on the road to Damascus, changes, negates this prayer in response to a culture that was hostile to women, and in the book of Galatians, writes: "For ye are all the children of God by faith in Christ Jesus. For as many of you as have been baptized into Christ have put on Christ. There is neither Jew nor Greek, there is neither bond nor free, there is neither male nor female: for ye are all one in Christ Jesus" (Galatians 3:26–28).

NOTES

1. *Children's Songbook* (Salt Lake City: The Church of Jesus Christ of Latter-day Saints, 1989), 120.

2. For a full discussion of this topic, see Jeni Broberg Holzapfel and Richard Neitzel Holzapfel, *Sisters at the Well: Women and the Life and Teachings of Jesus* (Salt Lake City: Bookcraft, 1993), 10–18.

3. Hesiod, *Theogony,* lines 550–601; see Hesiod, *Theogony, Works and Days, Shield,* trans. Apostolos N. Athanassakis (Baltimore: John Hopkins University Press, 1983), 27–28.

4. Posidippus, *Hermaphr,* as cited in Eva Cantarella, *Pandora's Daughters: The Role and Status of Women in Greek and Roman Antiquity* (Baltimore: Johns Hopkins University Press, 1987), 44, 195 n19.

5. Flavius Josephus, *Against Apion* 2.202; see William Whiston, trans., *Josephus: Complete Works* (Grand Rapids, Mich.: Kregel Publications, 1972), 632.

6. *Babylonian Talmud,* Menahoth 43b; see *Tractate Menahoth* 43b, vol. 23, in Isidore Epstein, ed., *Hebrew-English Edition of the Babylonian Talmud.*

7. Attributed to Plato or Thales, as quoted in Wayne A. Meeks, "The Image of the Androgyne: Some Uses of a Symbol in Earliest Christianity," *History of Religions* 13 (February 1974): 167.

8. Jeffrey R. Holland, *Christmas Comfort* [pamphlet] (Salt Lake City: Bookcraft, 1996), 3–4.

9. See Richard Neitzel Holzapfel, "The Hidden Messiah," in *A Witness of Jesus Christ: The 1989 Sperry Symposium on the Old Testament,* ed. Richard D. Draper (Salt Lake City: Deseret Book, 1990), 80–95.

10. See Mark 10:32–34.

11. The Synoptic tradition speaks of the house of Simon the leper—some have suggested that Simon was the father of Lazarus, Mary, and Martha, thus eliminating the seeming contradiction on the location of the event; see note 13, below.

12. See William F. Arndt and F. Wilbur Gingrich, *A Greek-English Lexicon of the*

New Testament and Other Early Christian Literature (Chicago: University of Chicago Press, 1957), 55.

13. John 12:3; see also Luke 10:39; John 11:32.

14. John 12:4–5; see Matthew 26:8 and Mark 14:4 for the inclusion of the other disciples in this protest. Judas is here identified as the son of Simon, which may make him the brother of Martha, Mary, and Lazarus; see note 10 above.

15. See Max Zerwick and Mary Grosvenor, *A Grammatical Analysis of the Greek New Testament* (Rome: Biblical Institute Press, 1981), 154; and William F. Arndt and F. Wilbur Gingrich, *A Greek-English Lexicon of the New Testament,* 254.

16. See also JST Matthew 26:9–10; JST Mark 14:8.

17. See John 12:3; Mark 14:3; Matthew 26:7.

18. See Arndt and Gingrich, *A Greek-English Lexicon of the New Testament,* 895.

19. See Joseph Plevnik, "The Eyewitnesses of the Risen Jesus in Luke 24," *The Catholic Biblical Quarterly* 49 (January 1987): 90–103.

20. See Luke 9:45; 18:34. Luke is careful to identify these women as companion travelers with Jesus (see Luke 8:1–3) *before* Jesus makes his first prediction of his death to his disciples (see Luke 9:23).

21. Some have seen Luke's phrase "two men," an added description of the angels, as a device that underscores the fact that the two were legitimate witnesses; see also Luke 9:30; Acts 1:10.

22. Josephus, *Antiquities* 4.219; see Whiston, trans., *Josephus,* 97.

23. Greek text of John 20:18. In Psalms we find, "I will declare *thy name* unto *my brethren:* in the midst of the congregation will I praise thee" (22:22; emphasis added).

24. See Gottfried Quell, *"Kurios," Theological Dictionary of the New Testament,* ed. Gerhard Kittel, 10 vols. (Grand Rapids, Mich.: Eerdmans, 1982), 3:1058–81, in particular 1060–62.

25. See "Apostle," Bible Dictionary, LDS Edition of the King James Version of the Bible, 612.

26. Luke 24:13, 15; a furlong, a Greek measurement still used in Roman times, was about six hundred feet, the length of the racetrack at Olympia. This clue helps us identify the location of the village from several possible sites. In all likelihood, Emmaus Colonia, situated one or two hours' walking distance from Jerusalem is the probable location; for another possible identification see "Emmaus," LDS Bible Dictionary, 665.

27. "And the one of them, whose name was Cleopas" (Luke 24:18) is not to be confused, as often is the case, with Cleophas of John 19:25, whose name is

of Semitic origin, whereas Cleopas is well attested as a Greek name (a short-ened form of Kleopatros—"illustrious father"); see Robert F. O'Toole, "Cleopas," *Anchor Bible Dictionary,* ed. David Noel Freedman, 6 vols. (New York: Doubleday, 1992), 1:1063–64.

28. See Adolf von Harnack, *The Mission and Expansion of Christianity During the First Three Centuries* (London: Williams and Norgate, 1908), 64–84.

29. Averil Cameron, "Neither Male nor Female,'" *Greece and Rome* 27 (April 1980): 60–68.

30. Origen, *Contra Celsus* 3:49; see A. Cleveland Coxe, ed., "Origen against Celsus," *The Ante-Nicene Fathers,* 10 vols. (Grand Rapids, Mich.: Eerdmans, 1989), 4:484.

31. *Babylonian Talmud,* Menahoth 43b; see *Tractate Menahoth* 43b, vol. 23 in Isidore Epstein, ed., *Hebrew-English Edition of the Babylonion Talmud.*

INDEX

patriarchal, 156, 169; of
knowledge, 200
Blessings: receiving, 139; temple,
297–98
Blindness, 41
Blood, Henry, 56
Blood, Mary Stretton, 54–56
Blood, William, 54–55
Bodies, 14, 274
Boggs, Lilburn, 266
Book of Mormon, the, 35
Boston Marathon, 246–47
Bread of life, 14
Brigham Young University, 247–48;
Jerusalem Center, 301
Brooks, Bob, 194
Budgets, 102; of time, 252
Burdens, 149
Burnham, George, 21
Burnham, James Lewis, 20–21
Burnham, Maria Antoinette, 20
Burnham, Mary Ann Huntley, 20–22
Burnham, Wallace, 21
Burn-out, 209
Bush, Mirabai, 90

Callings, 137
Calvin, John, 151
Cambodia, 97
Cancer, 5, 242
Cannon, George Q., 80
Capabilities, 67
Caregivers, 173
Carter, Gideon, 266
Cash, 230
Catholicism, 33
Certainty, sin of, 41–42
CHADD chapter, 199–200
Chains, snow, 72
Chandeliers, 292–93
Change: challenges in, 7; desire to, 16
Charcot's disease, 209
Charity, 50, 176
Children: Christ and, 76, 313–14;
obedience of, 79; listening to, 87;

turning, to Christ, 162–63; of God,
337
Christianity, 339
Choices, 15, 40, 212; appropriate, 114;
structure of, 199; consequences of,
201
Christensen, Doug, 99
Church Human Resources, 101
Church of Jesus Christ of Latter-day
Saints, the: membership in, 47–48,
78; writing the, story, 319;
Christianity and, 339
Circles, 311
Clarke, J. Richard, 258
Comfort, 331
Comforter, 10
Commandments, 140
Commendations, 49–50
Commitment, 198
Communication, 114, 240, 336
Compassion, 308
Compliments, 49
Condemnations, 49–50
Conflict, 111; resolving, 117–19, 170
Consecration, 311–12
Constitution, Beatitudes as, 325
Contention, 335
Contentment, 143
Control, 184, 191; and ADD, 203
Conversion, 33–37
Counseling, 42–43, 125
Countries, third-world, 103–4
Cowdery, Oliver, 269
Covenant: fire of the, 276; keeping,
311
Crisis, management by, 251, 256
Criticism, 117, 159–60, 176–77; and
ADD, 200; of handcart companies,
279
Crosses, bearing, 5
Cues, 188
Cutler, Ralph, 30
Cutler, Virginia, 30–32

Dailyness, 249